The Ubiquity of the Finite

D0897048

Studies in Contemporary German Social Thought
Thomas McCarthy, General Editor

Theodor W. Adorno, *Against Epistemology: A Metacritique*

Theodor W. Adorno, *Prisms*

Karl-Otto Apel, *Understanding and Explanation: A Transcendental-Pragmatic Perspective*

Richard J. Bernstein, editor, *Habermas and Modernity*

Ernst Bloch, *Natural Law and Human Dignity*

Ernst Bloch, *The Principle of Hope*

Ernst Bloch, *The Utopian Function of Art and Literature: Selected Essays*

Hans Blumenberg, *The Genesis of the Copernican World*

Hans Blumenberg, *The Legitimacy of the Modern Age*

Hans Blumenberg, *Work on Myth*

Helmut Dubiel, *Theory and Politics: Studies in the Development of Critical Theory*

John Forester, editor, *Critical Theory and Public Life*

David Frisby, *Fragments of Modernity: Theories of Modernity in the Work of Simmel, Kracauer and Benjamin*

Hans-Georg Gadamer, *Philosophical Apprenticeships*

Hans-Georg Gadamer, *Reason in the Age of Science*

Jürgen Habermas, *The Philosophical Discourse of Modernity: Twelve Lectures*

Jürgen Habermas, *Philosophical-Political Profiles*

Jürgen Habermas, editor, *Observations on "The Spiritual Situation of the Age"*

Hans Joas, *G. H. Mead: A Contemporary Re-examination of His Thought*

Reinhart Koselleck, *Critique and Crisis: The Pathogenesis of Modern Society*

Reinhart Koselleck, *Futures Past: On the Semantics of Historical Time*

Harry Liebersohn, *Fate and Utopia in German Sociology, 1887–1923*

Herbert Marcuse, *Hegel's Ontology and the Theory of Historicity*

Claus Offe, *Contradictions of the Welfare State*

Claus Offe, *Disorganized Capitalism: Contemporary Transformations of Work and Politics*

Helmut Peukert, *Science, Action, and Fundamental Theology: Toward a Theology of Communicative Action*

Joachim Ritter, *Hegel and the French Revolution: Essays on the* Philosophy of Right

Alfred Schmidt, *History and Structure: An Essay on Hegelian-Marxist and Structuralist Theories of History*

Dennis Schmidt, *The Ubiquity of the Finite: Hegel, Heidegger, and the Entitlements of Philosophy*

Carl Schmitt, *The Crisis of Parliamentary Democracy*

Carl Schmitt, *Political Romanticism*

Carl Schmitt, *Political Theology: Four Chapters on the Concept of Sovereignty*

Gary Smith, editor, *On Walter Benjamin: Critical Essays and Recollections*

Michael Theunissen, *The Other: Studies in the Social Ontology of Husserl, Heidegger, Sartre, and Buber*

Ernst Tugendhat, *Self-Consciousness and Self-Determination*

Mark Warren, *Nietzsche and Political Thought*

The Ubiquity of the Finite

Hegel, Heidegger, and the
Entitlements of Philosophy

Dennis J. Schmidt

The MIT Press, Cambridge, Massachusetts, and London, England

This book was set in Baskerville by Asco Trade Typesetting Ltd., Hong Kong and printed and bound by The Murray Printing Co. in the United States of America.

Library of Congress Cataloging-in-Publication Data

Schmidt, Dennis J.
  The ubiquity of the finite.

  (Studies in contemporary German social thought)
  Bibliography: p.
  Includes index.
  1. Metaphysics. 2. Hegel, Georg Wilhelm Friedrich, 1770–1831. 3. Heidegger, Martin, 1889–1976. I. Title. II. Series.
BD111.S323 1988   110   87-25973
ISBN 0-262-19270-5

For Lisa

Socordiam eorum irridere licet qui praesenti potentia aevi temporis memoriam extinqui posse credunt.

—*Tacitus*

Contents

(bot) p. 73 on FINITE TRACES.

p. 190ff.

pub. 1988

Preface

It is doubtful that philosophy has ever had such a unity that would justify talk about "the tradition" or "metaphysics" as if it were a whole cut of the same seamless cloth. Far too much chopping and cutting is required to seriously entertain the possibility that even a list of such interrelated thinkers as for instance Plato, Ockham, Aquinas, Ficino, Locke, Hobbes, Rousseau, Kant, and Hegel should be easily recognized as representing a unified "tradition." Drawing more lines to include Kierkegaard, Aristotle, Spinoza, and Vico stretches the credibility and even thinkability of the idea of a "tradition." The more names we add to the list fleshing out the constituents of this tradition, the more the very notion withers. "Der Teufel versteckt sich im Detail." Contention,—multiple and deep—not consensus, is the general tenor of the history of thought. Even if a retrospective look finds unified movements in which individual thinkers stand as representatives, it is unlikely that any individual thinker of any originality ever faced the future in terms of an effort to identify himself with a movement rather than the other way around. The philosophical imaginations that are at work in the twists and turns in the history of thought confront the details of issues in all of their particularity. Enduring contributions always get worked out, and must be reenacted, with a degree of specificity that resists easy schematization into a unified "tradition." It is precisely this resistance, standing in an uneasy relation with the effective history of such contributions, that keeps history alive and makes the notion of "tradition" problematic.

Nevertheless, one trademark of continental thought after Hegel is the tendency to speak of "metaphysics" as if it stood for a unity and the "tradition" as if it were singular. This does not signal a collective amnesia on the part of those working out of the continental tradition. Talk of the "tradition" does not mean that the long history of efforts to wrestle with phenomena, and to reflect upon the capacity and powers of reflection, has been reduced to a unified effort. Nor should the construction of such a tradition be the means whereby displaced and marginal texts and unclaimed heritages and ideas are once and for all excluded from an "essential" history. One of the other trademarks of recent continental thought, especially as it has been developed by feminist theorists, is the effort to enlarge our sense of philosophy's past and the tasks of its present. Speaking about the "tradition of metaphysics" is not the last gasp of historicism but one of the ways in which contemporary thinkers have sought to simultaneously establish and loosen the history of the discourse that is called philosophy. To speak of "metaphysics" and "the philosophic tradition," as this book will do, is not to suppose that the past history of thought has been sedimented and so presents a unified front but to ask whether the present of thought can identify itself in a unified way. The point is this: despite its richness and depths, despite its honesty and efforts, and despite its complexity and conflicts, it has become increasingly difficult for contemporary thinkers to hold onto what can be found in the history of thought as vital, tenable, and answering needs of today. We find ourselves in a moment in history in which we no longer seem to be able to find our own place: that which we want to value often seems to have no place, while many of the challenges of today come from quarters and raise questions that are unanticipated by the topics of the past. It would be foolish to attempt to pinpoint a single cause for contemporary upheavals or even to locate contemporary challenges in one region of life. Yet it does seem reasonable to say that technology has spawned many of the questions that dissolve more "traditional" frameworks for arriving at answers. It is not insignificant that the rapid developments in "medical ethics" take place at the same moment that we find the notion of "postmodernity" making deep inroads into several fields of questioning. Developments in medical technology are forcing ethical theorists to look for answers and solutions where, until recently, there were no questions. But there are other domains in which technology is providing a heat that melts long-standing assumptions—Walter Benjamin signaled this in his 1936 essay on "Art in the Age of its

Technological Reproducibility." So did Hannah Arendt when she began *The Human Condition* by pointing out that the first launch of an earth-born object in 1957 was an event "second in importance to no other." More recently, Lyotard is compelled to begin *The Postmodern Condition* by saying that "the nature of knowledge cannot survive unchanged" in light of recent technological transformations.

But the point is not simply a matter of technology. It is not the only domain of inventions and discoveries that seems to be outstripping inherited frames of thought. It is not alone in altering, or at least challenging, our perceptions of what is right, real, and meaningful— it is simply frequently more public in its effects. More important is to recognize that technology is the expression and product of a way of thinking and a set of values and that modern technology, which is a modification of the possibilities of human techne, is best understood in light of its values, imperatives, and conceptual underpinnings. To do this, to understand such distinctive and dominant features of modern life and culture, requires that the unsettled place of the present historical juncture be settled—if only for the present.

This is one of the points from which contemporary efforts to speak of the past as a unity can be understood. In confronting the past as a "tradition," and specifically as a tradition of "metaphysics," we are equally confronting ourselves. When a philosopher like Heidegger writes of the "history of Being as Metaphysics," or of "metaphysics as the forgetfulness of Being," and then calls for the "overcoming of philosophy as metaphysics," his primary purpose is not to homogenize or domesticate the past, or to demolish a presumed and already received pantheon, but to ask and challenge the present to find its own integrity against, or simply out of, the diversity of the past. That is why the project of overcoming metaphysics is part of the recovery of the task of thinking today.

This book is an attempt to confront the details of Heidegger's career-long efforts to think the tradition as a unity and so overcome it. My purpose is to take Heidegger seriously and to ask how far he has succeeded in this effort, and to ask how far he has succeeded thereby in contributing to our present understanding of the present and what is at stake in it. To what extent do his achievements toward this end of thinking "the tradition" match his claims? What, if any, hidden intentions and motivations are concretized in the issues over which Heidegger must confront the representatives of metaphysics?

Part of Heidegger's purpose in bringing philosophy to an end is to release thinking into the region of that which calls thought, a region that he contends has been suppressed and muted by the presumptions of metaphysics. But how far has this intention of emancipating thought had the unintended effect of refusing to release the full potential of the past? Does regarding the past as something from which we must be emancipated do justice to the radical senses of time and history that Heidegger himself articulates? Is Heidegger's attempt to overcome metaphysics radical enough to recover the topic of thought, the ontological difference, from its supposed abandon or suppression? Does a vision of the metaphysics of modernity, and of what lies before and after it, emerge from this project of destruction and release?

Such questions can only be worked out in the details of Heidegger's confrontation with metaphysics. Heidegger was well aware that the demonstrations and decisions called for by his project would have to be exhibited in the confrontation with individual "representatives" of metaphysics. To that end, at crucial stages in his critique of metaphysics Heidegger generally singles out a predecessor who he considers typifies that element of the tradition at issue, and frequently it is Hegel who is singled out as the representative of metaphysics par excellence. Whether or not this decision is the most interesting one, that is, the decision that discloses most both about Hegel and the problems that metaphysics poses, is one of the questions addressed throughout this book. Certainly it is not surprising that a contemporary German philosopher, especially one dedicated to establishing the lines of a "tradition," would pay special attention to reflecting upon and criticizing the reappropriation of history in Hegelian thought. It would be far more surprising if there was the lack of such reflections from a philosopher from Heidegger's generation and with his intentions. But what is surprising, and thus revealing about Heidegger, is the extent to which he resists Hegelian thought, preferring to separate himself from the rhetorical excesses of Hegel's description of the dialectic rather than drawing out the richness and complexity of that which the "Absolute" was an attempt to describe. The frequency with which Heidegger turns to Hegel as a representative of "the" tradition of "metaphysics" is striking, but equally striking is the detail of Heidegger's analyses of Hegelian texts and topics. These detailed and extended remarks on Hegel clearly reveal Heidegger's own prejudice that Hegelian thought embodies and gathers into a unity the characteristic prejudices of metaphysics and its tradition. Nevertheless, the confrontation between Hegel and Heidegger is a complicated matter—more complicated and more a matter of nuances than Heidegger generally concedes—and it is a dialogue that reveals much about both, as well as about the topics over which they confront one another.

It is important to bear in mind that confronting Hegel and Heidegger is not a matter of adjudicating a debate between competing or incompatible "positions." The idea of a "position" is always inappropriate in the dialogue between thinkers. In the case of Hegel and Heidegger it is better to characterize that which emerges as at stake: speaking and thinking the meaning of the finite. Both make sustained attempts to capture—without holding captive—the finite as that which both agree has eluded their respective predecessors. Both claim to be at the "end" of a "tradition" and to have ushered in that end by virtue of the rediscovery of the meaning of the first and ubiquitous topic of philosophy: the finite. Herein lies the hidden persistence—the appeal and the threat—of Hegelian thought for Heidegger's own concern: motivated by a sensitivity to the finite, yet governed by the prejudices that are destined to conceal the finite, Hegelian thought harbors both the threats and promises of metaphysics for the project aimed at getting over metaphysics and back to the task of thinking.

Acknowledgments

My debts to others are manifold and my gratitude for their friendship and criticisms is deep. Four in particular have left a deep mark on every page of what follows: Joseph P. Fell, Hans-Georg Gadamer, Stephen David Ross, and Jacques Taminiaux. Each in his own way has made a direct contribution to this book and has made it better than it would have been otherwise. Of course, no one is to be blamed that it is not better still.

Others have made valuable comments and offered support at various stages or on individual chapters of this book: Oliva Blanchette, Martin Dillon, Chris Fynsk, Werner Marx, Tom Nenon, and Basil O'Neill. Tom McCarthy's encouragement helped me enormously.

Last, because most important, I thank my wife, Lisa Fegley-Schmidt, whose belief that I had something to say helped me to try to say anything at all. Her patience, insights, and criticisms, along with her generous and unstinting efforts over the years, have been the sine qua non of far more than this book that is dedicated to her.

Abbreviations

Works of Hegel Cited

PG   *Phänomenologie des Geistes* (Hamburg: Meiner, 1952)

Enz   *Enzyklopädie der Philosophischen Wissenschaften* (Hamburg: Meiner, 1969)

WL   *Wissenschaft der Logik*, 2 Bd., (Hamburg: Meiner, 1971)

JS   *Jenaer Schriften* (Frankfurt: Suhrkamp, 1970)
     in *JS*:
        D   *Differenzschrift*
        GW   *Glauben und Wissen*
        NR   *Naturrecht*

FS   *Frühe Schriften* (Frankfurt: Suhrkamp, 1971)

PR   *Philosophie des Rechts* (Frankfurt: Suhrkamp, 1970)

VPG   *Vorlesungen über die Philosophie der Geschichte* (Frankfurt: Suhrkamp, 1970)

SS   *System der Sittlichkeit* (Hamburg: Meiner, 1967)

VGP   *Vorlesungen über die Geschichte der Philosophie*, 3 Bd., (Frankfurt: Suhrkamp, 1971)

JN   *Jenenser Naturphilosophie* (Hamburg: Meiner, 1967)

JSW   *Jenaer Systementwurfe I*, (Hamburg: Meiner, 1969)

VA   *Vorlesüngen über Äesthetik*, 3 Bd., (Stuttgart: Frommanns Verlag, 1953)

Works of Heidegger Cited

GZ   Bd. 20 *Gesamtausgabe*, "Prolegomena zur Geschichte des Zeitbegriffes" (Frankfurt: Klostermann, 1979)

L	Bd. 21 *Gesamtausgabe*, "Logik: Die Frage nach der Wahrheit" (Frankfurt: Klostermann, 1976)
GP	Bd. 24 *Gesamtausgabe*, "Grundprobleme der Phänomenologie" (Frankfurt: Klostermann, 1975)
ML	Bd. 26 *Gesamtausgabe*, "Metaphysische Anfangsgrunde der Logik" (Frankfurt: Klostermann, 1978)
GM	Bd. 29/30 *Gesamtausgabe*, "Die Grundbegriffe der Metaphysik" (Frankfurt: Klostermann, 1983)
HP	Bd. 32 *Gesamtausgabe*, "Hegels 'Phänomenologie des Geistes'" (Frankfurt: Klostermann, 1980)
HH	Bd. 39 *Gesamtausgabe*, "Hölderlins Hymnen" (Frankfurt: Klostermann, 1980)
VH	Bd. 55 *Gesamtausgabe*, "Heraklit" (Frankfurt: Klostermann, 1979)
F	*Frühe Schriften* (Frankfurt: Klostermann, 1972)
SZ	*Sein und Zeit* (Tübingen: Niemeyer, 1972)
KPM	*Kant und das Problem der Metaphysik* (Frankfurt: Klostermann, 1973)
EM	*Einführung in die Metaphysik* (Tübingen: Niemeyer, 1966)
W	*Wegmarken*: (Frankfurt: Klostermann, 1978)

in *Wegmarken*:

WM "Was ist Metaphysik?"
WG "Vom Wesen des Grundes"
WW "Vom Wesen der Wahrheit"
BH "Brief über den Humanismus"
HG "Hegel und die Griechen"

H	*Holzwege* (Frankfurt: Klostermann, 1972)

in *Holzwege*:

ZW "Die Zeit des Weltbildes"
UK "Ursprung des Kunstwerkes"
HBE "Hegels Begriff der Erfahrung"
SA "Der Spruch des Anaximander"

EH	*Erläuterungen zu Hölderlins Dichtung* (Frankfurt: Klostermann, 1971)

in *EH*:

HEH "Hölderlins Erde und Himmel"

FD	*Die Frage nach dem Ding* (Tübingen: Niemeyer, 1975)
S	*Schelling* (Tübingen: Niemeyer, 1971)
HD	*Was Heisst Denken?* (Tübingen: Niemeyer, 1971)

Abbreviations

N   *Nietzsche*, 2 Bd., (Pfullingen: Neske, 1961)

US   *Unterwegs zur Sprache* (Pfullingen: Neske, 1975)

TK   *Die Technik und die Kehre* (Pfullingen: Neske, 1962)

VA   *Vorträge und Aufsätze* (Pfullingen: Neske, 1978)

SG   *Der Satz vom Grund* (Pfullingen: Neske, 1978)

ID   *Identität und Differenz* (Pfullingen: Neske, 1978)

VS   *Vier Seminare* (Frankfurt: Klostermann, 1977)

GD "Grundsätze des Denkens," *Jahrbuch für Psychologie und Psychotherapie*, VI (1958)

ZF   *Zur Frage nach der Bestimmung der Sache des Denkens* (St. Gallen: Erker-Verlag, 1984)

Introduction

Philosophy, which once seemed to be overcome, remains alive, because the moment of its realization was missed.
—*Adorno*

However one wants to characterize it—whether as finitude, limit, mortality, opinion, partiality, mutability, or immanence—the first topic of philosophy has generally been taken to be something to be overcome. Even superficial reflection discloses the appearance of what seems to be given as somehow inadequate to the tasks of reflection, regardless of whether those tasks are theoretical or practical; the talents that are given with the given never seem to quite measure up to the tasks at hand, yet it is precisely such "givens" that wake thought and speech to the tasks of reflection. There are, and seem always to have been, events, experiences, phenomena, and ideas that puzzle us and solicit attention precisely because they seem to be inviting their own overcoming. Such topics are the ones that stir and provoke us; as soon as they are conceptualized, they represent a kind of challenge to thought and speech as holding out a promise beyond themselves. Since antiquity the effort of philosophic thought has been to follow this promise in order to see beyond the captivity of finite perspectives and prejudices of every sort—national, historical, egoistic, linguistic, physical—to a perceived or simply promised metaphysical region of free and abstract generality which is said to first grant thought its mandate to speak intelligibly about the world in which we find ourselves. The very language of philosophy, the way we talk about what is humanly right, real, and important—the language of ideas—seems to come from that region. For much of the past two-plus-millennia tradition of such reflections beyond the given, the terms and standards validating those reflections were defined by this region. Consequently, metaphysics, until recently at least, has been the mother tongue of philosophy, a language that makes up in clarity what it lacks in carnality. The seductions and pull of such a region are so strong and so complete that it includes a tendency to describe itself as another world altogether, one often detached from and at odds with the world to be interpreted. Hegel's celebrated remark that philosophy represents a kind of "inverted (or perverted) world" reflects this tension between philosophy and its first topic, and this tension is only exacerbated once it is finally recognized that the talent for philosophizing and the history of such achievements are themselves constitutive elements of that human world to which philosophy addresses itself. Despite this tension, philosophers have traditionally found it easier to locate and legitimate their own enterprise by disentangling philosophy from its topic and to embrace all the more tenaciously the prospects of overcoming its own starting point.

The diversity and richness of the history of thought notwithstanding, that history can be seen as guided by certain fundamental concerns and ideals, and even more by the common denominator of a shared perception of what inhibits the true talents and possibilities of thought. Plato, for instance, whose dominant legacy and metaphysical image is decisive for what follows, is said to have found this hostility between thought and its topic so great as to warrant a description of that initial topic as holding us as thinking beings prisoner in its chains. Only by dint of will and reflection do we come to break these chains and begin the long labor of ascent toward the infinitely bright light of the metaphysical region of the idea of the good where all of the finite and fleeting shadows of below are finally shown to be illusory. Education, knowledge, and the basis upon which the true leader—the philosopher-king—judges find their source beyond the limitations of the limited world of phenomena, a source mirrored in the special discourse and logic of question and answer pointing upward beyond particulars and their peculiar specificity. Generations of other thinkers interpreted this upward way as en route to God, and so saw fit to describe the attachment to the other, to the eternally true and infinitely good God, as a state of sin. When philosophy met and married religion, it was a rocky marriage but nevertheless quite natural: both come forward in response to a sense that what is given and found points beyond itself. Religious thinkers left their mark upon philosophy by intensifying the idea that the infinite stood for a kind of salvation from our own multiple forms of finitude and mortality. For such thinkers grace, faith, prayer, and occasionally reason offered a pathway to the infinite which alone rescued us from this mortal life. It is not surprising then that the history of philosophy and of its efforts to surpass and so understand the given in terms of the language and ideals of metaphysics lend themselves so readily to being characterized as "onto-theology." Whatever else it might be, metaphysics has traditionally been characterized by its embrace of some form of transcendence as the route to a full comprehension of the world around us, and transcendence has traditionally held open the promises and possibilities of the infinite where all limiting conditions of thought are left behind or comprehended and the ideal of the unconditioned is found.

Of course metaphysics is not simple or orthodox; if it were, it is doubtful that it would continue to exert such a claim upon thought. There have been would-be heretics to this rule of the unconditioned for whom the assumption of an other, ontologically prior and un-environed, world is not taken as so self-evident. Likewise, epochs in the history of thought have been defined by challenges to this meta-physical intoxication with the scope and powers of transcendence. The tensions and complexities inherent in the promises of philosophy when compared with its tasks have not escaped the notice of phi-losophy's most creative minds. Yet even those who in one way or another have loosened their attachment to the idea of transcendence and so have renounced this ideal of the metaphysical infinite—this includes most empiricists, Kant from time to time, and Nietzsche in intent, to mention but a few who face the issue in our post-Cartesian framework—generally only demonstrate that sobering up about transcendence and the denial of our full access to the infinite does not necessarily bring with it full release from its grip. Nor do the needs of the unconditioned ever seem to slacken. The empiricists, who never let go of the ideal of the unconditioned—they generally find it in the basic unit of experience rather than another world—can only find release from the idea of the infinite by abandoning the demands of thought that first called for an ontology and called the idea of the infinite into being. For them the refusal to grant thought the capacity to free itself from finite conditions not only entails the denial of the metaphysical way of answering questions, it also means that those all-embracing questions to which metaphysics addressed itself must be left unanswered. Kant, on the other hand, sought to restore the human need and right to raise those questions of "God, freedom, and immortality" on the basis of experience so that the critique of abstractive metaphysics could serve as the rehabilitation of a phenomenally and morally grounded metaphysics. Yet even in this effort to free metaphysics from the rationalist prejudice of his day, Kant pulled back from the original radicality and apparent finality of the limits outlined for reason in the first *Critique* and in Heine's unforgettable phrase resurrects the corpse of the transcendent deist God in the second *Critique*. The infinite and unconditioned were, for Kant, indispensable pillars in support of the moral vision he wanted to defend, and he reasserted their legitimacy as such. And Nietzsche, who went so far as to label the unlimited ambitions of metaphysics a "lie," suffered the deepest tug of the infinite in the rage against that which he denied; for him God's infinite absence in death meant that God's presence was felt all the more profoundly. Even the real test of *amor fati* in the absence of God's presence is described as a kind of infinity and unconditionality of the moment—the eternal recurrence of the same—a notion that asks if we can still love the moment, any moment, infinitely despite the loss of its traditional legitimation. The nihilism of which Nietzsche speaks is clear testimony to his recognition of thought's failure to live up to its own unconditional demands. It is not a consequence of renouncing those demands; quite the contrary, it is a matter of revaluing and reconfiguring them.

In the end there is a certain legitimacy to the view that the long and varied history of western philosophy ultimately "consists in a series of footnotes to Plato,"[1] for it is the record of thought's love affair with all that is represented by the idea of the infinite and unconditioned as the character of the truth to which transcendence delivers us. In the eyes of the tradition it was Plato who, especially in the "Allegory of the Cave" and Diotima's speech, once and for all displayed the erotic pull of the unconditioned for thought and the necessity of thought's dialectical ascent to the infinite. Plato was the first, but far from the last, to write of the special charm and possibility of thought and speech as apparently able to point beyond the limitations of their own topic. Since Plato the task and horizon of philosophy has traditionally come to be understood in terms of this infinite, even if the infinite is conceived and located in a variety of ways.

But ours is clearly one of those epochs that thrives by calling this alliance between thought and the infinite into question. Since Hegel, the last great speculative thinker of the infinite in the continental tradition (Whitehead stands at the similar end of another tradition), metaphysics has generally only fallen into disrepute and decline in the same tradition that once fed so eagerly upon the metaphysical ideal. Even the list of leading continental thinkers after Hegel yields names synonymous with the effort to reclaim philosophy from its metaphysical past: Marx, Kierkegaard, Schopenhauer, Nietzsche, Husserl, Heidegger, Sartre, Merleau-Ponty, Gadamer, Habermas, and Derrida are all names associated with an urgent call to a fundamental redefinition of philosophy, its self-understanding, and its horizon. This legitimation crisis into which philosophy's traditional self-understanding has entered has endured so long and shattered such essential philosophic assumptions that we are not taken aback when we read a remark that would have proved startling for most of philosophy's long history: that "the only real advance that metaphysics has made since the time of Hegel was its decline. It no longer claims to be a science, to say nothing of being the first among the sciences." [2] The air of crisis and urgency, which once filled the work of the early Marx, Kierkegaard, and Nietzsche, has dissipated and given way to a calmer reassessment of metaphysics and the task of thinking today. So it seems that the only surprise about assertions of the end of metaphysics is that they no longer surprise us.

Yet even while speaking of the death of metaphysics, few would deny the living effective history of over two millennia of metaphysics in language, culture, and even in the current shape of practical life. One does not get over metaphysics the way one gets over a cold or former opinions. Nor do many deny that something resembling the traditional conception of metaphysics is "a basic event" (*WM*, 120) determinative of human existence and its possibilities. Yet the fact remains: it is unthinkable that a philosopher after Hegel could make the claim, common until Hegel, that metaphysics as it has traditionally been conceived could ever be the legitimate expression of a realizable human hope. Today we hear a sort of naiveté, not optimism, in Hegel's celebrated remark that "the initially concealed and opaque essence of the universe does not possess the power to resist the courage of knowledge: it must yield itself to knowledge and give its riches and depths over to it" (*VGP*, I, 14). Nevertheless, the provocations and talents of human speaking and thinking that once gave rise to the eventual presumptions underpinning such hope for the metaphysical way of answering human questions still remain. The same untenability of staying put with the isolated moment, with any existing here and now, that propelled the dialectic of Spirit in Hegel's *Phenomenology* remains today, but no longer with the expectation of the eventual achievement of Spirit coming home to itself once again in the moment. What is at stake after Hegel is the question of the commensurability of the talents of thought and speech when measured against the provocations of existence. The crisis in European philosophy after Hegel arises from the confusions about just what can serve as a measure against which we might assess the possibilities and requirements of thought today. Events and ideas since Hegel seem at times to have conspired to render our traditional way of understanding events and the self-sufficiency of ideas ineffective, and because philosophy played a large and central role in this process of sorting out events and ideas, it is not surprising that philosophy would be numbered among the casualties of this seeming conspiracy. And so we find ourselves in a paradox: philosophy, perhaps even in its form as a metaphysical attachment to transcendence and the idea of the infinite, is certainly indispensable for the fullness of human life and experience, but today the prevailing claim is that philosophy, as it has been traditionally conceived, is nevertheless impossible. One hears echoes of Kant frequently today; philosophy's own history seems to have disclosed the dominant idea of philosophy as metaphysics as itself harboring an insurmountable antinomy between philosophy's need and its satisfaction. Occasionally one can even feel Kant's lament about the decline of metaphysics as having become remote from its own task and talents, yet one no longer seems able to share Kant's enthusiasm and hope that metaphysics stands for something to be rescued and rehabilitated. Today it is not the prospects but the end of metaphysics that shapes our concerns. The aporias of our own present, and the perceived failures of philosophy's past, leave many calling for a radical rupture with tradition and a new beginning as the only way of carrying on the best that philosophy has always harbored.

But what does this mean and entail? How does one legitimate the claim to be sufficiently distant from metaphysics to be in a position to speak of its end or even more to speak of the end of philosophy as such? What sort of "position" is it that provides a vantage point upon the long and varied metaphysical tradition so that that same tradition is revealed as, at bottom, always having forgotten something essential? How far can such a "basic event" in human life be dismantled, and what kind of redefinition of human being accompanies this end of metaphysics? Does avoiding excesses of metaphysical speculation mean that all vestiges of the metaphysical infinite must be left behind? What new self-understanding must accompany such a fundamental reevaluation of the horizon of human thought and speech? Before autopsies are performed and metaphysics can be buried, a careful look at these questions is called for: it still remains unclear whether our era is as free of the captivations of metaphysics as it understands itself to be. Are contemporary claims to radicality warranted? Are we radical enough to measure up to those claims? We still need to ask ourselves if we are sufficiently far from the end (s) of metaphysics to justify talk of a new beginning. The dissolution of modernity and its varieties of metaphysics has certainly begun, but it is far from finished.

The truth of the matter is that since Hegel the decline of metaphysics has meant its withering, but not yet its overcoming or abolition. The ideals and seductions of metaphysics are not so easily left behind. The end of metaphysics is a long process, one which yields new bearings for thought only slowly, for the idea of metaphysics itself has become a real factor in the very world it was established to interpret. But it is not simply as an entrenched factor of human history that metaphysics has shown itself to cling so tenaciously to life. It is not an object behind or before us to be gotten around or overcome; it is not like the set of keys or pocket knife we can misplace or replace; it is rather such a habit of the mind that the fight against metaphysics is equally a fight against ourselves. When looked at closely, we find that our contemporary self-understanding seems too deeply entangled in ideas, ideals, and the claims of the unconditioned to permit any easy divorce from such habits. Metaphysics might, in the end, be an impossibility, or even error, for us; but the possibility of attempting something like what metaphysics once was said to be remains as a basic fact that any future effort to come to terms with the place and possibilities of thought needs to confront. When we are honest about the ways we do in fact judge, act, and understand our world, that is, when we reflect, for instance, upon contemporary technology and the administration of states and peoples, we find the language and habits of metaphysics alive and well—even if unwelcome. While we find a basic flaw in what metaphysics has become, it is important that we recognize that the effort to overcome metaphysics, to answer to the task of post-Hegelian thought, while preserving the special genius of philosophic reflection, is no easy matter. It is also important to recognize that such an effort requires a serious confrontation with the past as both no longer tenable and not yet at an end.

Most of the serious contemporary efforts to break out of the empire of metaphysical reflection have recognized this need and so have established themselves in a confrontation with some exemplary representative of metaphysics. Hegel is the opponent of choice in the majority of these confrontations. Marx, Kierkegaard, Nietzsche, Dilthey, Heidegger, Merleau-Ponty, Gadamer, Habermas, and Derrida have all frequently singled out Hegel in their own efforts to criticize the metaphysical tradition. There are many reasons for this choice, but two closely related ones stand out as particularly important. First, Hegel is watershed figure, among the last self-acknowledged subscribers to the task and route of metaphysical speculation attached to the idea of the infinite and the ideal of the unconditioned. But Hegel is a Janus-faced figure who also calls for an end to metaphysics as it had been known, since he is intolerant of the ways in which his own predecessors finitized the infinite by opposing it to the finite. In this regard he is a predecessor to contemporary attempts to overcome metaphysics and so offers a critical wedge to this end within metaphysics itself. As such, Hegel is both a champion of metaphysics and easily won over as a champion of the effort to overcome its past. Second, more than being just another champion of the cause, Hegel is the self-avowed completer of metaphysics. He understands himself as having fulfilled the Greek metaphysical-conceptual task of uncovering the rational order lying behind both physis and human affairs. This is what he expresses when announcing that in the *Science of Logic* we are presented with "God ... as he is in his eternal essence before the creation of nature and of finite Spirit" (*WL*, 31). As such, Hegel represents metaphysical thought carried to its extreme. His claim, of course, is that he carries a real possibility of finite Spirit to its full and necessary infinite consequences. The claim of many of his successors is that he is the height of the metaphysical error.

Yet between Hegel and his successors there remains always the common denominator of the claim that philosophy as metaphysics has come to an end. But even on this point of agreement it must be said that the senses of "end" invoked are obviously quite different: for Hegel metaphysics has reached its end as perfection, it has come home to itself and rests in its telos; for his successors the end of metaphysics signals its demise and the disclosure of the fundamental error of its leading assumptions. The contemporary consensus, shaped in part by Hegel, is that philosophy as it has been carried out since its basic Greek formation is no longer the way it should be carried out henceforth. Post-Hegelian thought is marked by an unwillingness to accept the conception of philosophy that Hegel inherited from Kant as an ancient conception to be rejuvenated for a modern world; namely, that philosophy is, and should be, the queen of the sciences and so the science of what is fundamental. Unlike critical moments in the past when the call went out for a new foundation and new conceptual frame for the sake of an advance in metaphysics, the current call to acknowledge the untenability of that conception of philosophy and so the end of metaphysics claims to be of another order altogether, for it is equally a call to a fundamental restructuring of the self-conception of philosophy itself.

There have been several and assorted attempts to reclaim philosophy from metaphysics, but until Heidegger none had the conceptual and historical force, precision, and scope found in Hegel. Kierkegaard, Schopenhauer, and Nietzsche, for instance, while offering penetrating criticisms of metaphysics, were never able to burrow from within the conceptual frame of metaphysics itself. Their assault was carried not by a power to reshape and renegotiate the basic concepts of metaphysics such that metaphysics itself was rendered untenable; rather they rested their critique upon a poetic and literary force that clearly reached beyond the confines of the philosophic tradition but was taken as too reckless to touch those who had already made a commitment to metaphysics and what it represents. The lasting impact and yet to be discovered contributions of these thinkers is not to be diminished; quite the contrary, since it might be the case that they are in need of still greater appreciation. Clearly the force and radicality of their drive beyond traditional metaphysical categories—beyond either/or and good/evil—established standards for challenges to philosophy still to come. But these assaults on the metaphysical tradition by solitary thinkers, who were among the first thinkers of human solitude, might have touched upon something felt to be lacking in metaphysics, but they never succeeded in winning away from metaphysics that authority and seductive power characteristic of the metaphysical appeal to the infinite and unconditioned.

In the continental tradition it is perhaps Husserl who made the first serious bid to reclaim the grounds and concepts of metaphysics for something other than a metaphysical ontology. His rewriting of formal and transcendental logic, his rethinking of the Kantian and Cartesian subjects, his recasting of transcendence as intentionality, and his analysis of the contemporary crisis of the sciences are all efforts that belong to this post-Hegelian tradition of coming to terms with the possibility of philosophy after Hegel. Working squarely within the philosophic tradition, and addressing its ancient questions and concerns, Husserl sought to break through the conceptual frames of traditional philosophy in order to overcome philosophy's traditional neglect of the real phenomenal content of the world in all of its specificity and abundance. But Husserl's attempt to return to the phenomena as that lost to the metaphysical approach lacked the radicality and existential appeal long previously established as requirements for the overcoming of metaphysics. Despite the sensibility that motivated his battle cry of "back to the things themselves," and the effort to reestablish contact with a lived world by focusing upon the fundamental intentionality of consciousness, Husserl never succeeded in fully legitimating his own phenomenological ontology. The full force and weight of history and of language, issues that Hegel had already disclosed as unavoidable for challenges to philosophy's past, never quite emerge out of the Husserlian conception of the life-world. Even in his later works, after existentialism had made some productive entry into the avenues opened by phenomenology, the full sense of the existential dimension of experience and our entanglements in finite conditions as disclosed by Kierkegaard or Nietzsche is missing in Husserl. Nevertheless, even if his imaginative reach fell short of the task, Husserl's battle cry of "back to the things themselves," and his basic phenomenological assumptions, did provide key elements that had been lacking in earlier bids to overcome metaphysics: the conceptual rigor and phenomenological evidence that he established lent a precision, rigor, and authority to philosophizing not found since Hegel.

The idea of evidence is all important here, for with his self-imposed criterion of the apodicticity of the grounds of any phenomenological ontology, Husserl did not rest the validity of his claims simply upon the appeal to inwardness and its insights. Prior to Husserl there seemed to be no route by which any discourse that presented itself as outside or exempt from traditional standards of justification could legitimate itself. In particular, the demands of certainty and consistency, and the language of grounds repeatedly reassert their rights as incumbent upon speech and thought. While it became increasingly clear that it was precisely such traditional standards that needed to be called into question, they seemed to have taken on such an air of self-evidence that the only way to escape them seemed to require the abandonment of the idea of any standards and justification whatsoever. Among the first problems that confronted post-Hegelian efforts to break through to a new style of thought and speech was the problem of locating and legitimating such a nonmetaphysical discourse in the face of long accepted metaphysical standards of legitimacy. The antimetaphysical polemic of Kierkegaard, for instance, lived on its reassertion of the metaphysically neglected truths of inwardness and ambiguity but lacked the "grounds" needed to establish a full, alternative, nonmetaphysical vision founded upon that truth. Because they could not recover the legitimating grounds of discourse from metaphysics, because the very notion of legitimacy had become metaphysical, the critical intent in thinkers such as Kierkegaard, Schopenhauer, and Nietzsche was never able to give way to a discourse freed from its (anti) metaphysicalities. Nihilism remains as the only outcome of a critique still deeply entangled in the standards and language that are the target of that critique. Husserl's phenomenology, in particular its methodological concerns, turned itself directly to the task of justifying a set of possibilities for the legitimating grounds and alternative language of philosophy. That is Husserl's true legacy to Heidegger, for it is this pointed conceptual thrust to establish a new nonmetaphysical mode of discourse found in Husserl's early version of phenomenology that in Heidegger is wedded to the radicality of an existential analysis of human facticity. It is in this respect, as the wedding of two separate but mutually requisite post-Hegelian efforts to break through metaphysics, that Heidegger's own starting point in existential phenomenological ontology presents the first challenge to metaphysics since Hegel that not only sets itself up as antimetaphysical, but also as en route to legitimating a truly nonmetaphysical form of philosophic discourse. Speech and thought that define themselves as *anti*metaphysical fail to present a real alternative to metaphysics since they are defined by their antagonistic tie to metaphysics. That is why Heidegger is able to regard Nietzsche as the "last" metaphysician and to find him suffering from the most extreme metaphysical displacement of thought: Nietzsche's critiques of philosophy and religion, and his efforts to recover the life of the will-to-power in the agon of tragedy, ultimately receive too much of their shape from that which they are set against. Hölderlin is more radical that Nietzsche in this respect.

Like his predecessors in the effort to destroy the metaphysical tradition, Heidegger is concerned with reestablishing the importance and fundamentality of some essential and ineradicable, if only varyingly visible, "truth"—described by these thinkers variously as finitude, limitation, mortality, worldliness, facticity, immanence, or the ontological difference—that metaphysics traditionally sought to overcome as something holding thought captive. Recovering or rehabilitating this "truth" requires the destruction of metaphysics and its standards of truth. The "essence" of "truth" and "grounds" get rethought so that all their traditional trademarks—certainty, singularity, stability, unconditionality, and consistency—lose their hold upon thought. This effort to destroy metaphysics is the "negative" dimension of Heidegger's thought. But to a degree unprecedented in those who participated in this effort before him, Heidegger also sees his task equally as establishing a new ontology that finds its grounds outside those grounds that have necessarily metaphysical consequences. It is this second, "positive," dimension of Heidegger's project that has led him into a careful and attentive dialogue with leading representatives of the metaphysical tradition in his continual effort to disentangle his own discourse from metaphysics. And it is also this task that has spawned the greatest controversy and confusion surrounding Heidegger's work, for the effort to navigate beyond both nihilism and metaphysics is not easy: from the point of view of one, it always looks like Heidegger has fallen victim to the other. The project to overcome metaphysics without always speaking only against metaphysics required an unprecedented creative effort on Heidegger's part, not the least element of which has been the fashioning and finding of a language and legitimating measure appropriate to the task.

Despite the apparent lack of precedent for this project Heidegger generally regards four thinkers as speaking about living themes, preludes, and anticipations pertinent to his own understanding of the overcoming of metaphysics. Aristotle, Kant, Hegel, and Nietzsche are each life-long concerns for Heidegger, and each plays a central role in the development of his own efforts to recover and redirect thought. While from the outset Aristotle, Kant, and Nietzsche are typically regarded as witnesses to and partners in Heidegger's own project, Hegel is more frequently cast in the role of a counterfeit witness and so as an opponent to that project. In this way Heidegger reveals himself as belonging to the post-Hegelian era that early on recognized the need to confront Hegel. It is especially evident that during the first two decades of his long career Heidegger takes the Hegelian dialectic and the decisions to which it leads as an exemplary representative of the forgetfulness of Being. Yet at the same time Heidegger concedes that Hegelian thought, the first to usher in the end of metaphysics, frequently bears at least a surface kinship to the very phenomenological ontology that Heidegger himself tries to outline as the basis for the destruction of metaphysics. Hegelian thought is the end of metaphysics as its apotheosis, and it is this by virtue of its own rethinking and radicalizing of the possibilities and topics of thought. In his own phenomenology of Spirit Hegel is the first to take a retrospective look at metaphysics as a unity, and in doing that Hegel is the first to ask seriously about the possibilities of thought that is no longer speaking from within that unity. But while the ascendancy of metaphysics might no longer be at work in Hegel, his purpose is to preserve, rather than overcome, the fully ascended form of metaphysics. Hegel is the first to develop a clear concept of modernity, but unlike Heidegger his intention is to preserve the genius of modernity in that concept. That is why Heidegger says that the "overcoming of Hegel is an intrinsically necessary step in the development of Western philosophy, one which must be made if philosophy itself is to remain alive" (*GP*, 254). And that is why Heidegger devotes such enormous energies to working out the details of his own claims in a confrontation with Hegel. The largest and most basic Heideggerian concerns frequently arise out of the minutiae of Heidegger's critique of Hegel. The confrontation with Hegelian thought and texts must be seen as central to the development of Heidegger's own thought and texts. To neglect or underestimate the importance of this confrontation is to fail to recognize the extent to which Heidegger's work belongs essentially to the historical debate that is still being carried on today: the debate arising from the problems and unresolved questions of modernity and the claims of postmodernity. Heidegger, like the best of his predecessors in this debate, recognized Hegel as the Janus-faced figure he is and so as sitting squarely in the interstices opened up by the historical clash between modernity and postmodernity, metaphysics and its overcoming.

The speculative and synthetic nature of Hegelian thought enables it at least to claim to escape the traditional metaphysical prejudice in favor of some form of "ontological primacy."[3] With few exceptions, metaphysical thought has been guided by a first principle in the face of which all else is seen to be ontologically subordinate. The rewards of such an ontologically primary first principle, which can function as the adjudicating standard against which the real is measured, are quite clear: principles are the great talents of thought, and with them comes a certain clarity. But the danger of holding fast to such principles, of making principles rather than the phenomena to be explained the intractable topic of thought, should also be borne in mind: that the real puzzles and aporias before us are either squeezed into an unconditioned framework of principles or that intellectual contortions are required to hold all one's principles together. In this Descartes' discussion of the mind-body relation serves as a fine warning: the rigor of his principles led him into the absurdities of his talk of the pineal gland. The special challenge of Hegel is that he dedicates himself to overcoming any form of thought that attaches itself to principles over the phenomena that embody those principles and that thereby sets itself up as essentially other than its topic, and this means that Hegel's dedication to the infinite and unconditioned is not made at the immediate expense of the finite and limiting conditions. More than perhaps any other metaphysical thinker, Hegel makes many essential decisions on behalf of the finite, for he recognizes that merely leaving the finite behind leaves it outside of the infinite and as such leaves it as a limiting condition to the infinite itself. Hegel emphasizes that outside of the infinite the finite is fixed in opposition to its own intelligible basis, and an absolute ontological bifurcation rather than the real satisfaction of metaphysics is the result. Hegel does not want to sacrifice the finite and all of the aporias it carries upon some altar of unconditioned principles. Quite the contrary. The essential thrust of the dialectic is rooted in this intolerance for any species of exteriority and the inequality and domination that it produces. The dialectic of the master and slave is only the most celebrated attempt to disclose the essential instability and failure of any effort to organize or understand the world short of the infinite union found in the full complexity of Absolute Spirit. In Hegel the universal is not able to be thought apart from the particular but always only as the concrete universal; similarly, the infinite is not the finite infinite limited by being other to the finite itself but is the inner infinity of the relation between the infinite and the finite. By means of the unifying power and ineluctability of Absolute Spirit, Hegel seeks to overcome the traditional metaphysical prejudice in favor of an infinite and ontologically primary principle that is separate from the finite. Ontologizing the world in the infinity of Spirit's own concretization, Hegel is able to confront those concrete expressions of finitude that lie outside of the domain of traditional metaphysical reflection. Thus, to an extent not even found in previous critics of metaphysics—even one as radical as Kant—Hegel has much to say about human experiences of finitude such as time, nothingness, history, anxiety, repetition, circularity, work, language, culture, and the history of philosophy. Each of these topics, conspicuously absent in the largely conceptual enterprise that constitutes the history of metaphysics prior to Hegel, becomes a central concern for the philosophical upheavals that follow in Hegel's wake. This is another reason why the project to overcome metaphysics cannot avoid a confrontation with Hegel.

Heidegger recognized that Hegelian thought does not easily fit into traditional metaphysical molds, that Hegel's effort to think the finite in its infinite inner relation to the infinite posed a special challenge to Heidegger's own effort to legitimate a phenomenological ontology of finite Being. Contrary to Heidegger's understanding of the meaning of radical finitude, Hegel argues that the full reconstruction of the experience of finitude discloses it as always having been what it is by virtue of its relation to the Absolute, which first becomes visible once philosophy comes to an end but which was always already latently present, even before the culmination of philosophy in Hegel. For Hegel the evidence for this argument is, at least in part, historical: only after the dialectic of history has disclosed finite Being as such as that behind which thought cannot penetrate does the true inner infinity of finite Being itself first become visible. Only at this historically achieved point does the truth of finite Being, as itself disclosing the Absolute, become visible. Thus if Heidegger is to articulate an ontology of finite Being as such, then he must do so by reclaiming the idea of the finite from Hegel and by disclosing the fundamental finitude of the Hegelian system itself. This quarrel over the finite and its meaning, and the effort to show how even the dialectic of the finite and infinite ultimately falls back into a hermeneutics of finitude, remains the issue at the core of much of what follows after Heidegger. Gadamer himself, perhaps more than anyone else, working out of the center of this quarrel, put the question that Heidegger faced, which this book seeks to answer, succinctly: "Whether or not the all-encompassing dialectical mediation of all the possible paths of thought, which Hegel undertook, necessarily gives the lie to every attempt to break out of the circle of reflection in which thought thinks itself. In the end, is even the position which Heidegger sought to find against Hegel caught in the circle of the inner infinity of reflection? ... or is his questioning radical enough and comprehensive enough not to omit any of what Hegel asked and yet to inquire behind Hegel's position?"[4] In significant respects that is the historically couched form of the question confronting the continental tradition of philosophy today: our update on the ancient *gigantomachia peri tes ousias*.

In addressing himself to this question, in his own confrontation with Hegelian thought, Heidegger sometimes forgets his own counsel that "all refutation in the field of essential thought is foolishness" (*BH*, 333), and so it is easy to find passages in Heidegger's texts that treat Hegel as a sort of metaphysical straw man set up to be refuted. Frequently, Heidegger defines the thrust of his own thought in terms of what he regards as the clarity of its separation from Hegelian thought. Thus, as late as 1965, we find Heidegger saying that "[Investigation into the topic of thought] soon discloses that all thought is finite. Its finitude does not reside only, or even initially, in the limitations of human capacities, but in the finitude of the topic of thought itself. Experiencing this finitude is far more difficult than the hasty preparation of an Absolute" (*ZF*, 20). The context of this passage, which poses Heidegger's relation to the whole of philosophy, the "step back," to Hegel's dialectical mediation of history, makes it clear that this remark is directed against Hegel. For the most part however, Heidegger recognizes that his task is not to refute Hegel but instead to draw Hegelian thought into that experience of the finite from which the presumptions and claims of metaphysics are no longer possible. One of the most important ways in which Heidegger set about validating his own nonmetaphysical approach to finite Being is to be found in just such a painstaking effort to uncover and so recover experiences of the finite remaining as the residue of thought that has been seduced into the untenable conclusion of metaphysics. Likewise, the purpose in confronting Hegel and Heidegger in what follows is not a matter of proving or correcting the "mistakes" in Heidegger's reading of Hegel, or of letting one thinker "best" the other, but of asking just how far Heidegger has succeeded in undermining the all-embracing infinity of the Hegelian system. To what extent has Heidegger wrestled the finite away from its metaphysical interpretation given it by Hegel? To what extent has Heidegger succeeded in pointing to the insurmountable aporias of the ubiquity of finitude despite Hegel's demonstration of an intelligible pattern to such ubiquitousness of the finite? Is Heidegger able to distinguish between Hegel's sensitivity to the ubiquity of the *finite*, and Hegel's his attempt to disclose the intelligible pattern residing in it?

The confrontation between Hegel and Heidegger not only centers about essential philosophical topics raised by the notion of finitude but leads to questions about the possibilities and scope of philosophy itself. The question that ultimately surfaces in this confrontation is not simply one concerning the truth or truths of finite Being—its nature or "what"—but the question that asks how far finite Being points beyond itself, inviting thought to act and judge on the basis of principles that are grounded in such Being but are themselves nevertheless beyond the rough edges and obscurities that come under the heading of "finitude." How does the finite fight its own ubiquity? To what extent does the ubiquity of the finite exhibit an "intelligible pattern"? To what extent is any such pattern fated to ambiguity and concealment? To what extent is the discourse about such a pattern itself finite? The traditional attachment to the ideals of clarity, wholeness, and unconditionality have always militated against any tolerance for such ambiguities. Renewing the question of finite Being involves the question of the possible horizons of the thinking of such Being. In short, the issue at the end of every stage in the Hegel-Heidegger confrontation is just how far philosophy can continue to act and understand itself as it has traditionally done since Plato. Consequently, when Heidegger outlines and comes to terms with what he sees as the Hegelian achievement in the history of metaphysics, he is not simply cataloguing and judging the decisions of an important and influential thinker in a bygone tradition. Rather, he is trying to redefine the horizon of thought's own possibilities by demonstrating that Hegelian thought can only understand itself as infinite by having forgotten something essential about the finite that still lies at its basis. Heidegger's contention is that remembering the finite points to the inability of thought to ground itself in such a way that it can ultimately return to itself as unconditioned and so be the sort of master in its own house that Hegel finds it to be. Key, and often baffling, Heideggerian concepts such as the ontological difference, the fourfold, the clearing, and the event of appropriation are all efforts to articulate a discourse the fundamental character of which is precisely this commemoration of the essential and radical finite. Such concepts do not succeed in their task simply by their strangeness. It is quite true that "one does not simply transcend metaphysics by introducing a concept that makes no sense to metaphysics,"[5] but by recapturing phenomena as well as the force of the language that interpret such phenomena. If we are to take Heidegger seriously, then the question that must be asked is how far has he succeeded in validating the discourse of commemorative thinking [*andenkendes Denken*] and its corresponding ontology of the finite despite the competing and overlapping claims of the Hegelian speculative dialectic. To what extent does Heidegger's commemorative, meditative thinking escape the metaphysical assumptions and claims of the empire of infinite speculative thought? What sort of "evidence" can Heidegger appeal to in order to argue on behalf of the essential finitude of Being without laying claim to a privileged and unconditioned basis for such an ontology? Can Heidegger ever hope to develop a basis for such a nonmetaphysical ontology, or has he put himself in the position of constantly debasing the very possibility of his own discourse on Being?

Heidegger's destruction of metaphysics is not so simple, unambiguous, or so single-minded as many have found it. Overcoming the tradition is the signal of the full recovery, not the abdication of the riddles of the topics and tasks of thought. The destruction of metaphysics does not imply the denial or refusal of those fundamental transcendent experiences that have always been appealed to in the self-justifications of metaphysics. Essential experiences, experiences such as anxiety, language, love, imagination, hope, history, and perhaps even aspects of faith, remain—or at least have a potential place—at the basis of Heidegger's nonmetaphysical ontology. He does not deny such experiences of transcendence, but frequently appeals to them; yet rather than finding these experiences paths to metaphysics and the infinite, Heidegger argues that they too point to the fundamental tentativeness, provisionality, and incompleteness inherent in all experience. The verticality and ascendance of transcendence is never detached from the essential finitude of the jurisdiction and horizons disclosed by the phenomenological analysis of such experiences. Heidegger's further claim is that no ontology is possible outside the horizons outlined by the conditions of the possibility disclosed by this sense of finite transcendence, yet he also wants to argue that when properly thought the finite does not simply hold us captive, as had long been assumed by the metaphysical tradition. Rethinking the finite, the first topic of philosophy and that which calls for thought, is the task of philosophy as Heidegger sees it. But how does this notion of finite transcendence, and other distinctively Heideggerian expressions of finitude, cripple the march of the Hegelian dialectic as on the way to the Absolute? What precisely is the Heideggerian insight that not only refuses to be drawn into the teleological pull of the infinite but also reveals the "whys" and "wherefores" of the infinite itself as a forgetfulness and the extreme form of thought's own captivity? Such questions are directed to the point from out of which Heidegger undertakes his basic project of overcoming metaphysics. A project that has come to define the basic tenor of much philosophizing after Heidegger.

Heidegger makes it clear that while insight into the end of metaphysics does not entail the release from the claims of philosophy, it does require more than simply gerrymandering the traditional philosophic framework. There is a need to maintain a delicate balance on many points, one situated between or beyond nihilism on the one hand and metaphysics on the other. Hegel is not the only pole with respect to which Heidegger must situate his own thought: Nietzsche represents another outcome of metaphysics not fully commensurate with Heidegger's concerns. Time, history, Being and non-Being, the circularity of truth and originality, language, and identity and difference become some of the issues raised by Heidegger's effort to recast the topics and tasks of thinking after metaphysics. Each of these themes is approached in order to recover an essential experience of thought that is shut out by the metaphysical attachment to the infinite and unconditioned. The very matrix of these concerns, all directed to overcoming the paralysis of Being characteristic of metaphysical ontologies, has itself already had a real impact in redirecting the continental philosophic tradition. Nevertheless, we are still only between "two eves" [6]—that represented by being after both Heidegger and Hegel. Before we move too hastily forward and eagerly stake out our own "post-modern" ontologies and strategies, it is necessary to take yet another, more detailed look at the successes at deconstructing the tradition. The purpose of such a critical assessment of this project, of such a look back, is not at all to reclaim or rehabilitate the tradition as it saw itself (in fact the very claim that "the" tradition ever saw itself as such betrays a sort of contemporary naiveté); it is rather as a test and deepening of the radicality of contemporary efforts to confront modernity and metaphysics that such a detailed confrontation with the claims of Hegel, perhaps the most radical metaphysical thinker, are needed. If we are to avoid simply moving to a new metaphysics of the finite, then a radical test of the first, and still decisive, destruction of the tradition is requisite. Again it is Gadamer who anticipates the spirit of this project: "When science rises to a total technocracy and the corresponding 'night' of the 'forgetfulness of Being,' which was prophesied by Nietzsche, approaches, can one look back to the last glimmer of the declining sun in the evening sky, instead of turning around and looking for the first flickerings of its return?" [7] One might put the matter more forcefully: looking back is the requisite prelude to moving forward.

That is the real purpose of this confrontation between Hegel and Heidegger: to ask what Heidegger has left as a legacy for contemporary thought. Since Hegel philosophers have been faced with the challenge of Hegel who, thanks to his rare capacity "to think against himself, and to observe and record himself doing so," [8] seems to both invite and defeat efforts to overcome the empire of reflection he describes. Heidegger is among the most serious challenges to Hegel, to the same extent that Hegel poses a challenge to Heidegger's own effort to avoid entanglement in the excesses of thinking characteristic of metaphysics. The overlap of concerns coupled with ambiguous intentions and conflicting claims makes the confrontation between Hegel and Heidegger the site of multiple entanglements. Disentangling the issues and decisions is not a matter of staking out "positions"; it is even less a matter of finding one thinker right or the other wrong. Nor is the inability to disentangle Hegel and Heidegger the signal that Hegel was ahead of "his time" or that Heidegger is behind "the times"; it merely signals that the dialogue between thinkers—a dialogue that has its own rules and history—is always finally guided by the topics of thought. Yet only if we move forward carefully and patiently does the deconstruction and end of metaphysics pave the way to the context for the breezes of a genuine, if not entirely new, beginning that does not degenerate into a pretext for our own prejudices. Recuperating the finite and staking out the horizons of thinking and speaking disclosed by the finite at this historical juncture brings along a renewed conviction that there is no legitimacy to the seductive and long-standing prejudice that this present historical juncture—no matter when—represents a privileged place from which a full-fledged new beginning may be launched. In the end, the renunciation of this prejudice, the disclosure of the aporias of the finite as ubiquitous, as well as the atopological character of a thinking and speaking that tries not to deny this situation brings in turn the recognition that the special genius of philosophy ultimately only remains true to itself when it understands itself as being on but one of many edges from which one may speak and think of the finite. Philosophy's excellence leads to a twofold dissolution, or overcoming, of philosophy proper: first, by overreaching its own topic and legitimation; second, by reaching beyond its own horizons into other not always commensurate modes of speaking and thinking its own topic. The end of philosophy does not mean its termination but its self-opening up into its own plural modes and the larger modes of pluralities within and against which philosophic discourse is located. Such are the ends of philosophy disclosed by the confrontation between Hegel and Heidegger.

To that end, in what follows, Heidegger's critique of Hegel is allowed to determine the themes and issues in their confrontation. It is in the details and their chronological and thematic development that the confrontation between Hegel and Heidegger is to be worked out, for it is in the real complexity of the details, not in synthetic claims or criticisms, that the full meaning and scope of what is at stake comes into view. If Heidegger is to speak about the end of philosophy and to recover the full aporia of the finite from Hegel's claims to have disclosed the truth of the finite in the agony of the Absolute, then what must be disclosed in these issues is their variety, conflict, and lack of monolithic character. If Heidegger's critique of Hegel as representative of the forgetfulness characteristic of metaphysics is to have any force, then the confrontation with Hegel cannot merely be the confrontation with Hegel taken as a "representative." The most important reason for taking Heidegger's critique of Hegel as the unifying thread of this confrontation is that by making explicit the role that the confrontation with Hegel played in Heidegger's efforts to overcome metaphysics, otherwise submerged yet important themes in those efforts gain a new prominence. For instance, by following Heidegger's critique of Hegel, renewed emphasis falls upon the critique of technology and its relation to work and culture (see chapter 5) as well as the question of the relation of art (see chapter 3) and history (see chapter 6) to truth. Systematically reading Heidegger's reading of Hegel is a way of bringing into sharper focus precisely those issues that stand at the center of contemporary post-Hegelian, and specifically postmodern, attempts to realize the overcoming of philosophy as metaphysics. The price of such a hermeneutic decision is that themes that one might anticipate as of importance to the issue—such as Hegel's claim to have unified philosophy and theology—submerge and only play a background role. Nevertheless, the decision to follow Heidegger's critique of Hegel is also a way of presenting Heidegger's thought in terms of a unity of purpose evident only over the longest stretch of his career. But while Heidegger determines the topics of the confrontation with Hegel here, the final question at each stage of that confrontation is always directed at Heidegger upon whom some sort of "proof" is incumbent if he is to lay claim to have succeeded in pointing to a new context for a nonmetaphysical ontology of finite Being. Reading Hegel through the optic of Heidegger's concerns and holding Heidegger to the standards established by his own critique of Hegel is a way of rotating both positions along the axis of the other and so yields interesting portraits of each. But more important than the resulting portraits is that both Hegel and Heidegger want to lay claim to being at the end of philosophy, and neither can legitimate that claim except in the confrontation with the other. Ultimately the confrontation between Hegel and Heidegger focuses upon the rights, scope, and entitlement granted by the topics of philosophy to a thinking and speaking that describes itself as philosophic.

1

Time and the Thinking of Being

What is this dream of time, this strange and bitter miracle of living? . . . . Is it to feel, when furious day is done, the evening hush, the sorrow of lost, fading light, far sounds and broken cries, and footsteps, voices, music, murmurous, immense and mighty in the air?
— *Thomas Wolfe*

If metaphysics has been a hymn to the infinite, then Heidegger's intentions are matched in sacrilege perhaps only by Nietzsche, for from *Being and Time* forward his purpose has been to demolish and remove the traditional metaphysical idols in order to recover what he describes as the original experiences of the finitude of Being. Heidegger's claim is that this original experience, in itself quite slippery and not easily grasped, has progressively withdrawn from the central concerns of philosophy and has been further concealed by the expectations, language, and self-understanding of philosophy's own effective history. Embedded and entangled in its own preconceptions, philosophy has lost sight of those radical experiences of originary phenomena that continually inspire metaphysical speculation in the first place.

Against this tradition Heidegger argues that the destruction of those leading and basic metaphysical prejudices will clear the way to a renewed understanding of Being as finite, an understanding hostile to the basic framework of metaphysics. In light of these antimetaphysical intentions, it is quite legitimate to characterize *Being and Time* as a prolonged meditation on the insurmountable nature and meaning of a sense of radical finitude absent in the philosophic tradition. While it takes as its clue the essential finitude of the human way of being, it does not want to stop there. Not an existentialist study in the ambiguities of human existence à la Kierkegaard but intended as a phenomenological contribution to fundamental ontology in the tradition of Plato and Aristotle, Heidegger's argument here is that Being itself is fundamentally and insurmountably finite and that the essential element of all presence is that it comes to be and to pass away according to a temporal structure hitherto neglected or distorted by the post-Platonic philosophic tradition. Recognizing this temporality of Being, Heidegger claims, would reveal as intenable most of the guiding assumptions of philosophy as we know it. Furthermore, since the assumptions of this same tradition have been woven in the language and self-definition of philosophy, Heidegger contends that in order to think the meaning of Being as finite, we must first destroy the key operative concepts that have governed philosophy since Plato. His reasoning on this point, while controversial, is quite simple: since its inception philosophy has been governed—even in absentia—by the ideal of an infinite and omnipresent mind, and as the surrender to this metaphysical image, that is as ontotheology, it is blind to the true finitude of Being. Governed by the will to an absolute and unconditioned ground, philosophy, as metaphysics, becomes an expression of the forgetfulness of Being rather than the thinking of Being. In the metaphysical attempt to ground and thereby unravel and overcome the finite, it reveals its basic hostility to the original experience of Being, which is its own reason for being. Hence the call for the destruction of metaphysics and the attempt to recover the true "grounds" upon which it rests.

Thus, according to his own self-understanding, Heidegger has two related tasks in *Being and Time*: to provide the basic phenomenological evidence on behalf of the fundamental finitude of Being and to undermine the long established and instituted obstacles to the further thinking of Being by demonstrating the priority of his phenomenological ontology against leading and decisive representatives of the metaphysical tradition. In line with this twofold task Heidegger introduces *Being and Time* by announcing a two-part text with each part divided into three sections. The first part is largely dedicated to the phenomenological demonstration of the temporality of Being, while the second part was to have been given over to the task of reevaluating and deconstructing key elements in the metaphysical tradition. But it is important to bear in mind that the published portion of the text only covers the first two sections of part one, and so there is an essential incompleteness in the claims of the first part as well as a virtually complete absence of the effort to further defend those claims by showing them to be both prior to, and incompatible with, the grounds of metaphysics, as metaphysics conceives those grounds. Compared with the unblushing promises and anticipations of the introduction, the text as we have it is but a torso. Given what *Being and Time* itself teaches regarding the projective structure of any interpretation and the guiding role of prejudice in understanding, it seems only in the spirit of Heidegger that this truncation of its own project should be raised as the leading issue in any consideration of that project. If there is a real flaw in the conception and carrying out of the phenomenological project outlined in *Being and Time*, then that flaw itself deserves further attention.

Strangely, Heidegger remained rather silent on this matter.[9] Later in his career, when he spoke of *Being and Time* as still belonging to the very metaphysical tradition it was to topple, he said that initially external circumstances intervened—namely, a German species of publish or perish—leading him to publish the first two sections prematurely, yet with the full intention of later publishing the entire work as projected. But some years later, following further circumstantial delays in the announced project, he began the celebrated "turn" in his thinking, and only after this turn was he able to fully realize that the existential starting point of the text was insufficiently radical and so still trapped within the framework of thought that it sought to undercut. But there is something not very satisfactory about this answer. It leaves *Being and Time* as an important, but misfired, attempt at the new brand of philosophizing that Heidegger called for and only later developed. Heidegger's own later remarks on *Being and Time*—namely, that it is "subjectivistic," "voluntaristic," and "too Kierkegaardian"—are too vague to be of any help when trying to understand why this book, which perhaps more than any other single work of this century has defined the topology of continental philosophy, failed to measure up to its own announced intentions. In the end, any critical interpretation of Heidegger's position in *Being and Time* must look for the source of the disjunction between Heidegger's intention of remembering the finitude of Being, which did not alter in an essential way in the course of his career, and his claims and real achievements in that text. In many ways Heidegger's later career is best understood as a response to what is disclosed by the failure of that first attempt to dismantle metaphysics and so make way for an ontology that remembers the radical finitude of Being.

In *Being and Time* Heidegger claims to have demonstrated that any and all possible ways of understanding or comprehending the world are founded in the temporal openness of Dasein. The bulk of the second section of the text is dedicated to providing the phenomeno-logical evidence and argument for this claim announced in the first section. But Heidegger has also contended that his conception of the temporality of Dasein is a more original and primary phenomenon than can be grasped from the vantage point of metaphysics. That is why the second section (the final section of the published text) concludes with a chapter in which Heidegger's motive is to compare his notion of time as witnessed in the finite temporal structure of Dasein with what he claims is the traditional metaphysical concept of time as infinite. His argument is that no thinker has yet adequately escaped the metaphysical prejudice in favor of omnipresence and eternity, and that this prejudice has blinded philosophers to the original temporal finitude of all Being as presence. In other words, Heidegger's claim is that because the finite temporal openness of Dasein is the precondition and foundation for any thought at all, and because this "original time" has gone unthought, the foundation upon which the metaphysical thinking of Being has been built and from which it receives its structure has gone unthought throughout the history of metaphysics. This is why Heidegger calls metaphysics "the forgetfulness of Being," where Being is understood as appearing within the horizon of this finite temporal openness. The unpublished portion of the text was to carry the implications of this discovery one step further and demonstrate how the rethinking of this original temporal horizon of any comprehension of Being is simultaneously the destruction of the grounds and very possibility of metaphysics. While the full execution of this second step remains absent from the text, the last published pages of the text do serve as a preliminary trial of this confrontation between Heidegger's phenomenological ontology and metaphysics.

More than merely "rounding out" the treatment of time in *Being and Time*, these last pages of the text are intended to form the authentic reappropriation of the ordinary understanding of *Being*[-in-the-world] in the largest, most fundamental context of primordial *time*;

that is, they are intended to explode the restrictive naiveté of the traditional concept of time and thus open up anew our access to the question of the meaning of Being by outlining the horizon for any understanding of Being at all. The last pages of the text, which were to provide the hinge for the reversal of Being and time to time and Being, are thus central to the whole of Heidegger's project in *Being and Time*, that is, the fight against the thinking of Being according to what Heidegger describes as the model of things that are (omni)present at hand. In many ways the question of the relation of Being and time appears nowhere more pointedly and surfaces so clearly in no other place in the text. Originally intended as a linchpin in the larger project of the text, the final chapter of the published text only functions as a pivot that does not move, as the finish, but not the end or conclusion, of the work that appeared. This section of the text is unusual in that it is concerned with the nuances of a concept in another thinker and in that it gives the appearance of being involved in a careful reading of other texts. For a book devoted to diagnosing and overcoming the errors of metaphysics, the last section of the text stands out amidst a conspicuous absence of references to the texts and thinkers of that tradition. It is also the first extended treatment of Hegel by Heidegger in any published work.[10]

It is crucial to the project to destroy metaphysics that Heidegger not only demonstrate the priority of his conception of time as well as the link between Being and time, but also that he defend the claim that his notion of time is unique in the history of thought. Since he has argued that the recognition of the essential temporality of Being destabilizes the grounds of metaphysics and renders its fundamental assumptions untenable, it is necessary that Heidegger separate himself from even the semblance of an accord with any metaphysical conception of time. Such a sweeping claim does not imply that Heidegger's intention is to treat the history of metaphysics as a seamless monolith in every respect. His lecture courses of this period, which are frequently careful studies in landmark figures in the Western tradition, indicate that he is well aware that the history of metaphysics is a history rich in diversity; however, in *Being and Time* he is especially concerned with what is lacking everywhere in that history: a real sense of the ineradicable radical finitude of Being, one that is first disclosed by the temporality of factical Dasein and manifests itself as an active hermeneutical, historical, and temporal sense.

Few in the history of metaphysics grant time and history such a central role as does Hegel, who sees himself as tracing the infinity of Absolute Spirit and so as the "completer" of the task of metaphysics. So it is not surprising that Heidegger chooses to confront Hegel at this most crucial moment in his effort to destroy what Hegel claims to have completed. It is difficult to imagine another thinker who goes as far as Hegel toward thinking Being as fundamentally linked with time and history and so seems to pose a challenge to Heidegger's claim to a unique insight into this link. In this respect Hegel represents a special threat to Heidegger's claims in *Being and Time*, and that is one reason he is singled out in this crucial passage. No one before Hegel gave both time and history a more active and essential ontological role than it finds in Hegel. Heidegger later argues that Kant demonstrated a real and radical sense of the meaning of time in the transcendental schematism but that Kant ultimately shied away from the implications of this in the second edition of the *Critique of Pure Reason* and, furthermore, that he lacked a real understanding of history. After Hegel few exceed his efforts to think Being along with time and history. Among those who sought to match Hegel's efforts, there is Marx, who, besides working largely in the framework of a Hegelian understanding of history, would surely resist being regarded as a metaphysician. There is also Bergson, who is treated and dismissed in a footnote in the section on Hegel. Husserl and Dilthey might of course be mentioned; but for Heidegger, neither surpassed the radical claims that Hegel seems to make. Finally, it appears that Heidegger never read Whitehead, and so he is exempt from consideration on that score, though it is likely that Heidegger would have found in him simply another brand of Hegelianism.

But Heidegger does not merely confront Hegel on this issue simply for the lack of a better representative of a metaphysical conception of time that has the appearance of Heidegger's own conception of time. By confronting Hegel in such a crucial passage, it could be said that Heidegger also tacitly acknowledges the debt of the concept of phenomenology as developed in the first pages of *Being and Time* to Hegel's *Phenomenology*, where Hegel develops a "doctrine of internal relations,"[11] which takes meaning into the real internal constitution of beings. In a lecture course of the same period Heidegger acknowledges this debt more explicitly by saying that "usually one says that contemporary phenomenology has nothing to do with Hegelian phenomenology. But the matter is not that simple. With some caution we can say that contemporary phenomenology has very much to do with Hegel; not with the phenomenology, but with that which Hegel designates as logic. With certain reservations this is to be identified with contemporary phenomenology" (*L*, 32). Thus, Heidegger is recognizing a proximity of his thought with that of Hegel, the "completer" of metaphysics, precisely at the high point of Heidegger's own attempt to "destroy" metaphysics. This proximity, however, poses a real threat to Heidegger's efforts to dismantle metaphysics, and so it is crucial that Heidegger separate himself from Hegel if he is to legitimate the radicality and originality of his phenomenological evidence for an ontology of finite Being. For these reasons Heidegger is expressing a kind of dismay when he says: "Our interpretation of the temporality of Dasein *seems to be* in accord with Hegel with regard to the *results* of that interpretation and the way in which world-time belongs to temporality" (*SZ*, 405). The proximity with Hegel on other matters notwithstanding, Heidegger cannot tolerate even an apparent accord with Hegel's concept of time.

Indeed there is a clear appearance of an accord between Hegelian and Heideggerian concepts of time in that for both Hegel and Heidegger time is essential, not accidental, to the nature of beings, not only in the sense that from its first appearance a thing must be understood as the bearer of as yet unrealized possibilities but also in the sense that a thing is unintelligible apart from its history. Furthermore, neither regards the present, the place of the appearance of things, to be intelligible as a simple immediacy; rather, the present is understood as the mediated product of history. For both, a thing is what it is across time and history and cannot be understood apart from its future possibilities. Thus, for instance, we find in both Hegel and Heidegger many parallel remarks such as Hegel's: "It [the future] is the essence of the present" (*JN*, 203); and Heidegger's: "The meaning of temporality is the future" (*L*, 265). It is quite obvious that both Hegel and Heidegger are in accord in granting time, especially the future, a fundamental nonaccidental role in the world. But this accord, which Heidegger calls an "apparent *accord of results*," is never developed or investigated; instead the attention is given to what Heidegger describes as the "fundamental *opposition* of *principles*," which underpins this accord and so separates his phenomenological ontology from Hegel's metaphysics. Thus, despite the acknowledged proximity to Hegel, Heidegger is claiming not only to be in disagreement with Hegel but to be working according to fundamentally different principles. The appearance of an accord notwithstanding, Heidegger calls Hegel's concept of time "the most radical form of the vulgar understanding of time" (*SZ*, 428) and says that "nothing is to be learned about temporality from Hegel" (*L*, 257).

In order to make sense of Heidegger's argument, one must first understand his distinction between "vulgar" time and "primordial" time.

I

The meaning and significance of time for Heidegger in *Being and Time* is guided by the fundamental effort to renew the question "about the meaning of Being" (*SZ*, 1). In order to gain access to this question of the meaning of Being, the existential analysis of that being with an understanding of Being is undertaken. While this approach admittedly bears the deep imprint of Kant's transcendental method, Heidegger takes great pains to distinguish the different foci and results of his concerns and those of Kant. While Kant's analysis is of the knowing subject, Heidegger's starts with the concrete life of affective Being-in-the-world. The problem of knowledge plays a relatively small role in the problematic of *Being and Time* because knowing is analyzed as only one of the derivative modes in which the possibilities of Being-in-the-world can be actualized.[12] This living being, which is not merely a knowing subject but the not yet fully actualized being for which Being is a question, Heidegger calls Dasein. Thus, "the fundamental discipline of ontology is the analytic of Dasein" (*GP*, 26). Taking Dasein in its everyday life as the starting point for ontology is necessary, Heidegger argues, because the possibility of any ontology is always referred back to that ontical being. Against the traditional metaphysical contention that ontology must be self-grounding (a contention with which Hegel wrestles in the beginning of the *Logic*[13]), Heidegger insists that ontology does not admit of a purely ontological grounding.

The essential result of Heidegger's analysis of Dasein is that "the constitution of the Being of Dasein is founded in temporality" (*GP*, 323), that "temporality discloses itself as the meaning of authentic

Care" (*SZ*, 326), and that "time . . . is really Dasein itself" (*L*, 205). The existential analytic of Dasein, undertaken in order to gain access to the meaning of *Being*, leads to the notion of *time* as the condition of the possibility and horizon through which the question of Being can be understood at all. But before any comparison of Hegel's concept of time with Heidegger's can be undertaken, more must be said about the analytic of Dasein and the special notion of time that it discloses.[14]

Dasein, as Being-in-the-world, is that being whose very Being is at issue for it. It is that being which asks the question of the meaning of Being because its own way of Being is always questionable for it. This fundamental characteristic of the Being of Dasein Heidegger calls *Care*. Now Care is not to be understood in the everyday sense that "human life is care and toil" (*L*, 227) but as saying that Dasein is never something merely present-at-hand or a matter of fact. The meaning of Care as the Being of Dasein is that "that which concerns it" is never "established or fixed." The word "Care," which is the translation of Heidegger's word *Sorge*, should not be misleading. *Sorge* means "worry" as much as "care," and this dual sense of the word is important in Heidegger's investigation of the phenomenon it names. Heidegger argues that the Care structure of Dasein, its essential openness and restlessness, underpins and is the fundamental determining feature of human existence. All that Dasein does or can do is pervaded by an awareness, usually submerged from view, that what it is to be is always an as yet undetermined issue for it. As always en route to something and always not yet finished, the essential element of Dasein's existence is the ineluctable care and worry that it has about its own existence. The significance of this phenomenon of Care for the effort of *Being and Time*, to reawaken the question of Being, is clear: Care is the fundamental way of characterizing that being which is unique by virtue of its relation to Being, and so the structure and meaning of Care will be that which must be interrogated in order to gain access to this sense of Being which Care discloses.

Being and Time begins with the announcement of the reason for and preliminary justification of the analysis of Dasein, which, according to Heidegger, is the *phenomenological* disclosure of the radical experience of Being that lies behind all subsequent metaphysical speculation on the part of Dasein. This phenomenology of Dasein does not begin with Dasein as engaged in metaphysics, but with Dasein where we first find it: in its *everydayness*. In its everydayness Dasein does not first understand itself in its fundamental meaning as Care, rather the first and foremost concern of Dasein is with that which is nearest to it. An analysis of this concern with its environment reveals that Dasein always finds itself as a unity dispersed in-a-world and already alongside and part of that which it finds in its world. The basic character of the everydayness of Dasein reveals that this being with an understanding of Being and a proclivity for speculation is not for the most part attending to Being as such, but is rather to be found in the concernful intercourse (praxis) with things (pragmata) (*SZ*, 68). In other words, in the first glance of the phenomenological analysis of Dasein, it is not revealed as concerned "everyday" with Being.

But Dasein is never inextricably stuck in the realm of praxis; it does not live by bread alone—perhaps even when there is none. Nor does it have the way of Being of things present in the world; even other living and dynamic beings give no sign of the concern with speaking and thinking with what is not immediately present—the special excellence of Dasein's dynamic being.[15] Rather, the analysis of Dasein reveals that it is quite unpredictable as to how it will be, and this unpredictability appears to be a consequence of the fact that Dasein has moods. What is important about this phenomenon of mood is that in and through its changing disposition something essential about Dasein is disclosed to itself. In and through its varying dispositions Dasein first finds, in a multiplicity of ways, that its own existence is always at stake, so that Being is for it a burden (cf. *SZ*, 134). Being is an issue for Dasein because, as having-to-be, it has already begun to be but has not yet resolved itself. In the instability of moods, Dasein's own essential facticity first becomes evident to it. But, having said this, Heidegger asks whether there is a fundamental or privileged disposition in which Dasein is delivered over most completely and directly to its own facticity such that the issue of Being as such comes into view. Such a disposition would be one in which the question of Being itself would be most pressing and apparent and one in which the everyday concern with pragmata—a concern that only masks the question of Being—slips away. According to Heidegger, anxiety is just such a disposition. In anxiety Dasein is brought face to face with the issue of Being itself by discovering itself as potentially *non-Being*, and in this way the question of Being is raised as a fundamental question. In short, Dasein is distinctive in that it always and inevitably faces Hamlet's question: to be or not to be.

The analysis of anxiety is one of the ways in which Heidegger further legitimates his claim that Care is the defining hallmark of the Being of Dasein: anxious, Dasein understands itself as an open issue. But this existential analysis alone is not yet sufficient for the task that *Being and Time* has before it as fundamental ontology. Thus far Heidegger has demonstrated that the issue of Being is accessible through Dasein because Dasein is that being which must come face to face with its own immanent potential for non-Being. Were Heidegger to stop his analysis of Dasein at this point the text would be more appropriately entitled "Being and Nothingness," a text that would not yet be in the position to complete the phenomenological destruction of metaphysics but would remain the expression of existential philosophy which it is all too frequently said to be. Although the idea of nothingness quickly becomes a central concern for Heidegger in the years immediately following the halting of the project of *Being and Time*, in this text the theme of nothingness is conspicuous by its almost total absence. Sartre recognized this and sought to carry out his version of phenomenology by developing the idea of nothingness as the largest context for the thinking of Being. Heidegger, on the other hand, wants to demonstrate the essential finitude and historicity of Being and to do this independently of every absolutizing tendency such as the all-embracing idea of nothingness invites. That is why he pushes the topics of anxiety and nothingness further in order to disclose the temporality of Dasein as the most compelling, and least liable to absolutism, evidence for an ontology the trademarks of which are finitude and history. To move in this direction, Heidegger asks the question that opens up the topic of the second section of the text in which the issue of time is introduced: Does the existential interpretation of Dasein as Care fulfill the demand of an original and fundamental ontological interpretation to have thoroughly presented the essential wholeness and concreteness of Dasein? In other words, Heidegger points out that the idea of Care alone does not yet allow us to speak of Dasein as the kind of whole that it uniquely is, and the risk of having omitted something essential about Dasein as providing the access to the question of Being jeopardizes the ontological claims that rest upon this existential analysis. Although Care is the essential feature of Dasein's way of Being-in-the-world, it only permits us to speak of Being-in-the-world as at stake and not yet as essentially whole. Therefore the full analysis of Dasein requires an analysis of that which brings Being-in-the-world as Care to a close: death.

Heidegger has already described Dasein as the being whose way of Being is to be incomplete, to be always underway in choosing how and what it will be in the world, and to be anxiously aware of itself as a future-directed Being-toward-death. As this futural Being-toward-death, and aware of itself as such, Dasein always understands itself as projecting ahead of itself in the present. Its present is never a sheer present, a closed-off isolated moment, but is essentially an openness to the future. Dasein's way of being present can only be an issue for it because it always understands itself as an anticipation of what it is not yet. The most distant, yet inevitable, not yet present future is Dasein's own death, and this then is the decisive element determining the context not only of Dasein's own self-understanding but equally of its very way of understanding anything whatsoever. The assumption here is that all understanding is contextualized and that Dasein's ever-present awareness of itself as the certain possibility of non-Being, that is as dying, forms the largest context for its understanding of itself as Being-in-the-world and of Being in general.

The case for the anticipatory and retrospective structure of understanding is an obvious one: an essential way in which we understand anything present to us is by asking what that thing has been and can be. Heidegger is not alone in arguing this case. Hegel, Aristotle, and Husserl make this hermeneutical principle the guiding assumption of their analysis of understanding. Heidegger's distinctive contribution to the analysis of the temporal structure of understanding is that he holds that the self-understanding of Dasein as the certain possibility of *non-Being*, that is as finite, forms the largest context for any present whatsoever. As such, Dasein's present understanding is what it is as situated within the whole context of Dasein's own temporally anticipated finite Being. Its every present, which as having always been opened up in its past as a possible future is always understood as such a possible past in choosing its future, is thus a futural-past-presentness that discloses its present "there" Being within the whole context of its temporal Being. The meaning of the Being of Dasein, Care, is made possible not merely because it is a finite being in the sense that it eventually comes to an end in some future present but because Dasein always discloses itself as already finite by being beyond itself in its present to itself in its futural finitude. The present "there" and "here" (*da*) of its Being (*Sein*) is disclosed in and through a temporal context; the present, in opening Dasein to what it is, opens itself to the arrival of that which Dasein's future brings with it: a world. Thus to speak of the finitude of Dasein's understanding is not merely to speak of the limits of the capacity to know in the Kantian sense but signals a fundamental finitude, one that is aware of non-Being itself as always already entering into the very fabric of any understanding at all. It is Dasein's understanding of itself as finite, not simply the limits of its ability to transcend the constitutive elements of its present, that lets Heidegger describe Dasein as a finite transcendence. The temporal openness, this finite transcendence of Dasein most evident in Dasein's special, anxious, relation to death, is the precondition for the appearance of anything. Thus, "temporality is the ground of the possibility of this structure of Care itself" (*L*, 410), and time is revealed as the horizon of any thinking of Being.

This temporally structured openness of Dasein, which Heidegger calls primordial time, has been revealed as the ontological possibility and meaning of Care as the Being of Dasein. Consequently, this same temporal openness that Dasein is, is simultaneously the precondition for, and the horizon of, that understanding of Being that distinguishes Dasein. Ultimately, "all ontological propositions are *temporal propositions*" (*GP*, 460). In the last section of *Being and Time* Heidegger moves to demonstrate that this "ground" and "horizon" of thinking has been forgotten by metaphysics (cf. *SZ*, 2), which has always conceived time not in this "primordial" sense but in a "vulgar" everyday manner.

II

Thus far, Heidegger's attempt has been to demonstrate that this primordial time, this futural-past-presentness that Dasein itself is (cf. also *GZ*, 267, *GP*, 323, and *L*, 205), is the condition of the possibility that there is an awareness of something like Being at all (cf. *L*, 410). The place of the appearance of Being in the world is a temporally defined place. It is in this sense that Heidegger can claim that time, as the possibility of the appearance of Being, is the (as yet unthought) "ground" of the thinking of Being. What is surprising in this is not that Heidegger claims to have uncovered a "new" ground of thought, for the history of philosophy is full of such claims. Rather, the distinctive element here is the way in which the "ground" itself is conceived. There is nothing unshakable or certain about temporality that would let it function as a firm foundation or principle of principles. Quite the contrary, primordial time itself is nothing and represents nothing. It does not ground in the sense that it gives "reasons" for Being but by opening up the place of the appearance of Being. Time itself "is" not anything but simply provides the horizon for anything that is at all. Heidegger emphasizes this by saying that "temporality 'is' not a being. It is not, rather it temporalizes itself" (SZ, 328); that means that it "grounds" only as disclosing the temporally defined horizon, or place, for the appearance of a world the basic articulation of which is itself temporal. Time "grounds" in that it opens and "times." Primordial time is therefore an ecstatical conception of time. This is why Heidegger insists on calling the past, present, and future temporal ecstases—openings—rather than the isolated "moments" of time; the past, present, and future are not instances of time but different ways of speaking about the constitution and direction of Dasein's openness to Being. As such temporality is the essential meaning of Dasein's primordial 'being-outside-of-itself' that grounds in providing the historically active and finite *opening* for the appearance of Being in the world. It is a ground not in the sense of an unshakable absolute which is a priori "there" in the world "for all time"; nor is time an absolute or static "open" as an independent stage upon which things come and go. The a priori of temporality is an "a priori perfect" (SZ, 85).[16] Measured against the expectations of the modern metaphysical conception of ground as a stable fundament, this ecstatical opening up of a world is a quite groundless ground.

Heidegger does not explicitly address the question of the peculiar character of this ground until the 1929 essay "On the Essence of the Ground" where he analyzes it primarily in terms of the freedom and transcendence of Dasein, and this in turn as further evidence for the fundamental finitude of that being whose Being outlines the horizon for the general question of Being as such. Here his concern is rather to make clearer and sharper the radicality of his notion of primordial time and to defend the claim that such a sense of time has yet to be thought in the history of metaphysics. This radicality is best seen by opposing Heidegger's concept of temporality to the so-called "vulgar" conception of time Heidegger claims has guided the history of metaphysics.

This "vulgar" conception of time is most clearly evident in the "everyday" understanding of Dasein. Dasein lives in an everyday world full of concerns with the pragmata of its world in which "All concernful reckoning, planning, preventing, and taking precautions always says, (whether audibly or not) that something is to happen *'then'*—that something else is to be attended to *'beforehand'*, that which has eluded us *'previously'* must be made up for *'now'*" (*SZ*, 406). In Dasein's everyday concerns, where it is pressed upon by *immediate* needs, it always understands itself with regard to a "moment in time," and this "moment," in turn, is situated with respect to the present "now." In this everyday way of Being of concernful praxis "the present has a special weight" (*SZ*, 407). Heidegger has already demonstrated that in the final analysis Dasein's openness to its world is grounded in temporality, so the claim that even the everyday "concern of circumspective common sense is grounded in temporality" (*SZ*, 406) is not surprising. But there is an important difference between the authentic time that is disclosed in the privileged disposition of anxiety and the time of Dasein's everyday reckonings: primordial time discloses the relation between *Being and non-Being*, while vulgar time is guided by praxis and the *beings* of everyday concern. Furthermore, the fundamentality of the future as the place of possibility, which distinguished "primordial" time, is shifted in everyday time to the "mode of a making present which retains and awaits" (*SZ*, 406). In its everyday doings with its world Dasein situates itself proximately and for the most part with regard to things which are present to it, and so this present moment has a privileged position in Dasein's everyday understanding of its world. So dominating is this "making present" that it comes as the present now, to be understood as the only moment of time which *is*. Hobbes gives clear expression of this view when he says that "The *present* only has a being in nature; things *past* have a being in memory only, but things *to come* have no being at all; the future being but a fiction of the mind" (*Leviathan*, bk 1, chap. 3). The enduring present thus comes to be understood as the essence of time. The ordinary understanding of the past is of "nows" that have been but are *not* any longer; of the future as of "nows" that will be but are *not* yet; and of the present as the now that *is*. The present now thus comes to be commonly ("vulgarly") understood as the Being of time that stands out against the other moments of time that are not and so have no "Being." The everyday understanding of time as the Being of the present thus brings with it the opposition of Being and Nothing. It now becomes clear how the everyday understanding of time brings with it a pre-conception as to what Being may be: whereas Heidegger's notion of temporality develops the question of Being through its connection to our understanding of the presence and significance of non-Being, the everyday conception of time immediately raises the opposition of Being and Nothing.

In the analysis of Dasein, Heidegger develops a concept of time that opens access to the issue of Being insofar as it is a "human," "lived" time, which is future-directed, ecstatic openness first revealed in Dasein's way of Being as Being-toward-death. Primordial time is thus a *finite* time which reveals the finitude characteristic of Being itself that can be revealed to Dasein, and only as finite, as not fully disclosed as a whole, does it open up Being as a question at all. The vulgar interpretation of time, on the other hand, by being led in the interpretation of its world by the concernful attentiveness to things already present-at-hand comes to judge the present now as the reality of time; and, because it does not draw its sense of time from its own finitude, it conceives of time as an enduring present, i.e., as infinite. The full phenomenon of "lived" time, that is, the full variable time of Dasein as the moody thinker who has already recognized its death and already remembered its birth, is transformed into an "empty" calculable time, that is, "a free-floating self-contained flow of present at hand nows" (*SZ*, 424). Purged of history, finitude, its affective life, and openness, this "empty" time is not the original temporality of Dasein but the derivative and abstractly measurable time of the anonymously enduring "everyone."

The vulgar notion of time, as a measurable sequence of an uninter-rupted flow of present nows simultaneously passing away and coming along, governs our everyday understanding of our environment and is the result of our concernful orientation that loses itself in beings present-at-hand. Though Heidegger does not make note of it at this stage, his later critiques of calculative thinking and the metaphysical-technological conception of nature will both have roots in, and be a continuation of this critique of vulgar time. Likewise, the later critique of technology must be understood as part of Heidegger's lifelong project to overcome metaphysics. It is interesting to note the extent to which *Being and Time*, which ends with a consideration of the philosophies of nature found in Aristotle and Hegel, fails to escape the technomorphism of the metaphysical conception of nature despite the effort there to outline a way of thinking the Being of nature freed from the traditional framework for doing so (cf. *SZ*, 211 where Heidegger speaks of the need to make inroads into a way of thinking nature outside the present-at-hand/ready-to-hand matrix outlined to that point in *Being and Time*).[17] This is a topic to which we will return when considering the question of technology in chapter 5. At this stage however Heidegger is content to remark that: "The hallmark of the vulgar concept of time is that it understands time from the point of view of now" (*L*, 244).

The intended differences between Heidegger's conception of time and what he presents as the vulgar conception of time are clear, and since Heidegger claims that time is the possibilizing horizon of any comprehension of Being at all, the importance of establishing his sense of temporality as primordial time is also quite clear. But the real significance of these differences is that Heidegger claims that this so-called "vulgar" conception of time, characterized as the place in which present-at-hand things now come to be, is not only the concept of time that guides the everyday, fallen, orientation of Dasein as worldly absorbed, but that this is the same conception of time which characterizes and determines metaphysics itself. The effort of this section was to demonstrate "that temporality ... is the origin of the vulgar concept of time" (*SZ*, 404), and it is in this way that this section attempted to establish the priority of Heidegger's ontology with regard to the entire history of metaphysics. It is here that Heidegger tries to justify his claim to have thought the ground of Being more originally than metaphysics had been able. But has he done this yet?

The differences between Heidegger's conception of time and the everyday conception are readily apparent, but to this point his defense has for the most part consisted in some sort of vague appeal. One could argue against Heidegger that he has only succeeded in setting up a straw man opponent, and that the history of metaphysics obviously has various and differing concepts of time, many of which seem to bear a strong resemblance to his own concept of temporality. Furthermore, Heidegger has yet to say what real difference such a thematized conception of time makes. In order to fully legitimate his claim to have overcome metaphysics, Heidegger must first respond to a number of questions: What, if anything, does this notion of temporality open up with regard to the meaning of Being that had been closed off by the traditional concept of time? What, if anything, does it conceal that the tradition had been able to disclose? Can the real difference in his concept of time be demonstrated even at a point where there seems to be a concept of time in the history of metaphysics that is similar to Heidegger's own?

Heidegger claims that since its inception the history of metaphysics has been governed by the conceptualization of this everyday, "vulgar," sense of time. Metaphysics, says Heidegger, as the inquiry into the *on he on*, Being qua Being, orients itself to beings that occur within the world, and it does so by considering them from the point of view of the temporal mode under which they are encountered; that is, the present now. In other words, a special understanding of Being and time serves as the guiding principle, the *arche* of metaphysics, one which is fundamentally opposed to the principles of phenomenological ontology. Phenomenology is thus opposed to metaphysics in principle, so that the effort to dismantle metaphysical principles is part and parcel of the idea of phenomenology. Recognition of this need to destroy the tradition of philosophy as metaphysics is one of the most significant ways in which Heidegger advances the idea of phenomenology as it was developed by Husserl.

Surprisingly, Heidegger devotes only one page of the text to the justification of his massive claim that the entire history of metaphysics has accepted Aristotle's definition of time given in the *Physics*: *touto gar estin ho kronos, arithmos kineseos kata to proteron kai hysteron.* Heidegger's argument is that since Aristotle time has metaphysically been conceived fundamentally as reckonable motion, that is, as countable movement within space. "All further discussions of the concept of time have clung in principle to the Aristotelian definition, i.e., in taking time as their theme, they have taken it as it shows itself in circumspective concern" (*SZ*, 421). The claim is, therefore, that the history of philosophy has attempted to think Being within the horizon of a derivative, everyday, inauthentic concept of time, and consequently that the ground of the thinking of Being, lying outside of the metaphysical framework, had never been opened up to metaphysics. Because it was unable to resist the seductions of the present, and because the peculiar weight of the present gets thematized and given an active role in the metaphysical pre-understanding of Being, the metaphysical framework becomes an obstacle rather than route to its own topic. Thus in *What is Called Thinking?* Heidegger contends that "in the guiding determination and the inner core of metaphysics, something essential in the essence of Being remains unthought. This unthought in all metaphysics is pointed to in the question of *Being and Time*. Metaphysics rests upon this unthought" (*HD*, 42). The clear implication is that this unthought ground of all metaphysics first comes into view through an understanding of time that is deeper, more primordial, than this "everyday" metaphysical conception of time. Understanding the radical and insurmountable openness and finitude of time as the horizon for any appearance of Being in the world is thus the first step in reversing the long history of the forgetfulness of Being. According to Heidegger, the result of the foregoing analysis of Dasein is precisely this disclosure of the special relation of Being and time.

In turning to his confrontation with the metaphysical conceptualization of this "vulgar" sense of time, Heidegger notes that there is at least a tacit recognition of the temporality of Dasein in the metaphysical tradition, for "even if the vulgar experience of time proximately and for the most part recognizes only the (vulgar) world-time, it nevertheless ascribes to it a *special* connection to 'soul' and 'spirit'. . . . Thus the interpretation of Dasein as temporality does not, in principle, lie outside of the horizon of the vulgar concept of time" (*SZ*, 427). This remark will later take on an increased significance as Heidegger comes to the recognition that the metaphysical tradition conceals within itself the seeds of its own overcoming. It will also take on an increased significance when Heidegger's later self-critique turns upon the view that the notion of Dasein developed in *Being and Time* was not sufficiently freed from the metaphysically conceived subject. But in *Being and Time*, Heidegger's concern is to hold the notions of "Dasein" and "subject" as far apart as possible and to show that even if an intuitive sense of the relation of Dasein and temporality does manifest itself in the history of metaphysics, the true meaning of this sense has never been recognized in that history. Heidegger then cites some classical texts on the idea of time from Aristotle and Augustine[18] to document his point before noting that "Hegel had already made the explicit attempt to demonstrate the connection of the vulgar concept of time and Spirit . . . and so is appropriate to clarify indirectly our interpretation of Dasein as temporality and our exhibition of temporality as the source of world-time" (*SZ*, 427–8).[19] This express Hegelian effort to demonstrate the fundamentality of the connection of time and Spirit appears to have some special accord with the role played by the connection of temporality and Dasein in Heidegger's destruction of metaphysics, and it is in order to destroy this semblance of an accord between his conception of time and Hegel's that Heidegger first encounters Hegel.

III

Thus far Heidegger has differentiated his notion of time as the ecstatico-horizonal temporal openness of Dasein from what he calls the vulgar-metaphysical notion of time. However, the significance of the difference between these two conceptions of time first begins to show itself in the way in which these concepts are developed with regard to something like a *subject*. Here Hegel becomes the natural counterpoint in Heidegger's analysis because, for Hegel, not only do history and time play an essential role in the understanding of Being, but both have an essential relation to the essence of the subject conceived as Spirit. But it is equally important to at least note a further accord that Heidegger does not point out; namely, that because both he and Hegel bring time and history so fully into the idea of the subject, both come close to abandoning the very idea of a subject whatsoever. Neither Dasein nor Spirit is best understood as what is commonly called a "subject," and both are defined essentially by their respective relations to time and history. Heidegger acknowledges this by saying that "History, which is essentially the history of Spirit, runs its course 'in time' ... Hegel is not, however, satisfied with asserting that the innertimeness of Spirit is a fact, rather he attempts to understand the *possibility* of Spirit 'falling into time'" (*SZ*, 428).

Thus, in Section 82 of *Being and Time* Heidegger turns to a confrontation with Hegel by posing two questions:

1. "How does Hegel delimit the essence of time?" (*SZ*, 428)
2. "What belongs to the essence of Spirit which enables it to fall 'into time'?" (*SZ*, 428).

Both of these questions concern the same topic: the kinship of time and Spirit.

This kinship of time and Spirit is obviously significant for Hegel. Hegel's philosophy is a philosophy of Spirit, and because Spirit manifests and develops itself through a historical process, time must be able to take (*aufnehmen*) Spirit up into this process. For this to happen, Spirit must be akin to time and in an essential relation with it, for if Spirit is to be absolute, if it is to have no other to it, it must not be taken in by something other than itself. Nevertheless, Heidegger claims that the investigation of the kinship of time and Spirit for Hegel will serve the purpose of clarifying the inner connection of time and the meaning of what is (Spirit) in contradistinction to that relation of time and Being which Heidegger has exposed in *Being and Time*. Hegel is chosen as the opponent here because, among metaphysical concepts of time, the explicit significance of time for Hegel has let there be an apparent similarity with Heidegger's interpretation of time. Despite the complexity and importance of a confrontation with Hegel on these issues, Heidegger admits that his analysis of Hegel "does not even claim a relatively complete treatment of the allied problems in Hegel, especially since 'criticizing' Hegel will not help us" (*SZ*, 428). At this point in the development of Heidegger's thought the confrontation raised with Hegel considers Hegel as not having reached beyond the prejudices of the tradition he intends to complete and so as paradigmatic of a way of thinking that, as governed by an inauthentic concept of time founded in our everyday concern with things, is fundamentally incapable of thinking Being in any way other than according to the frozen and restrictive model of the present now. In *Being and Time* Hegel is considered not as a witness to the connection of time and Being as developed in the text but as a counterfeit witness, as a fraud; that is, as appearing to be in accord with the analytic of Dasein, but as nevertheless testifying to that which that analysis has exposed as the forgetfulness of Being. In the context of Heidegger's concerns in *Being and Time*, especially the concern with establishing his own originality as opposed to the tradition, it should be clear that the threat harbored in Hegel's "fraudulence" is not that Hegel might be read as somehow testifying to the finitude of Being, but that the *contrast* that Heidegger wants to establish between phenomenology and metaphysics might be mitigated. To some extent this contrast is necessary, since Heidegger's own sense of the meaning of Being as finite has not yet fully emerged independently of that contrast.

In order to defend this charge, Heidegger undertakes the "comparison of the existential-ontological connection of Temporality, Dasein and World-time against Hegel's conception of the relation between Time and Spirit" (*SZ*, 428). There are two phrases in this title which already make clear what one can expect in this confrontation with Hegel. First, the phrase "Comparison ... against" announces the intent of the section. Heidegger wishes to distinguish himself over and against Hegel; this reflects the opposition in principle of which Heidegger spoke earlier (*SZ*, 405). The second set of words, "Connection" and "Relation," also reflect this opposition which Heidegger wishes to heighten: when he speaks of his own characterization of time and the "subject," Heidegger uses the word *Zusammenhang*, that is, he hints at the idea of something which is the *internal relation* of time and the subject; however, in mentioning Hegel he uses the word *Beziehung*, indicating that which has only an *external connection*. In other words, in Heidegger's view the claim that Hegel makes to have exposed and systematically thought the real inner relations of time and Spirit is not achieved but rests upon a derivative and external fraudulent relation. Despite the apparent radicality of the concepts of time and history in Hegel, and despite the apparent centrality of their role in his system, Heidegger intends to demonstrate that even in the case of Hegel we find a restrictive concept of time at work, concealing something essential to the question of Being. With this indication of his intentions Heidegger begins his analysis of Hegel.

IV

Heidegger begins his investigation into the kinship of time and Spirit by unpacking the essence of time according to Hegel. To that end Heidegger turns to the second part of Hegel's *Encyclopedia*, the "Philosophy of Nature," whose first division considers the "Mechanics," the first section of which is an investigation of "Space and Time." Heidegger emphasizes that Hegel remains true to the vulgar conception of time by considering time as a "natural" event, and that Hegel is true to the metaphysical formulation of this vulgar notion of time insofar as he thematically treats time as a topic within the philosophy of nature. Heidegger does not mention that Hegel's intention in this text is to display time in its still alienated form. This framework of

Hegel's philosophic interpretation of time serves as the most significant factor in Heidegger's uncovering Hegel's concept of time.

In the *Encyclopedia*, space and time are not merely externally listed alongside one another; rather, Hegel investigates the idea of time after having considered space and justifies this sequence as *dialectically* necessary. That is, Hegel considers time after space because space, if dialectically thought, that is, if thought according to its own innermost structure, reveals itself in its truth *as* time. Thus, in order to develop Hegel's concept of time as found in the philosophy of nature, it is first necessary to turn to Hegel's concept of space. Space is defined in *Enz* #254 as follows: "The first or immediate determination of Nature is the abstract universality of its Being-outside-of-itself, the undifferentiatedness of this is space. It is the ideally side-by-side, because it is Being-outside-of-itself, and is continuous because this outsidedness is still wholly abstract and has in it no determinate differentiations." Space is characterized as an abstract, undifferentiated continuity. For Hegel space is not the joining together of already differentiated points; rather, it first appears as an undifferentiated void and emptiness, and the first definition of space, the point or Being-for-itself, is simply the negation of this empty space. Though differentiable by points, space itself is an "indifference." The point, insofar as it differentiates the indifferent and abstract continuity of space, is the *negation* of space, but since the point is itself still of a spatial nature (as a relation to space), it is not yet the dialectical truth of space, that is, it has not yet explained the essence of space. In order to think space dialectically, and so, according to Hegel, grasp its essential truth, one must not let this "punctuality" (*Enz*, Zusatz, #254) of space remain in this state of static indifference, for this first determination of space must be surmounted; that is, the first negation must itself be negated. In being negated, the point relates itself to what it is not, to what is outside of it (other points), and so determines itself as a relation of points, and ultimately as lines and then as surfaces. In this negation of "punctuality," the point emerges from its indifference of being-alongside-of-one-another by positing itself as for-itself. The result of this process sets space in motion: "Negativity, which as point relates itself to space and develops in it its determinations as line and space, is however in the sphere of Being-outside-of-itself just as much for-itself and its determinations ... thereby it appears equally in opposition to that which sits tranquilly side-by-side. As thus posited for itself, it is time" (*Enz*, #257). Thought dialectically, space is disclosed as a movement.

In the transition from space to time, Hegel introduces the words "for itself." These words are the key to understanding the way in which Hegel makes any dialectical transition, and the transition from space to time is no exception. The "for itself" is, for Hegel, always to be understood in relation to its counter-concept, the "in itself," which is the given, static, immediacy out of which the "for itself" returns as the process of surpassing (*Aufhebung*) this tranquil uncomplicated immediacy. The words "for itself" indicate the dialectical unfolding and uncovering of the true condition of the possibility of that which had been taken as the given immediacy. The dialectical analysis of immediacy (in this case, space) always reveals itself as an already mediated immediacy. Thus the "for itself" must always be understood as an uncovering of the hidden precondition for the concept as given, "in itself." By describing the transition of space to time in terms of the move from "in itself" to "for itself," Hegel makes clear that time is the truth, the condition of the possibility, of space. When it is no longer regarded in its indifference in itself, space reveals itself for itself as motion. Space, in its truth, *is* therefore time. Heidegger explains this transition by saying: "This negation of the negation as punctuality is, according to Hegel, time. If this discussion has any demonstrable meaning, then it can mean nothing other than that the positing-of-itself-for-itself of every point is a now-here, now-here, etc. Every point 'is' posited for itself as a now-point.... The 'now' is the condition of the *possibility* of the point's positing itself-for-itself" (*SZ*, 430). Understood in this way, time is measured movement through empty space.

In formulating Hegel's concept of time Heidegger focuses on the following passage from *Enz*, #258: "Time, as the negative unity of Being-outside-of-itself, is likewise thoroughly abstract, ideal. It is that Being which, in that it is, is not, and in that it is not, is: it is intuited becoming...." Time which, for Hegel, first appears as the truth of space is itself determined as "intuited becoming." The terms that Hegel uses in his definition of time as "intuited becoming" are, for Heidegger, further proof that Hegel's concept of time in its abstract form is ultimately in accord with the vulgar concept of time as a natural succession of "nows." The term "intuition" speaks for this interpretation because it refers to an immediate contact with something present now. The term "becoming" provides further testimony for Heidegger's reading of Hegel because, as Hegel demonstrates in his *Logic*, becoming is the transition from Being to Nothing or Nothing to Being; in other words, becoming is the passing away of either Being or non-Being, and in either case it is the "now" of this passing away, which is the essential moment of this transition. It is the "now" which "in that it is, is not, and in that it is not, is ... " (*SZ*, 430). But Heidegger does not mention that the "now" for Hegel is therefore that which "is" both Being and Nothing. Only in the "now" is the apparent opposition of Being and Nothing surmounted, and as such it is the essential moment of time for Hegel. As pointing to the identity of Being and Nothing, Hegel's sense of the "now" obviously begins to move away from the simple and full instantaneous present that Heidegger would have it be. Even the natural scientific conception of time outlined in the *Encyclopedia* characterizes time as a complex moment of what is and is not, rather than as the moment of pure unadulterated presentness. Nevertheless, Heidegger seems to want only to mitigate this complexity. Furthermore, this identity of Being and Nothing, which the concept of time expresses for Hegel, should be the occasion for Heidegger to separate his own characterization of that identity as it is disclosed in anxiety from Hegel's account of it, but this crucial issue is never raised nor addressed in *Being and Time*. As we will see in chapter 2, this unasked question of the identity of Being and Nothing becomes the leading question for Heidegger in the years immediately following *Being and Time* and in the texts which culminate in the celebrated "turn" in his thought. One might argue that the failure to address this question explicitly is one of the basic failures of the project to overcome metaphysics as outlined in *Being and Time*. At this point however Heidegger simply wants to disentangle himself from Hegel as far as possible, and so he quotes Hegel: "Thus in a positive sense one can say of time that only the present is, the before and after are not; but the concrete present is the result of the past and it is pregnant with the future. The true present is thus eternity" (*Enz*, Zusatz, #259). This is then a conception of time that far from being radical and novel in the history of philosophy appears quite similar to the one expressed in the *Timaeus* where Plato says that "time is the moving image of eternity" (37d).

With this Heidegger says that "it does not require a comprehensive discussion to make clear that Hegel's interpretation of time moves wholly in the direction of the vulgar understanding of time. Hegel's characterization of time in terms of the now presupposes that the now remains leveled off and covered up in its full structure in order to be intuited as an 'ideal' present-at-hand" (*SZ*, 431). In other words Heidegger's claim is that Hegel has concealed the full meaning of time as the ecstatical openness revealed by the temporality of Dasein and that Hegel has consequently concealed the ground and horizon of any understanding of Being at all. This is the first prong of Heidegger's attack on Hegel; the second prong appears in the second question that Heidegger puts to Hegel. Since Heidegger argues that the connection between Spirit and time is an external, not a real internal, connection, he must ask what it is that enables Spirit to 'fall' into time thereby creating the semblance of a real relation between Spirit and time.

Even before approaching this question, Heidegger announces its answer: "The most appropriate expression of Hegel's concept of time lies in the definition of time as the *negation of a negation*. . . . Here the sequence of nows is formalized and leveled off in the most extreme way. It is solely from the standpoint of this formal-dialectical concept of time that Hegel can produce any connection between time and Spirit" (*SZ*, 432). Hegel's concept of Spirit, according to Heidegger, is not intrinsically temporal and historical but is only formally and artificially identical with the structure of time as Hegel understands it. The dialectic of time and Spirit thus comes to be regarded by Heidegger as the height of artifice.

V

Like Heidegger, Hegel regards thinking that remains on the plane of abstraction as deficient. It is important then that the essence of Spirit be conceived such that it is possible for it to actualize itself concretely 'in' time and history. In light of this requirement Heidegger's decision about the essence of Spirit at first seems quite strange, for it puts Spirit on a plane that seems devoid of any sense of concreteness and of both time and history: "The essence of Spirit is the concept . . . (i.e.) the form of self thinking thought itself: the *grasping of oneself* as the conceiving-of-the-not-I" (*SZ*, 433). This characterization of the essence of Spirit as the concept is, however, able to account for the necessary relation between Spirit and history, for what this description of Spirit says is that it is the conceiving of the negation of the "I"; in other words, it is the *negation of a negation*. In the concept, the self is conceived as able to conceive both itself and its other, as such it is able to know itself and, as independent of something other than itself, it is free. However, this absolute self-identity of Spirit with itself, the freedom of Spirit, is not an immediate nor given identity. It is rather a mediated and achieved identity, which is realized through the process that Hegel calls "World-history." History is, for Hegel, the process of Spirit coming to know itself; that is, it is the process of Spirit overcoming (negating) itself as other (a negation) to itself. History is Spirit coming to self-manifestation and self-realization through this concrete process of the negation of a negation.

This is what Heidegger has in mind when he comments that "because the restlessness which Spirit develops in bringing itself to its concept is the *negation of a negation*, it accords with Spirit, as it actualizes itself, to fall 'into time' as the immediate *negation of a negation*" (*SZ*, 434). Thus time, which was previously disclosed in the analysis of space as being the negation of a negation, and history, as the actualization of Spirit coming to know itself as itself, both possess the same abstract dialectical structure as Spirit. Heidegger argues that the apparent kinship of time and Spirit for Hegel is to be found solely on the grounds of this common formal structural characterization. Or, in Derrida's paraphrase of Heidegger, that the dialectical Spirit is but "a tributary of the vulgar concept of time." [20] But even the effort to establish a formal identity between Spirit and time in order to permit the concretization of Spirit in time and history must be recognized as some sort of response to the fundamentality of the relation of Being and time. Thus Heidegger ends his confrontation with Hegel by saying that "whether or not Hegel's interpretation of time and Spirit and their connection is correct and rests upon ontological foundations which are primordial can not yet be discussed. But the very *fact that* a formal-dialectical 'construction' of this connection can be ventured *at all*, discloses a primordial kinship of the two. Hegel's 'construction' was prompted by his arduous struggle to conceive the 'concretion' of Spirit" (*SZ*, 435). Despite Hegel's intention of giving Spirit a real temporal structure, it is now clear why Heidegger announced that his concept of time is fundamentally opposed in principle to Hegel's: Heidegger's claim is that the concretization, the making real, of Spirit is an achieved one, which does not recognize the original, ineluctable and primordial, temporality of 'Spirit' itself as given. Hegel's talk of the concrete universal and the embodiment of Spirit in world-historical individuals is regarded by Heidegger as artificial and merely formal. Heidegger's own presentation of the 'kinship' of time and Dasein, on the other hand, "starts with the 'concretion' of factically thrown existence itself in order to reveal temporality as that which makes such existence possible. [Properly understood] 'Spirit' does not just fall into time, rather it *exists* as the primordial temporalizing of temporality" (*SZ*, 435–6).

This, then, is the outcome of Heidegger's analysis of Hegel's concept of time: Hegel does not begin with a concept of Spirit that is genuinely temporal and so must attempt to achieve or construct a process whereby Spirit is able to be concretized. Whereas Hegel must involve himself in the reconstruction of the odyssey which leads to the fullness of the present moment of Spirit, Heidegger's project requires the deconstruction of the present in order to disclose its essential finitude. If thinking is to live up to its task, then it must not be guided by the will to reconstruct an unconditioned ground that accounts for Being as a whole but by the willingness to let the finitude of the temporal horizon of Being be. Thus Heidegger claims that Hegel, who makes the claim to have retrospectively thought the relation between Being and thought absolutely, seeks to defeat, or at least neglects, the finite temporal openness that has been revealed as the ground of the thinking of Being. The entire effort of *Being and Time* is to demonstrate that any attempt to think the ground of what is, any philosophy, must begin by exposing that which opens up the possibility of a ground at all. This opening up, which *Being and Time* reveals as the ecstatic-horizonal finite temporality of Dasein, is itself a "groundless ground" that opens up a sense of Being quite different than the way in which Being had been conceived in the history of metaphysics. It is a groundless ground in that time is no-thing upon which 'that which is' rests. As inherently mutable and unstable, time grants Being but does not function according to any of the other traditional, or at least post-Cartesian, criteria of a ground. As nothing, and as disclosing the relation between Being and Nothing, time is a ground that resists the demands and requirements of metaphysics, which since Parmenides has found Nothing the way of deceit. Because this "primordial time" that is the horizon of the meaning of Being has hitherto gone unthought, Heidegger claims that the entire history of metaphysics rests upon an unthought ground and hence that metaphysics at bottom is the "forgetfulness of Being." Despite the importance of time and history in Hegel's thought, which gives it the semblance of an accord with Heidegger's position, Hegel, who claims to have thought the ground of Being absolutely, is taken to be the height of the forgetfulness of the true ground.

Heidegger's presentation of the kinship of time and Spirit in Hegel can be summarized in three stages:

1. Time, which is presented as "intuited becoming," is conceived by Hegel as the negation (passing away) of a negation (the now-point), and so as oriented upon the "now" as the truth of time, it is presented by Heidegger as concealing and levelling off the ecstatic-horizonal openness of primordial time.

2. Spirit is conceived as the negating (overcoming) of a negation (non-Spirit).

3. According to Heidegger, the kinship of time and Spirit is found only on the basis of this formal identity of each as the negation of a negation (i.e., as dialectical). Dialectic is thus criticized as a formalist position, and the dialectical history of Spirit (i.e., the phenomenology of Spirit) is presented as founded upon a metaphysical concept of time expressed as the negation of a negation.

In short, Heidegger's analysis of Hegel in *Being and Time* tries to outline a mechanical, empty, formal concept of time which, as a conceptualization of the everyday "vulgar" sense of time oriented upon the present now, does not permit Hegel to think the meaning of Being in any way other than the everyday inauthentic manner of the "they." This, in part, is the basis for Heidegger's harsh judgment of metaphysics as inauthentic, fallen, and empty.

It must be emphasized that even by his own standards Heidegger's effort to set himself apart from metaphysics and so overcome it stands or falls with the justification of his ecstatic notion of time as something hitherto unrecognized in the history of thought. The critical question to be put to this section of *Being and Time* is whether or not he has done this. If we trust Heidegger's presentation of Hegel on this topic, then there is little doubt that Heidegger has succeeded in separating himself from Hegel. But Heidegger has drawn the line between them so sharply that one wonders where there could have even been the semblance of an accord with Hegel. The presentation of Hegel's concept of time smacks too much of the presentation of a straw man, yet this pivotal section of the project of *Being and Time* is too crucial to permit such haste, and so a second, more critical look to Hegel is called for in order to see if Heidegger has in fact succeeded in disentangling himself from the semblance of an accord with Hegel's concept of time and so preserved the claim of uniqueness for his own notion of time. To this end, it is necessary to re-ask two questions:

1. Does Hegel conceive of *time* as the negation of a negation which is "intuited becoming"?
2. Is *dialectic* (the kinship of time and Spirit) merely a formalistic position?

Both questions drive Heidegger into the core issues of Hegelian thought.

VI

In order to answer the first question, we have two alternatives: we could either argue that Heidegger's analysis of Hegel's concept of time as presented in the *Encyclopedia* was incorrect, or we could challenge the attempt to present Hegel's concept of time as found most clearly developed in the "Philosophy of Nature." The second alternative, to challenge the appropriateness of the place in which Heidegger finds Hegel's concept of time, is tacitly suggested by Heidegger himself when he opens his analysis by saying that the framework within which a philosophic interpretation of time is carried out determines the character of that concept. In turning to the analysis of the "Philosophy of Nature" in the *Encyclopedia*, Heidegger turns to an apparently obvious place to examine Hegel's concept of time, for here the discussion of time's role in nature is explicitly and thematically considered. In this sense Heidegger lets himself be guided by his own prejudices about the shape of metaphysical thought, which he finds has never recognized the fundamentality of lived, ecstatic time of the subject but has simply modeled even its account of lived time upon its preconceptions of a calculable "natural" time. Since Aristotle's *Physics*, the place to treat the question of time and movement has been in the framework of discussions of nature, and in this Heidegger finds Hegel no exception. But might it not be the case that, besides the considerations of the special "naturphilosophische" account of time as movement in nature, Hegel also develops another, more fundamental concept of time and its relation to thought, and that this other sense of time is the one operative within his system? Those special aspects of time as it is related to the study of nature are directly and thematically addressed by Hegel, and this invites attention to such passages; the general role of time in the Hegelian system, on the other hand, provides a more exhaustive and significant framework within which one would find the meaning and role of time in Hegel's ontology. Two such fully developed alternative presentations of Hegel's concept of time, by Koyré and by Kojève, have already been worked out and, not surprisingly, come to results that are quite different from those found in Heidegger's analysis of Hegel. The intentions driving Kojève's interpretation of Hegel are not fully commensurate with Heidegger's own. Kojève's attempt is to rehabilitate the master-slave dialectic and the left-Hegelian reading of history, while simultaneously pruning the dialectic of its theological dimensions yet preserving the possibility of absolute knowing. Nevertheless, it is also clear that Kojève is equally motivated by the desire to demonstrate that the Hegelian dialectic propelling both history and time is not toppled, but rather confirmed by Heidegger's analysis of the relation of Dasein and temporality. Kojève's purpose, like Heidegger's, is to participate in the critique of metaphysics but, unlike Heidegger, his purpose is to preserve Hegel from that critique. In light of these purposes Kojève's presentation of the Hegelian concept of time offers an alternative to Heidegger's own; an alternative that furthers, rather than stifles, the confrontation between Hegel and Heidegger. The influence of Heidegger upon Kojève is well known, as is the influence that Kojève had upon the development of French phenomenology as it was forwarded by Sartre and Merleau-Ponty. This relation of influences, and so the possibilities of the dialectic as contributing to the developments of phenomenology, sits at the center of the point from which French and German inspired work in the phenomenological tradition diverge.

After his translation of the section on time in Hegel's *Jenenser Logik*, Koyré announces that "it is the 'notion' of time as abstract and empty which Hegel tries to destroy by showing to us how time constitutes the living reality of Spirit. Deduction of time? Construction? Both of these terms are improper."[21] Rather than finding the significance of Hegel's concept of time within the framework of nature, Koyré contends that "the Hegelian time is, above all, a *human* time, *the time of the person*, which is this strange being who is insofar as he is not and is not insofar as he is.... And it is because Hegelian time is *human* that it is also dialectical and ... historical."[22] Koyré not only identifies Hegelian time as a human time, he also argues that the kinship of time and Spirit, rather than being a merely formalistic one, is a phenomenally real identity that is to be explained in the living dialectic of the human way of Being. Koyré's article serves as a preliminary challenge to Heidegger's reading of Hegel, but it ends before we are presented with a detailed analysis of this temporal dialectic of the human way of Being. However, Kojève's more extensive interpretation of Hegel, which was inspired by Koyré's provocative essay, does outline and develop just such an analysis of the temporality of this human dialectic. Whereas Heidegger finds the framework of Hegel's concept of time within the philosophy of nature, Kojève focuses his analysis on a text which does not extensively consider the concept of time as such, the *Phenomenology of Spirit*. Looking to Kojève's own interpretation of Hegel we find an alternative, and clearly more empathetic reading of the question of the relation between time and Spirit as Hegel conceives it. The other face of the Janus-faced Hegel becomes more evident by developing the basic elements of Kojève's text—the face of Hegel that always has an eye on the need to surpass the tradition of metaphysics as it has been conceived hitherto.

VII

The differences between the *Encyclopedia* and *Phenomenology* as frameworks for a presentation of Hegel's concept of time are readily apparent. Already in the "Preface" to the *Phenomenology* Hegel criticizes the mathematized, empty concept of time as paralyzed and abstract. Such a conception of time is inadequate to the task of philosophy because it is unable to capture "the pure restlessness of life" (*PG*, 39) and has never recognized that "time ... is the existing concept itself" (*PG*, 38). In short, any ontology adequate to its own topic must recognize the concrete temporal life of Spirit.

The final comment on time in the *Phenomenology*, that "time ... is the existing concept itself," is one which occurs both at the beginning (*PG*, 38) and very end of the text (*PG*, 558); perhaps the most important remark about time in the *Phenomenology*, it is also the most puzzling. Moreover, besides sounding strikingly similar to Heidegger's own remark that "time is really Dasein itself" (*L*, 205), it also clearly points to a concept of time quite different from the empty and formalistic one that Heidegger ascribed to Hegel. The meaning of this difficult, yet important, claim becomes more accessible by thinking about this notion of the "pure restlessness of life," which Hegel implies a true concept of time must be able to capture. The restlessness of life, the motor of the *Phenomenology* as the odyssey of this restlessness, describes the essential spiritedness of Spirit.

For Hegel, human life, which most clearly embodies the special excellence of Spirit, is never a static nor merely animal-like life. The human way of Being is never to simply "happen" or "occur" within time; rather man is unique in that he works, he plans and plants for the future, takes risks or is cautious, remembers the past beyond his own private life, and is anxious in the face of death. In other words man, this being that "is" Spirit, is distinctive in that he relates himself to time and history. In arguing that the person is never present as a completed self-identity, it is clear that Hegel would have no difficulty agreeing with Heidegger's insight that man is that being who always faces the question of having to be or not to be. Man is never simply conscious of what is present; rather, he lives in the present as expressly relating himself to himself as what he has been in the past and can be in the future. Human being is distinctive in that it is always living in a context—indeed several contexts—larger than the given immediacies of its private life, and the largest context, which is the condition of the possibility of all other contexts, is time itself. Furthermore, human being is also always aware of itself as defining itself within this temporal context. The way of Being of human Being is thus a self-consciousness of an always on-going, perpetually unfinished, self-relatedness. This lack of permanent self-identity Hegel describes as temporal and as an "inner" difference, and this difference is said to be the essential element of who we are as Spirit. Yet it is only as the effort to overcome this difference that man exists and can be understood. The urge to restore and achieve the sense of wholeness, to work through all the stages of this sense of incompleteness and

imbalance is a basic human urge, one that not only develops dialectically but reveals the basic dialectical structure of Being human. This
urge manifests itself as what Hegel calls the "restlessness of life," and
any concept of time must be able to take account of this disquiet that
underlies the journey of man qua Spirit in the world. In the section
of the *Phenomenology* entitled "Self-consciousness" Hegel gives this
restlessness a name: *Desire.* It is within this central notion of Desire
that one finds a framework for a presentation of Hegel's concept of
time, which is quite different from the one Heidegger articulates as
the Hegelian concept of time in nature.

In examining the Hegelian concept of Desire, it is important to
note that the Desire that marks the human way of Being is not merely
the natural desire, which is the desire merely to preserve life. Something other than sheer self-preservation is at stake in human life.
Human desire does not simply desire that which is present at hand,
rather it desires that which *is not*. "Desire is directed toward an entity
that does not exist.... Desire is the presence of an *absence* ... to act
in terms of ... a desire (as human desire) is to act in terms of what
does *not* (yet) exist, i.e., in terms of the future. The being that acts
thus, therefore, is in a time in which *the future takes primacy*." [23] Desire
is the negating (overcoming) of a present which is the negation
(absence) of that which Desire desires. As such, Desire, the first name
for the way of Being of human being, is another name for the dialectic
founding the identity of Spirit and time; the dialectical structure of
Desire outlines a temporal process and opening up of a world. As
such, Desire is another name for the "restlessness of life"; it is "the
portentous power of the negative" (*PG*, 29) underpinning and defining Spirit as the Being of the real.

Like Heidegger, Hegel takes the living, concrete, and temporally
dynamic appearance of Spirit in the world as his ontological clue.
Of course Hegel does not undertake the same sort of existential-
ontological analysis of Desire as Heidegger does of Care. Nevertheless, Hegel does develop a concept of time that is fundamental to the
horizon of Spirit and that is first articulated in the analysis of the
vital, temporal openness that is the special excellence of human
Being. Desire is a movement that originates out of the *future* as the
effort to make the absent future a *present* presence by having negated
the real present and produced its *past*. Like Care, the temporal
structure of Desire is thus the opening of the present as the arrival of

the future in the present out of the past. Like the temporal structure disclosed by Care, Desire leads to a concept of time in which each moment is what it is by virtue of containing its own other (different moments) within it. The present is a futural-past-presentness, and it is only as this relation to the future through its past that the present is intrinsically temporal and historical. Rather than "falling" into time and history, Spirit, which has this temporal structure, *is* time and history. That is why Kojève contends that "without man, nature would be space, and *only* space,"[24] and so even the analysis of time as it appears in nature is ultimately only intelligible on the basis of Spirit, which is recognized as there "in" nature. This is the sense of the passage in which Hegel says "time ... is the *concept* itself which *is there*" (*PG*, 558). Thus even the "natural" time which Heidegger finds presented in the "Philosophy of Nature" can be explained only as disclosed on the basis of the temporal structure of Desire, as the process of opening up a world by negating. The identity between Spirit and time, that which enables Spirit to fall 'in' time, is, as Heidegger said, the dialectic; but contrary to Heidegger's decision about the dialectic, it is not so clearly such a formalistic and empty mechanism of nature. While Heidegger wants to describe the dialectic as an empty sophistry, Hegel's discovery and analysis of the dialectic is, in large measure, a reply to the same living phenomenon that provides the basis for Heidegger's analysis of the relation of time and Being: the temporal structure of the human way of being as an open futural-past-presentness. Hegel is attempting to present and work out of human dimensions of time understood as essential to the philosophic horizons of Spirit. He does not stop with, and more important, does not start with, what Heidegger describes as the traditional conception of time. Of course this does not mean that Hegel has won the day in the confrontation with Heidegger, but it does mean that Heidegger has not backed up the charge that Hegel's dialectic is merely an artificial formalism. The temporality of Care and the temporality of Desire each open up upon a world that is fundamentally historical, each is oriented toward the still absent future, and each leads to a discourse about Being that is related to Nothing rather than defined in opposition to it. If the dialectic of Spirit that is disclosed by the temporality of Desire is a construct, then the structural features it has in common with Heidegger's own emerging ontology of finite Being indicate either that Heidegger is not yet sufficiently distant from metaphysics or that Hegelian thought has something to offer to Heidegger's own intentions. The book on the dialectic cannot be closed so easily on the basis of Heidegger's analysis of Dasein.

Returning to the first question with regard to Heidegger's Hegel critique, it becomes obvious that there can be—in fact must be—a way of reading Hegel's concept of time in a way that is quite opposed to the reading Heidegger offers at the end of *Being and Time*. In opposition to Heidegger's claim that Hegel follows Aristotle in understanding time as a natural event abstracted from the living history of Spirit and as being primarily oriented toward the present "now," it is possible to find in Hegel the presence of a human time that is an ecstatic time oriented primarily toward the future. Although Heidegger intended to oppose his concept of primordial time to Hegel's vulgar concept of time, it now appears that the apparent kinship between them is a genuine and real one. In both Hegel and Heidegger time is in an essential sense conceived of as human time; for both, the present is both open and historical in being a futural-past-presentness; and, for both, time is an ecstatical arrival of the future.

The very presence of an existential ecstatical concept of time in Hegel, despite Heidegger's attempt to dispel any appearance of kinship between himself and Hegel on this matter, is of course quite damaging to the project of *Being and Time* to destroy metaphysics. This section on Hegel was pivotal for Heidegger's plans, and yet, Heidegger's own explicit claims to the contrary, it fails to adequately separate Heidegger's position from Hegel who is portrayed as the metaphysician par excellence. In a very real sense it is the unanticipated result of this encounter with Hegel that led Heidegger to abandon the announced project of the book, leaving significant questions unanswered and the achievements of *Being and Time* entangled in the same metaphysics it set out to destroy. Heidegger's hope and expectation in this section was that in the confrontation with Hegel he would encounter a representative of that most extreme and seamless forgetfulness of the grounds of the thinking of Being, yet in this confrontation Heidegger obviously met more resistance than he anticipated, and so it is at this point that Heidegger finds it necessary to reassess his approach to metaphysics. Against his own intentions Heidegger has begun to discover that metaphysics has perhaps always concealed within itself something akin to the remembrance of Being that phenomenology calls for, and that it is not a one-sided forgetfulness of Being. Likewise, the nonmetaphysical mode of discourse that Heidegger hoped to give voice to is called into question by this more than apparent kinship with the Hegelian dialectic. The recognition that even the conceptual frame of metaphysics harbors the resources for its own critical destruction is what set Heidegger's post-*Being and Time* career off on an unprecedented dialogue with the leading thinkers of the metaphysical tradition. After this encounter with Hegel at the pivot point of *Being and Time*, Heidegger's attitude toward the problem of metaphysics and toward his predecessors undergoes a clear shift; metaphysics, as the title of his Kant book (1929) indicates, is no longer the clear enemy of thought, but poses a genuine problem for thought. The problem with metaphysics is that it is too often a covering up of the original experience of the finitude of Being; the problem posed by metaphysics is that this original experience circumscribes the horizon and possibility of the very idea of metaphysics as inviting a turn away from that same experience. Metaphysics is one of the possible ways of thinking and speaking disclosed by finite Being, and so it might be that the recovery of finite Being only deepens the problem of metaphysics. Heidegger is not yet ready to pronounce the project to overcome metaphysics as a response to the original experience of Being a failure. But the meaning of this approach to the history of thought is reassessed, and the idea of carrying out this project via a revision and analysis of the subject rethought qua Dasein is ultimately abandoned.

While the project to destroy metaphysics by means of a rethinking of time as the horizon for any thinking of Being is suspended for the moment, the questions that have precipitated out of the confrontation with Hegel need to be addressed if Heidegger is to be in a position to develop an ontology of Being as finite. The key distinction upon which the ontology of *Being and Time* rests is the first to be called into question: the idea of a "primordial" time, which provides a more original horizon for understanding Being than the "vulgar" concept, no longer seems to be adequate to its task. The concept of time derived from an analysis of the authentic, anxious self-presence of the human subject qua Dasein is not as novel as Heidegger claims it is, nor do the basic features of this concept prove so obviously hostile to the ground of metaphysics. Too much of the traditional shape of the "subject" remains even in the notion of Dasein to let it serve as the route by which Heidegger can overcome the obstacles to thinking the true finitude of Being. The case of Hegel is especially interesting in this regard, for not only do we find an ecstatic, existential notion of time at work in his phenomenology of living Spirit, but it is expressly on the basis of this human concept of time and the idea of history it leads to that Hegel claims to have thought the ground of Being absolutely.[25] Heidegger's claim that such a concept of time gives direct testimony to the essential finitude of Being is not able to carry the elemental force it needs.

So the question arises: does such an existential ecstatic notion of time necessarily require or even permit the openness and self-difference which characterizes the special restlessness of human being to be overcome and elevated into the self-identity of thought thinking itself absolutely; or does such a notion of time exclude such a possibility? Does the more radical thinking of time uncover a "primordial phenomenon" that is the thinkable all-embracing ground of what is; or does the more radical thinking of time discover the impossibility of a final "ground" that it can think, pointing instead to the ground-lessness of every ground?

The structural and substantive similarities between the Hegelian and Heideggerian concepts of time are clear. And this similarity means that the concept of primordial time is not the acid bath that works against metaphysics, since it seems amenable to the very meta-physical development it was brought forward to dissolve. Heidegger's attempt to deliver the fatal blow to metaphysics in one fell swoop itself falls to the complexities of the possibilities opened up by finite Being. However, the essential difference between these structurally similar concepts first becomes visible in the respective conceptions of the subject as the basis upon which each concept rests: for Hegel this basis is Desire as the living activity of *negating*; for Heidegger it is Care which, as the Being of Dasein, comes face-to-face with its future as *non-Being*. Thus the difference between these two "existential" con-cepts of time seems to be this: for Hegel time is opened up in and as the activity of negation; for Heidegger it is first revealed in the free recognition of non-Being. This means of course that the focus of Heidegger's project to destroy metaphysics has now shifted from an analysis of the concept of time to the meaning of nothingness. Not surprisingly then, the first extended text published after *Being and*

Time, namely, "What is Metaphysics?", has as its dual topics both metaphysics and the topic of nothingness. Furthermore, Hegel, who is mentioned twice in this text, is the only thinker who comes into focus as being directly addressed here, and once again Heidegger finds it necessary to defend his new position against the semblance of an accord with Hegel on this matter. It is now clear that the confrontation between Hegel and Heidegger, which began over the concept of time, will only be resolved by determining the difference between the real activity of negation and the meaning of the recognition of non-Being. Heidegger's contention is that no matter to what extent a mode of thought recognizes negation and is permeated by it, it never reaches the meaning of the disclosiveness of nothingness that belongs to the being of Dasein. The confrontation between Hegel and Heidegger has not been settled; its center has been relocated. The basic point of contention that Heidegger wants to emphasize remains the same: whether the essential horizon open to the thinker and first subject of philosophy can support the basic ideals of philosophy carried on as metaphysics.

2

On the Identity of Being and Nothing

Everywhere journeying, inexperienced and without exit, he comes to nothing.
—*Sophocles*

Guided by the ideals of plenitude, omnipresence, and divine Being, metaphysics has found it difficult, if not impossible, to give an account of non-Being as meaningful. Beginning with Parmenides, nothingness has been conceived traditionally as the great enemy of the truth of Being. In the words of the Stranger in Plato's *Sophist*, non-Being is *alogon*, that is, it is unreasonable and contrary to the Logos (238 c), and consequently unthinkable and unspeakable. This essential opposition and clear hostility between the metaphysical conception of Being and nothing has been a lasting hallmark of the Greco-Western philosophical tradition, and is clearly a fundamental tenet supporting the idea of metaphysics as such. This was already evident as a result of Heidegger's analysis of the ontological consequences of the so-called "vulgar" conception of time as carrying with it an inherent opposition between the idea of an enduring, eternal, and substantial present as the place of true Being and the transitoriness of the past and the unreality of the future as no longer and not yet Being. For long stretches of the tradition philosophy even lacks the words for what Heidegger wants to address as "nothing": the *me on* of Greek thought, and the *privatio* of the medieval world do not carry the same radical existential force of Heidegger's notion of *das Nichts*. The disappearance of the real is not a thinkable topic from the standpoint of the common understanding; so unthinkable that it serves as one of Berkeley's proofs for the necessary existence of an omnipresent perceiving mind.[26] The experience of the reality of nothing, which is not the same as the negation of things but is the discovery of the character of Being as finite, has been suppressed in the history of philosophy, only showing up in other guises such as that thought under the heading of "the problem of evil." But, Heidegger contends that even in such concealed showings the full felt force of nothingness has yet to be adequately taken into account.

In making the charge that the history of metaphysics has been guided by an unwillingness or inability to find non-Being as anything other than unreasonable and unspeakable, Heidegger is making a somewhat less controversial charge than when he indicted the entire history of metaphysics as having been governed by a single, vulgar, inauthentic concept of time. Here perhaps, in taking up the themes of non-Being and metaphysics, Heidegger will be able to put his finger on that enduring and essential element of philosophy as metaphysics that he finds so alien to what he sees as the task of thought. Heidegger did not change his intentions in moving from *Being and Time* to "What is Metaphysics?"—he is still bent upon destroying the habits of metaphysics as an approach to the question of Being in order to be able to develop an ontology of finite Being freed from the entanglements in the forgetfulness of Being—however, between these two texts the central target of his attack upon metaphysics has changed from the issue of time to that of non-Being. This new effort to raise the question of Being via the topic of non-Being is, in Heidegger's own self-understanding at this stage of his career, still en route to a radically new beginning for thought. In significant respects this intention can only remain because Heidegger has not yet learned the full lesson of the failure of *Being and Time* to defend its own position against metaphysical tendencies: still aiming at this "new beginning," Heidegger has not yet recognized that metaphysics is not the sheer and unadulterated forgetfulness of Being, but that it conceals, often despite itself, a remembrance of the aporetic character of Being which provides the resources for the critical overthrow of the excesses of the metaphysical infatuation with infinite Being. The effort to radically rupture and break out of tradition and history does not accord at all with the hermeneutics and sense of history developed in *Being and Time*. Later in his career, after the full ambiguities of thinking and speaking become evident to him, Heidegger will devote much energy to locating himself ambiguously within tradition and history as a way of critically confronting metaphysics. Nevertheless, in the years before the celebrated "turn" Heidegger's confrontation with metaphysics is always initiated from the perspective of a self-proclaimed outsider. In this respect his early critique of metaphysics closely resembles that of the first great critics of Hegel and metaphysics: Kierkegaard and Nietzsche.

There are several passages in a number of texts in which Heidegger specifically addresses the question of the identity of Being and Nothing. This is the central theme of the 1955 text "Zur Seinsfrage" in which Heidegger tries to express the mutual embeddedness of Being and Nothing by writing "B̶e̶i̶n̶g." In "Zur Seinsfrage," which as its title indicates is still on the way to an ontology of Being as finite, Heidegger raises the question of non-Being in the context of asking about nihilism and the global spread of modern technology. Both of these themes later become the focus of the effort to come to terms with the history of metaphysics. But immediately following the suspension of the announced plan of *Being and Time*, the confrontation with metaphysics and the question of nothingness are developed out of the language and requirements established in that text. Seen in this context, it is evident that there are important respects in which the relation between Being and Nothing is developed with different motivations in "What is Metaphysics?" and "Zur Seinsfrage." Consequently, for an examination of the problem of metaphysics as it is bequeathed to Heidegger from *Being and Time*, the 1929 text "What is Metaphysics?" is the best starting point, for here the concept of nothingness is developed as an explicit effort to articulate a problem in metaphysics that the topic of time failed to make fully visible.

I

The text "What is Metaphysics?" was originally delivered in 1929 as Heidegger's Freiburg inaugural lecture at the university there. It proved to be a key text for Heidegger's own development, and it is one to which he would return and develop throughout his career, for in 1943 he would add an afterword to it, and then in 1949 an introduction. The initial, central portion of the text was composed along with a contribution for a *Festschrift* for Husserl entitled "On the Essence of Ground." The title of this companion piece and the fact that the introduction that was appended to the text of the original lecture was entitled "The Way Back into the Ground of Metaphysics" give us some clue that we have not left the question, first raised but left unanswered in *Being and Time*, of the character of the ground and horizon of any thinking of Being, but that here we are deepening this question of ground. As in *Being and Time*, there is a dual intent here: to display and destroy the essential grounds of metaphysics and to "reground" the question of finite Being phenomenologically.

At the outset, Heidegger tells us how we should not read the text; it is not, he says, a text about or within the tradition of metaphysics. Instead he announces that his purpose is to confront a specific and fundamental question of metaphysics in order to separate himself as sharply as possible from the metaphysical conception of Being and so further clarify the basis of the destruction of the history of metaphysics begun in *Being and Time*. Here again the intention is to point to and analyze a key characteristic of the grounds of metaphysics that is shown to be untenable once it is measured against a metaphysically neglected, yet essential, element of the horizon opened up to Dasein as the one who asks and speaks about the question of Being. There is a clear continuity here with the last section of *Being and Time* in which Heidegger attempted to distinguish himself from Hegel in the attempt to legitimate his destruction of the ground of metaphysics.

The essay, which was delivered to a general academic audience, is divided into three sections: "The unfolding of the metaphysical question," "The working-out of the question," and "The response to the question." The first section makes a direct bridge to the final section of *Being and Time* in that it opens up with a reference to a celebrated remark by Hegel: "Philosophy—seen from the point of view of healthy common sense—is, according to Hegel, the 'inverted world'" (*WM*, 103). In once again broaching the question of metaphysics in the context of a confrontation with Hegel, Heidegger is beginning to establish the precedent for what will become a career-long trait: Hegel's thought stands for metaphysics carried to the extreme of its own possibilities, but at the same time, Hegel poses a genuine resistance and challenge to the project to destroy metaphysics as a way of philosophizing. Hegel has clearly become the bête noire of Heidegger's project to overcome metaphysics, and so Heidegger has once again found it necessary to commit himself to pointing to the differences between himself and Hegel. Nevertheless, in giving Hegel the first words of this text that addresses the problematic of metaphysics, Heidegger perhaps betrays a growing admiration for Hegel which, even if it did not show through in the published text of *Being and Time*, surely would result from that first confrontation with Hegel where Heidegger found in Hegelian texts a genuine thinker quite different from the neo-Hegelianism surrounding Heidegger at that time. But this quotation from Hegel at the outset of Heidegger's inaugural lecture is not yet the basis for a careful analysis of a Hegelian position; it is rather a springboard for Heidegger's own unfolding of the idea of metaphysics. Thus Heidegger explains this inversion (or better—perversion) that philosophy represents by saying that there is a double peculiarity inherent in all philosophical-metaphysical questions: first, they always inevitably inquire into Being as the ultimate whole and unity of the entire problematic of any metaphysics; and second, the inquirer, being at the core of this problematic, is placed into question. That is what Heidegger means when he says that "metaphysical questioning must be put as a *whole* and has always to be based on the essential situation of questioning Dasein" (*WM*, 103). Though Heidegger does not present a new or modified analysis of Dasein in "What is Metaphysics?", Dasein itself is still seen as our access to the question of Being announced in *Being and Time*. In important respects Heidegger is still working within the transcendental framework of the investigation into the way of being in Dasein. Here the leading question is: "What essential things happen to us in the ground of our Dasein insofar as science becomes our passion?" (*WM*, 103). The starting point of this investigation is not Dasein in its everydayness but Dasein as knower; specifically, Dascin as guided by the ideals and laws of science, the queen of which is metaphysics. Here the emphasis shifts from Dasein as an exemplary starting point for thinking and speaking about Being as finite to Dasein as the thinker and speaker of Being. These two aspects of the Dasein-analysis belong together and are only distinguished for analytical purposes.

In order to answer this question Heidegger discusses more precisely what science represents: "In all the sciences we comport ourselves to beings" (*WM*, 104). In "doing" science we comport ourselves to beings by asking about them *as* beings. In the practice of science the effort is to abstract or prescind from our everyday unreflective involvement with the pragmata of the world of praxis in order to come to a clearer view of what constitutes a thing as that sort of thing. There are obviously many different senses in which one can speak of a "scientific" approach to the world in which we are involved, but the science that claims to most completely prescind from the everyday world is the "science" of metaphysical reflection. Philosophy involves a kind of knowing—a *Wissen*—and so it seems necessary that it permits the organization of that knowing into a science—a *Wissenschaft*.[27] Nothing seems to speak against the possibility of realizing the full orderly unity of such knowing gathered into a systematic whole. This way of presenting the idea of science and philosophy as a science is quite in accord with Aristotle's definition of *prote philosophia*, which presents the inquiry into the *on he on* as one of the fundamental questions of the science of metaphysics. Science, Heidegger repeats, is the inquiry into "the being itself—and nothing else.... *But* remarkable: just at the point the scientific person makes sure of his surest possession he speaks of something else. Only what is to be researched and nothing else.... But what about this Nothing?" (*WM*, 105). Heidegger introduces the word "nothing" here first in the lower case, then capitalized.[28] This capitalized "Nothing" is the first introduction of the concept of nothingness, which is the specific metaphysical question to be considered in the essay. This is quite transparently an artificial transition that Heidegger makes here, for he introduces the concept of Nothing merely as the hypostatization of the word "nothing," which functions grammatically in the preceding sentences as a negation. In its first appearance "nothing" is determined here simply as the denial and limit of "what is"; it is here the opposite of what "is." Such an understanding of "nothing" is quite in accord with the traditional, "logical" definition of nothing as "the negation of the totality of beings: that which simply is not" (*WM*, 107). But Heidegger's motivation is to push the issue further and ask whether this facile answer really explains how such a concept is to be thought. Is the idea expressed by the word "nothing" simply a logico-grammatical function, or does it point to something more fundamental still? In the language of science we use the word "nothing" to name "that which is simply not." But how are we to understand what "that which is simply not" is, and is this even the best way to understand what it means that we can speak of nothing and that we can ask, as Leibniz did, why there is something and not rather nothing?

For the logic of science such questions seem to be nonsense, for to ask "what *is* nothing?" immediately inverts [*verkert*] the concept into its opposite, i.e., into something that is. To ask about the concept of nothing immediately leads to a violation of the fundamental rule of thinking, that is, the law of *noncontradiction*. Thus, Heidegger explains that for a type of thinking that holds logic to be the highest court of appeal the question of Nothing cannot be thought; it is, as Plato said, *alogon*: unreasonable and unspeakable. Such a type of thinking, characterized by its attachment to the principles of logic, Heidegger here calls *Verstand* ("understanding" or the "intellect"), a word which has played several and important roles throughout the history of German philosophical language, but also in everyday speech, which refers to *gesunder Verstand* (healthy common sense). However, Heidegger argues that even everyday common sense and the philosophical intellect and understanding cannot avoid pointing toward the question of the Nothing, because it appears whenever the scope of the inquiry found in science is made clear; namely, that it concerns "beings themselves . . . and over and above that *nothing*" (*WM*, 105). But despite this tacit nod toward the question of Nothing in order to account for the limits to its own field of inquiry, metaphysics, the inquiry into the *on he on* which abides by the law of noncontradiction, conceives of Nothing simply as negation, that is, as a limit to the field of its own reasonable concerns. Beyond these limits Nothing is simply not intelligible. As an example Heidegger might have pointed to Kant with the same lack of charity with which he pointed to Hegel's concept of time, for Kant only seems concerned with the question of nonbeing when he makes negating judgment one of the logical functions of understanding in judgments (cf. *KRV*, sec. 9), and negation one of the categories of the understanding (cf. *KRV*, sec. 10).[29] The *Critique of Pure Reason* seems a typical representative of the failure to think the meaning of Nothing as other than logical negation. When operating according to the logical principles of the intellect, metaphysics thus conceives the meaning of Nothing solely as the function of negation, that is, as a denial of Being.[30] Separating Being and Nothing in this way is equally a means of rejecting the finite character of Being itself.

At this point in the text, Heidegger asks the question that is meant as a challenge to such thinking: "Is there Nothing because there is nothing, i.e., negation? Or is the reverse true? Is there negation and nothing only because there is Nothing?" (*WM*, 107–8). This question whether negation is the origin of nothingness or whether the matter is inverted is not a matter of a mere inversion of the order of ideas.

Rather, Heidegger implies here that the way of thinking that he calls intellectual understanding, which he claims is the way of thinking characteristic of metaphysics, is not an original or fundamental way of thinking. This is basically the same accusation that Heidegger makes in *Being and Time* against metaphysics, except there the narrowness of the metaphysical field of vision is attributed to a vulgar concept of time. Heidegger's task there was to have demonstrated his destruction of the history of metaphysics by demonstrating the priority of his concept of time, but in the confrontation with Hegel at the end of *Being and Time* that question is transformed into the question of the priority of his concept of Nothing over the logical-metaphysical concept of nothing understood as negation. Therefore, when Heidegger says that "We contend that Nothingness is more original than nothing and denial" (*WM*, 108), he is continuing his project to destroy metaphysics by demonstrating that it is founded upon an oblivion to its own topic. Once again metaphysics is said to represent a way of asking the question of Being that masks rather than reveals the truth of Being as finite. It is still Heidegger's task to disclose the metaphysical flight from the finite as possible only in conjunction with the covering up of a basic phenomenon that is constitutive of the asker of the question of Being, namely, Dasein as Being-in-the-world. Here the specific charge is that metaphysics has yet to grasp the significance of saying that in Dasein's concern with knowing and science it has to do with the whole of what is to be inquired into and that beyond beings there is "nothing" else. Metaphysics, as Heidegger now intends to characterize it, stands for the willful refusal to ask beyond and about its own limits and this "nothing" else casually referred to in announcing the topic of intellectual inquiry.

II

"If Nothing itself is to be interrogated then it must first be given. We must be able to encounter it" (*WM*, 108). The first question to be raised is how we encounter Nothing. We already know that from the point of view of science, which is the logical study of things encountered in the world, it is not found alongside the things of the world. We know that nothingness does not have the character of a something, for if it did it would not pose a problem for the conceptualizing of the talents of the intellect. What then is the "ground experience of Nothing" (*WM*, 109), and where and how do we encounter it?

Though "What is Metaphysics?" does not make direct reference to *Being and Time*, the answer to this question in both texts is one and the same: *anxiety* first reveals the true and deeper meaning of nothing-ness.[31] "The disposition in which we find ourselves not only discloses according to the mood we are in what is in totality, rather this disclosure is the ground event of our Da-sein. . . . This event is possible only in the fundamental mood of anxiety" (*WM*, 110). In anxiety, which Heidegger claims is so basic and essential to the Being of the inquirer into Being that it is the happening of the ground of Dasein, everything that "is" falls away and *nothing* matters. Anxiety reveals nothingness insofar as the things from which we take our everyday, concernful, pragmatic orientation in the world sink back into empty, undifferentiated equivalency and nothing remains from which we may take our bearings; indeed there is a sense in which not even we remain. In the anxious event Dasein is individuated, but in a very peculiar way, since this individuation is not the coming-into-the-fore of anything like an ego. Unlike fear, in which the particular, personal, ego-bound I is threatened by the world around it and so held onto ever more tightly, in anxiety there is no split between Dasein and its world. There is no place to retreat to, no outside world threatening an inner one. It is in this sense that anxiety reveals the two topics of metaphysics—the whole of what is and the inquirer into this whole— as united in one and the same fundamental event. Anxiety is therefore distinctive in that it is a disposition that reveals totally and so univer-sally; that is, it is the slipping away into nothing of the whole manifold of what is, as well as the questioner into this manifold, in such a way that Nothing is revealed as belonging to the reality of what is (the Being of beings). Thus, Heidegger says, "Nothing is revealed in anxiety as *at one* with what is in totality" (*WM*, 112). Anxiety is not the result of a denial or annihilation of what is via some sort of act of negation we decided to carry out. Though acting upon us as subject to anxiety, anxiety itself is not a subjective act that we may will to happen. Indeed, in anxiety our own subjectivity is fundamentally altered to the point at which the authentic meanings of what is one's "own-most" is revealed as essentially individuated, yet nonetheless belonging to a "world" that in turn is disclosed by our own anxious projection. Asking about the "knowing subject" and its relation to "the world" from the point of view of the possible experience of anxiety requires that we abandon the traditional terms under which the subject-world relation has been discussed. It then becomes clear that the lived experience of this sense of Nothing is more fundamental than the intellectual act of negation; it is something which overcomes us, and that is why we speak of anxiety "attacks." According to Heidegger, such an experience of Nothing reveals the essence of Nothing as "Nihilation: it is neither an annihilation of what is, nor does it arise from a negation. Nothing does not let itself be reckoned in terms of annihilation or negation at all. *Nothing nothings of itself*" (*WM*, 113). This Nothing, which anxiety reveals as belonging to the Being of what is and which was disclosed in *Being and Time* in its *connection* to Being, is now defined as *nihilation*. But instead of making the meaning of this primordial sense of Nothing clearer, it seems to become even more obscure when it is said of this Nothing that it "nihilates" and "nothings."

In order to understand what Heidegger is driving at with talk of the Nothing that nothings, it is helpful to recall what this has to do with the question of Being and the destruction of metaphysics. "The essence of this primordial nihilating Nothing lies in this: above all, it brings Dasein face to face with what is as such ... [it is] that prior condition of the possibility of the revelation of what is at all" (*WG*, 114). In *On the Essence of Ground*, the companion essay to this text, Heidegger calls this possibility of the revealedness of beings "*The disclosedness of Being* ... [and this is] ... called ontological *truth*" (*WG*, 130). Nothing as nihilation is the original opening, or most fundamental horizon, within which something may come to our attention at all. Unlike the logical concept of negation, which is a function performed upon something already disclosed, the phenomenological conception of nothingness is intended to point more clearly to the very possibility of any disclosure at all. Heidegger's analysis of nothingness needs to make a clear distinction between this "primordial" nothing and negation. He cannot do as Sartre did in *Being and Nothingness* and identify nothing and negation as part of one and the same event. For Sartre both nothingness and negation are aspects of the negativity of consciousness, which infects and pokes holes in the positivity of the real and so produces nausea.[32] But Heidegger's point is not an existential one; it is not concerned simply with the life of Being-in-the-world as consciousness but primarily with developing an ontology of Being itself as finite. That is why Heidegger claims that the original sense of nothingness tells us something about ontological truth. The existential framework of the analysis of anxiety that was highlighted in *Being and Time* is played down in this later text in order to sharpen the contrast between Heidegger's own sense of non-Being as opposed to the metaphysical conception of non-Being understood as negation. As the undetermined and free possibility of the revealedness of beings, nothingness is the horizon of the disclosedness of the true ontological ground of beings, that is, of Being.

It is clear that when Heidegger contends that the traditional metaphysical way of thinking, which he characterizes as "intellectual," has not adequately thought the question of nothingness, he is also claiming that such a way of thinking ignores the ineradicable affective life of the thinker and so is incapable of comprehending the grounds of ontological truth. This is the reason the question about nothingness is the special metaphysical question that Heidegger chooses to continue his destruction of metaphysics; this question is special not in its particularity but in its universality and fundamentality. His claim is that insofar as Dasein comports itself to things in the world, it can do so only insofar as it has already held itself into Nothing and insofar as it remains able to do so. Thus only as able to recognize nothingness, which is possible because Dasein is able to know itself as essentially and inevitably nihilated Being and so *finite*, is Dasein able to comport itself to things in the world: "In the Being of beings there happens the nihilating of Nothing" (*WM*, 114). In *Being and Time* Dasein revealed itself as that being which always relates itself to beings simultaneously in terms of and influencing its developing understanding of Being. Now in "What is Metaphysics?" the origin of this access to Being that Dasein has is found to be intimately linked with the possibility of non-Being, and this in turn is thought in the notion of nothingness, which Heidegger has worked out in opposition to the notion of nothingness understood as negation. The recognition of nothingness, which is made most visible in the felt remembrance of Dasein's own finitude and in the sorrow of the loss of one's fellow Dasein, is the condition of the possibility of Dasein's openness to what is.

Despite the fundamentality and universality of this encounter with non-Being as determinative of Dasein, non-Being does not easily lend itself to conceptual analysis. In a very real sense non-Being is as Plato described it: *alogon*, namely unthinkable and unspeakable. Language itself—especially the language of concepts—seems disinclined to articulate the full force of the felt "presence" of non-Being. But the lack of any real metaphysical recognition of this basic event in any understanding of Being is not simply to be attributed to this lack of amenability to reason and speech by that disclosed in anxiety and named by non-Being. There is rather a more telling reason for the absence of any serious attention to nothingness in the history of metaphysics, and that is what Heidegger points to when he says that "it—Nothing in its nihilating—refers us straight away to what is" (*WM*, 115). This Nothingness, which grounds Dasein's access to the Being of beings, is itself a *self-concealing ground*: it opens us up to the encounter with things in the world, an encounter that simultaneously grabs our attention and concern, and invites us to ask the question "what is it?", making this the first question for thinking. Thus it is not only the case that non-Being is contrary to rational thinking and speaking, but it also invites such thinking to actively forget the true role of non-Being in itself in the appearance of Being. Lacking substance and all of the other idols that build the governing prejudices of the metaphysical conception of Being, the fleeting and unreasonable disclosure of nothingness revealed in the experience of anxiety has slipped out of the history of metaphysics, thereby permitting Heidegger to label that history "the forgetfulness of Being." Yet this limited experience, which is so intimately linked with our own experience of mortality, is too powerful to completely ignore, and so the concept of negation as a sharp demarcation between Being and Nothingness has filled the conceptual void and come to play a central role in logical, metaphysical thought. But, as Heidegger has argued, negation is not nothingness, and the conception of Being that can be developed on the basis of each is quite different: whereas the idea of negation preserves the positivity and pure presence of Being, the experience of non-Being points to a radical finitude that belongs to every authentic experience of Being. As incapable of grasping this anxious experience of non-Being, the history of metaphysics has become one long flight from finitude.

With this Heidegger contends he has justified his claim to have thought Nothing more originally than the understanding and its logic are able to conceive of it and to have explained the reason for the transformation of Nothing into negation. Thus he concludes that

"Nothing is the origin of negation, not the other way around" (*WM*, 116). His justification follows once more and in a forceful passage: "More abysmal than the mere propriety of thinking negation is the harshness of opposition and the sharpness of loathing. More responsible is the pain of refusal and the mercilessness of an interdict.... The permeation of Dasein by nihilating comportment points to the perpetual and darkened revealedness of Nothing, which only anxiety reveals in its originality" (*WM*, 116). Even when science has become Dasein's passion, the careful look to the concrete existence of Dasein discloses a more fundamental insight into the limit of Being than is expressed in the key logical function of negation. Pain, loathing, refusal, loss, as well as anxiety are all experiences that point to and document a more radical sense of the finiteness of Being than is expressed by the willful activity of negation.[33] Experiences of the fragmentation of one's world and place in it, of the singularity and frailty of life, can be analyzed by reference to the paradigm case of anxiety, but that does not mean that every experience of fragmentation and finitude must be traced back to its anxious roots. What is common to all such disclosures of Being as finite is that they are all dispositions that point simultaneously to the immensity and frailty of life. Moreover, none of these basic human experiences is fully within the control of our will, and as being at their mercy in a significant respect, they give us evidence not only of the finitude of Being, but of the will as well.[34] Yet it is precisely such experiences that cannot be grasped by the logical concept of negation and by any sort of intellect guided by that concept as the true concept of negation.

The differences between the results of Heidegger's attempt to think the meaning and role of non-Being for Being and the concept of Nothing as negation articulated by the metaphysical intellect are clear: whereas Heidegger's concept of Nothing, as nihilation, is first revealed in a *disposition* that happens to happen (for no particular reason), the understanding's concept of nothing, as negation, is first apparent in the *activity* of denial performed by the subject (in saying: "it is not that"); whereas Heidegger's concept of Nothing is revealed in its *belonging* to the fabric of reality, the understanding's concept of nothing is conceived of in the *denial* of what is; whereas Nothing as nihilation is the *opening* up of the world of beings, nothing as negation *presupposes* beings as already there in the world; and finally, whereas Heidegger's notion of Nothing is *experienced*, the understanding in asking the question "what 'is' it?" of nothingness finds that the question immediately violates the logical law of noncontradiction—it *conceives* of nothingness merely as the negation of what already is. Consequently, the logical understanding is unable to uncover what Heidegger contends is the more original sense of Nothing, which is of the very essence of Being. Yet this question "what is it?", which is asked in the natural attitude of the understanding, is the question that sets Greek philosophy apart from previous attempts to understand what is, *ti to on*. Furthermore, the question about beings is the guiding question of metaphysics as philosophy. On this basis, Heidegger is able to characterize the way of thinking of metaphysics as *Verstand*, and it comes as no surprise when Heidegger reminds us at the end of the text that even a cursory glance at the history of metaphysics indicates that the idea of non-Being has been conceived merely in its opposition to Being; that is, as negation. Yet, this need to rethink the true problem of Nothing, which goes unthought in metaphysics, is not merely a matter of arriving at a clearer conception of the meaning of negation as a special problem of metaphysics; rather, the approach to the question of nothingness, absent in metaphysics, "first awakens the true metaphysical point of view in the question about the Being of beings" (*WM*, 118). In other words, it is first in addressing the question of non-Being that the real problem of metaphysics, a problem to which it is blind, comes into view.

There is, as Heidegger reminds us, only one serious exception to this forgetfulness of the belonging-together of Being and nothingness: Hegel. Once again, at the height of his effort to separate himself from metaphysics and to prove to have thought Being more originally than yet thought in the metaphysical tradition, Heidegger finds himself compelled to acknowledge an apparent accord of results with Hegel and to try to disentangle himself from this seeming kinship with the metaphysician par excellence. Heidegger acknowledges Hegel's apparent recognition of the place of non-Being in any authentic ontology by quoting the beginning of the *Science of Logic*, a text which carries in its title two words as a badge of honor that for Heidegger represent a great error in the history of thought. There Hegel begins his account of Being by saying that "Pure Being and pure Nothing are the same" (*WL*, 67). Heidegger admits that such a claim is in accord with the results of his own interrogation of nothingness and is, therefore, quite 'correct'. However, Heidegger denies that Hegel's remark is the recognition of the original truth that Heidegger has described, for "Being and Nothing belong together, but not because they both agree in their indeterminateness and immediacy—as in the Hegelian concept of thinking—rather, they belong together because *Being in its essence is finite* and reveals itself only in the transcendence of Dasein holding itself out into Nothing" (*WM*, 119). Once again, Heidegger contends that an apparent accord between his own thought and Hegel's is merely formal, that Hegel's remarks are "correct" but still do not point toward the same original evidence and insight of Heidegger's own remarks.

III

While in *Being and Time* Heidegger recognizes the need to offer at least a somewhat detailed defense against the appearance of a kinship between his own position and Hegel's, in "What is Metaphysics?" Heidegger is content simply to assert that Hegel's conception of the identity of Being and Nothing is merely a formal identity bearing no real resemblance to Heidegger's own presentation of the belonging together of Being and non-Being. Only a brief paragraph is offered as a means of separating himself from Hegel. But, as was the case in *Being and Time*, this brief passage is crucial, for part of Heidegger's purpose is to demonstrate that his insight into the primordiality of non-Being has never been recognized in the history of metaphysics. His contention is that no true taking account of the realization of nothingness that is disclosed by such lived experiences as anxiety, pain, refusal, or loss would be able to provide the basis for any metaphysical ontology. From the perspective of an authentic recognition of non-Being, metaphysics, despite its long history and diversity, is a monolith and a massive flight in the face of nothingness. Metaphysics exhibits a kind of fear in the face of anxiety and its disclosures. Hostile to the very grounds of metaphysics, nothingness is thus able to serve the project to destroy every metaphysics and to render its basic assumptions untenable.

One of the most long-standing and fundamental laws of metaphysical thought that falls to any demonstration of the identity of Being and non-Being is the law of noncontradiction. Among the basic laws of logic and the intellect, the law of noncontradiction stands so inviolable throughout the history of metaphysics that it stands above our own profoundly felt subjective experiences of non-Being as belonging together with Being. Such a notion of the belonging together of a concept and its opposite, especially when that notion is based on a subjective experience, is intolerable when logic is the highest court of appeal; to say that Being and non-Being are the same is perhaps the most basic violation of the supreme law of thought and is, says Parmenides, the path to illusion. But Heidegger wants to challenge this rule of the law of noncontradiction. Yet Hegel does too, for he not only speaks of the identity of Being and non-Being, he also establishes the persistent violation of the law of noncontradiction as the life-blood of his entire system; namely, the dialectic.

So the threat that Hegel once again poses to Heidegger's project to destroy metaphysics is perhaps more serious than Heidegger's remarks and slender defense against a semblance of accord with Hegel acknowledges. Furthermore, when Heidegger chose to characterize metaphysical thinking as "*Verstand*," he undoubtedly intended that choice to reawaken Kant's distinction between "*Verstand*" [intellect] and "*Vernunft*" [reason], and he could not fail to recognize that rethinking this distinction is one of the ongoing concerns of Hegelian thought. It is quite well known that, to a large extent, Hegel won his system in working out a critique of the Kantian conceptions of the understanding and reason. It is all the more surprising then when, in the same year as "What is Metaphysics?" and the critique of the understanding that Heidegger develops there, he casually writes: "In the second edition of the *Critique of Pure Reason* did not Kant restore to *Verstand* a position of dominance? As a consequence of this did not metaphysics become, via Hegel, in a more radical way than ever, logic?" (*KPM*, 237). It appears that in this other text devoted to Kant Heidegger is still concerned with accusing Hegel's thought of being the most radical form of this deficient mode of thought called *Verstand* in the history of metaphysics. But despite Heidegger's claims to the contrary, all the signals of a real proximity between Hegel and Heidegger on this point are present. If Heidegger is to be in a clear position separate from Hegel's, then there are three questions that Hegel must fail to be in a position to answer:

1. Does Hegel criticize thought that subscribes to the law of non-contradiction as its highest tribunal?

2. Does anxiety and its fundamental disclosure of non-Being play a central role in Hegelian ontology?

3. Does Hegel conceive of nothingness primarily as negation and so in opposition to Being or as a "nihilation" belonging to the truth of Being?

IV

Hegel's critique of Kant and of the Kantian concept of the intellect is significant throughout his entire career and has been well documented by Hegel scholars.[35] From the time of earliest writings in the Tübingen period forward each and every Hegelian text can be interpreted as an overcoming of the Kantian antinomies in the agonistic resolution represented by the Absolute. In its early form, Hegel's critique of the intellectual understanding centered about the notion of positivity and Hegel's own passion to destroy the positivism of the metaphysics of his day. For Hegel the most virulent form of that positivism is found in Kant's development of the antinomies, for there Kant pushes thought right to the point of its own dialectical sublation only to retreat in order to preserve the logical laws of thought. Consequently, the antinomies are a special target of Hegel's critique. But this critique of Kant and of the logical intellect goes through rather clear transformations before the distinctively Hegelian element develops and does not first reach its mature formulation until the two texts *Differenzschrift* and *Faith and Knowledge*. In those texts we find the horizon of logic measured and shown lacking against the needs of philosophy and the claims of the Absolute. In the introduction to the *Differenzschrift* Hegel says that "Diremption is the source of *the need of philosophy*. . . . In culture that which is the appearance of the Absolute has isolated itself from the Absolute and fixed itself as something independent. Nevertheless, this appearance cannot deny its *origin* and must proceed from it to constitute the multiplicity of its limitations as a whole" (*D*, 20).

The purpose of this passage is to announce the task of thinking as Hegel sees it. More precisely, Hegel contends that thinking comes into its own once it sets itself to its task of overcoming the deep bifurcation (or diremption) that lies at the basis of all positivity. Where phenomena and key elements in cultural life are not yet recognized as internally related and constituting a world, then philosophy's first task is to demonstrate the myopia of such a comprehension of the world. The problem with such thinking is that it regards Being as essentially fragmented, and beings as an ensemble of independent and limited positivities. Operating according to such an assumption about the nature of Being and of things, the logical understanding articulates the world according to increasingly defined and refined concepts. In short, such fragmented and fragmenting thought understands the world by means of the limitations which it introduces into its world. For Hegel speculative philosophy must surmount the opposition of reified concepts if it is to fulfill its task and promises. Consequently, Hegel characterizes the logical understanding as that way of thinking which stubbornly refuses to set itself to the speculative task of constructing the Absolute for consciousness (cf. *D*, 25). In opposition to his predecessors, who he argues have one and all operated within the purview of the understanding, Hegel contends that we only begin to approach an authentic comprehension of the reality of our world by means of the higher faculty of reason that has surpassed the limitations of logical concepts. The basic difference between these two attitudes of thought is quite clear: whereas the understanding is the name for a way of thinking which posits oppositions, the sole interest of reason is "to surmount such reified oppositions" (*D*, 21). Any philosophy bound by the positivity and rules of the understanding represents an obstacle to be overcome by any authentic conception of the real.

Though it is the sole interest of reason to surmount the rigidified oppositions posited by the understanding, this is not so because reason is blindly opposed to conflict and opposition as such. Rather Hegel conceives of reason always as in the service of the living reality of life itself (*D*, 113) and "one factor of life, which eternally forms itself against itself, is the necessity of diremption" (*D*, 21). Nevertheless, the essential problem for philosophy is not principally that of trying to draw the lines and distinctions which separate and limit aspects of the real, for such analytic distinctions are easily and quite inevitably made. That is what Hegel means when he says that diremption is necessary in the process whereby life eternal reforms itself. The difficulty comes in trying to see through to the essential unity and internal relatedness of these apparently separate and independent realities. However, for that genuine philosophical insight, the rules that have traditionally guided thinking about the real are inadequate and one-sided. Obedience to the law of noncontradiction, refusing to surpass the level of oppositions created by this law, is equally the refusal to follow the talents of thought to their true conclusion. It is important to note that, while Heidegger regards the understanding as clearly hostile to authentic thought, Hegel regards the understanding merely as inadequate and so does not view the relation between the understanding and reason merely as an antagonistic one; rather, reason is described as the dialectical overcoming of the logical intellect which "originated in reason" (D, 22). Concealed within the intellectual understanding there lies "the secret effectiveness of reason" (D, 26), and this of course means that the seeds for an overcoming of the one-sidedness of the intellect lie dormant in the intellect itself. This is one reason why Hegel, like Heidegger, turned back into the history of philosophy, seeking to recover and preserve something essential to his own project of thinking the Absolute. For Hegel the history of philosophy exhibits its destiny as the essential development of thought coming to the realization of its full, yet hidden, potential.

The paradigm case of one who developed a concept of the real and of experience which recognizes the need for the Absolute, but whose thought tied itself ever more tightly to the logic of understanding, is Kant. The basic thrust of the Kantian critical philosophy is to point to the equal necessities of mutually incompatible metaphysical assumptions. In the "Antinomy of Pure Reason" Kant discloses the interest that reason has in overcoming the conditioned and self-contradictory limitations of the understanding, but Kant balks at taking the speculative synthetic step Hegel makes when dialectically uniting these contradictions. For Kant the law of noncontradiction remains a supreme and inviolable law for the knowing subject despite the demand made by the "unavoidable problems set by pure reason itself" (KRV, B 7) that the "unconditioned" is "required to complete the series of conditions" (KRV, B xx). It is this recognition of the interests and demands of reason that so inspires Hegel, but it is Kant's insistence that the dialectical reconciliation of the contradictions raised by these demands can never be speculatively completed that makes Kant the real enemy of the Hegelian project. In his moral philosophy Kant argues that the practical interests of reason point the way to a categorical imperative, but only an imperative, not a necessity, and only practically, not theoretically. But in Hegel's eyes Kant does not represent a formidable opponent, for Hegel argues that insofar as the understanding comes to recognize its relation to the Absolute, which it is the task of thinking to construct, the understanding destroys itself. His reasoning on this point is quite simple: for any conditioned truth to be both intelligible and enduring, the conditions that determine it must be brought into view. But for that to happen, the understanding must begin the process of going beyond the limitations of its grasp to a fuller and deeper conception of what is true. Thus the limits of the understanding cannot hold fast if we are ever going to give an account of the intelligible structure of the world. Affirming this intelligible structure, disclosing the essential identity of thought and Being, is a firm and guiding prejudice of Hegelian thought. There is a strong conviction in Hegel, one that calls Aristotle's faith in the essential intelligibility of the cosmos to mind, that, despite its richness, nature "does not possess the power to resist the courage of knowledge" (VGP, I, 14). Therefore, it is crucial that Hegel defend this claim that reason gives the understanding "the law of self-destruction" (D, 28), so that the understanding is only a moment in the development of Absolute knowing, and as such the understanding dialectically considered is, in its truth, reason.

However, the danger with the understanding is its "stubbornness" (D, 26); namely, that it refuses to destroy itself because, as the activity of positing and preserving oppositions, it follows the law which fixes oppositions, the law of noncontradiction. Of course one of the oppositions to which it holds fast is its own opposition to its subject matter. This holding on to contradictions as mere opposition results in the "entrenchment of subjectivity" (GW, 290), which produces a "formal idealism, which in this manner posits on the one hand an absolute point of *egoity* and its understanding, and on the other hand an absolute *multiplicity* or sensation, i.e., a *dualism*" (GW, 314). As such a dualism, the understanding "enables the opposition of determination and undetermination, of finitude and infinitude to persist alongside of one another still not unified, and it enables Being to hold fast against the equally necessary non-Being" (D, 27). Thus, abiding by the law of noncontradiction, the logical understanding is incapable of grasping the original identity of Being and non-Being, and thus it is unable to achieve the Absolute. The outcome of an understanding that does not dialectically destroy itself is an antinomy, and this means that the only relationship which the understanding has to the Absolute is not knowledge but faith in something beyond itself. As such the understanding fails the philosophic task as Hegel conceives it: to lift everyday modes of understanding out of their fragmented world of conflicts and confusions, thereby elevating it to true knowledge of the essential wholeness of both the real and truth itself.

Hegel is quite insistent when arguing on behalf of the ineluctability of the unconditioned for philosophy: "When reason recognizes itself as absolute, *then philosophy begins*" (*D*, 45). He is also quite unequivocal when he argues that the laws of traditional logic, which form the backbone of the understanding, are simply incapable of answering the call of philosophy. The stubbornness of the understanding is its blindness to the *origin and need of philosophy*. This origin and need of philosophy is twofold: "The first is *the Absolute itself*; it is the goal that is sought; it is already at hand—otherwise how could it be sought? Reason only produces it insofar as it liberates consciousness from limitations; this surmounting of limitations is conditioned through the presupposed unlimitedness. The other . . . (is) the stepping out from totality of consciousness . . . the diremption in Being and Non-Being" (*D*, 24). Thus, the understanding is only capable of holding onto the apparent opposition of Being and non-Being and so is incapable of attaining the Absolute insofar as it has not yet recognized its own origin in an essential unity with Being. Hegel's argument is that the fundamental dialectical unity of the ground of both thought and Being is more original than the fragmented world view of the intellect. The true, yet nonapparent, ground of the world as plurality of individuals disclosed by the understanding is a place in which nothing in particular stands out as independent of that ground, but in which we find the essential unity of Being and Nothing itself. The Absolute is the overcoming of the aporias of particularity (such as one finds outlined by Leibniz) and the disclosure of the indeterminate origin and intelligibilizing ground of any particularity as such. Thus Hegel says that "The Absolute is the night, and the light is younger than it, and the difference of the two, as well as the stepping out of the night by the light, is an absolute difference,—the Nothing, the first, from out of which all Being, all multiplicity of the finite, has arisen" (*D*, 25). This incapability of the understanding to overcome the level of diversity and opposition is a consequence of its blindness to the Absolute, the Nothing out of which all Being and the multiplicity of things first appear. This blindness is in turn a consequence of the attentiveness of the intellect only to the diversity of things before it. Thus Hegel describes the understanding as working on the level of *Vorstellung* (representation) in which the frozen relation between things is one of comparison, domination, and causation; that is, from the point of view of the intellect, the relationship between things is an external one of seemingly independent beings. For the intellectual understanding, the deeper grounds and essential unity of the real are absent.

This then is Hegel's critique of the understanding: as the logical activity of dividing, separating, and so positing oppositions, it is incapable of grasping the true internal relation between things. This inability means that the logical understanding is only capable of grasping the totality of things as an endless multiplicity of finite entities in their opposition both to each other and to the infinite; it never conceives of the true infinite unity and systematic whole within which the truth of things is first discovered. Such a discovery is possible only for reason itself, which is able to overcome the level of opposition because it has remembered the unlimited and indeterminate origin, the *nothingness*, out of which opposition first arises. In contrast with the unifying power of reason, Hegel later characterizes the understanding as "the activity of cutting ... the enormous and astonishing, or rather the absolute power ... *the portentous power of the negative*; it is the energy of thought, of the pure ego" (*PG*, 29). The understanding is thus the activity of the knowing subject in its own individuated subjectivity. Reason, on the other hand, as interested not in preserving but in overcoming oppositions and achieving systematic wholeness, is the negation of this negating activity. As such, it is not bound by the individual subjectivity of the knower, nor is it bound by the intellectual rules of knowing. But this larger horizon of reason, the condition of surpassing the level of individuated subjectivity, is attained only with the recognition of the unreasonableness of holding fast to this individuality conceived by and for itself. Letting go of this subjectivity as a determinate something is the turn to the insight into the original identity of pure Being and pure Nothing as thoroughly indeterminate. Thus, as the positing of *oppositions*, the understanding is the power of the determining negative and so is to be destroyed, that is, it is to be negated as itself insofar as it is blind to the primordial nothingness which is its true origin. This means that for Hegel nothingness is more primordial than negation, and that the overcoming of the understanding, the negation of this nega- tion, that is, its dialectical overcoming, is possible only on the basis of having already recognized the Nothing which first makes negation possible. The intellectual understanding is only able to be en route to the higher truth disclosed by reason by opening itself to the insight that its own origin, and the origin of its great power of negation, rests upon the more original unity of Being and Nothing. Negation, the motor of the dialectic and the great talent of the intellect itself, rests upon "the Nothing, the first, from out of which all Being, all multi- plicity of the finite, has arisen" (D, 25). And since Hegel claims to be the first in the history of metaphysics to have conceived of the truth of dialectic, we may assume that Hegel would characterize all phi- losophy before him as representative of the intellectual understanding, that is, as blind to the original unity of Being and nothingness which grants the possibility of dialectic.

In summarizing Hegel's critique of the logical understanding, we may say that it is a way of thinking which

1. characterizes the tradition of metaphysics (before Hegel);
2. is a way of thinking which separates and takes the opposition between things as its model;
3. holds logic and its law of noncontradiction as the highest court of appeal;
4. conceives of Nothing as mere negation;
5. is blind to the original nothingness which it presupposes.

Despite the very different implications each draws on the basis of their respective efforts to overcome this limited logic of the understanding —Hegel emphasizes here the need for the infinite, while Heidegger finds testimony for the finite—Hegel's basic characterization of the metaphysical understanding and of its peculiar blindness is quite clearly in accord with Heidegger's. Yet, this initial similarity notwith- standing, Heidegger has still not lost his claim to be the first to recognize the role of non-Being in any authentic theory of Being, for Heidegger's critique of the understanding referred us to a very special sense of Nothing; namely, nothingness as it is experienced in anxiety. Heidegger makes clear that the full force and meaning of Nothing as original is first felt, rather than being known, and that attempts by the intellect to conceive this primordial Nothing are ultimately in vain. Since Hegel's critique of the understanding seems so couched in the conceptual language and logic of a dialectical epistemology, it would not seem likely that such a conceptually resistant experience as anxiety would play a role in Hegel's critique of it. So the question is then whether Hegel's critique of logic's restriction of non-Being to the function of negation does in fact rest upon the recognition of the same humanly felt experience of which Heidegger speaks, or whether there is finally a real difference in the evidence and argument that each gives when criticizing the previous history of metaphysics. Since Heidegger has already contended that nothingness is only disclosed in the human experience of the disposition of anxiety, we must not only ask how Hegel treats anxiety, but we must ask whether anxiety or some felt experience of equal originality plays a real role in the disclosure of this primordial Nothing, this "secret abyss, which is the birthplace [of truth]" (*GW*, 431).

V

For Heidegger anxiety is the disposition in which Dasein finds itself when coming face-to-face with death, so it is not insignificant for his confrontation with Hegel that, following the passage in which Hegel describes the understanding as the "portentous power of the negative," we hear that "Death, if we wish to name that unreality so, is the most terrible, and to hold fast to what is dead demands the greatest force. Powerless beauty hates the understanding because the latter requires of it what it cannot perform. But the life of Spirit is not a life which shuns death ... rather it endures death and in death maintains itself; ... it is this power only insofar as it looks the negative in the face and dwells with it. This dwelling is the magic power that converts the negative into Being" (*PG*, 29–30). In other words, only by looking the unreality and non-Being death in the face, and only by being capable of dwelling with it, is one able to recover the true sense of the real life of Spirit. That deficient way of conceiving the real, the logical understanding, is then deficient by virtue of its incapacity to confront and recognize the meaning of death. Death does play a role in Hegel's account of the revelation of the origin of the life of Spirit out of the secret abyss of Nothing, and this is the first indication that the sense of this nothingness goes beyond the concept of logical equivalence with Being; but Heidegger has claimed that it is only in anxiety that the true depth and universality of Nothing are revealed, so the real issue here is whether or not Hegel's concept of nothingness has its roots in such an anxious experience.

References to anxiety are few in Hegel; however, one of those few references is to be found in one of the most significant passages in his work: the dialectic of the master and slave. The basis of this dialectic is the desire for recognition; in other words, this celebrated passage is founded in a key development in what Hegel characterizes as the way of Being of human being: Desire. More precisely: this struggle for recognition, which initiates the dialectic of the master and slave, occurs only because the human way of Being is not satisfied by the merely immediate and unconscious way of Being of natural life, nor can it be satisfied when treated as such an immediate life. Rather, the special excellence of human being is to be a transcendence beyond the natural, immediate, given present. Thinking through the require-ments of this excellence shows that achieving it inevitably entails the willingness to risk and even sacrifice one's natural life. The paradigm case of such a transcendence that meets the sort of resistance that might require the risk of death is found in the confrontation of initially independent, potentially conflicting wills. When two people, both desiring to establish themselves as living more than a merely natural life (that is, as for itself as well as in itself) encounter each other, Hegel argues that they necessarily must be willing to risk their own life before the other, for this risk of one's natural, biological life is ulti-mately the only way to achieve the desired recognition when the conflict of wills cannot be resolved otherwise. In this mutual process of risking life, one of the antagonists might not display a fear of death or at least—perhaps because he has not yet faced the true meaning of death—is ready to risk death in the confrontation, while the other "has ... anxiety ... about his entire essence for he has the fear of death, of the absolute master. He has been shaken in his very being and has shattered all that was fixed" (*PG*, 148). The antagonist who does not experience such radical anxiety in the face of death is then in the position to dominate the will of the other and so become the master, while the one who experiences genuine anxiety refuses to risk his life, withdraws his will from the potential non-Being of death, and so must eventually be willing to subordinate his will to the other, becoming a slave as a result. From this starting point in this confrontation with death, Hegel moves to demonstrate the ultimate futility of the position of the master and to show that only the slave is able to attain the liberated standpoint of self-consciousness. The details of this dialectic of liberation have been presented many times and need not be rehearsed here. What is important in Hegel's analysis of the mediating transformation of the understanding into reason is that anxiety plays an essential role in it. The complete dissolution of all fixity and anxiety about the whole of one's Being is, for Hegel, the precondition for the uncovering of Being which can only be accomplished by reason. The path to the fulfillment of the promise of reason, the path that overcomes the inadequacies of the logical intellect, passes through the shattering felt experience of anxiety. Any way of thinking that does not originate in, and pass through, the experience of nothingness disclosed in anxiety is incapable of reaching the level of reason's knowledge of Being and instead remains trapped in the limited logic of the understanding. Thus, for Hegel, like Heidegger, insight garnered from experience of anxiety is a precondition for the overcoming of that ontologically deficient way of thinking which each characterizes as the logical and representing understanding.

Clearly, both the Hegelian and Heideggerian critiques of the traditional metaphysical understanding paint quite similar portraits of what the limitations of the logical understanding are, and both touch upon the same fundamental points in their respective efforts to overcome this mode of thought. But, despite this similarity, Heidegger has contended that the identity of Being and Nothing which Hegel recognizes is not the same as the identity to which Heidegger refers (*WM*, 119). In order to decide about this issue we must consider the third question which we need ask of Hegel: does Hegel conceive of nothingness primarily in terms of its opposition to Being (i.e., as negation), or in its belonging to Being (i.e., as nihilation)? Has Hegel recognized the true scope and meaning of the non-Being disclosed by anxiety; that is, has he conceived it as the merely other to Being or as belonging to the very fabric of the real itself?

VI

Since Hegel's critique of the understanding made clear that it was its inability to overcome the level of opposition that prevented it from thinking the Absolute, and since this was seen to be a consequence of the blindness of the understanding to the original nothingness which all negation presupposes, it would seem that we have already demonstrated that the answer to the first part of our question must be answered by saying no, Hegel does not conceive of nothingness primarily in opposition to Being and so as negation. Indeed, in light of the beginning of Hegel's *Logic*, "Pure Being and pure Nothing are the same" (*WL*, 67), it is clear that Hegel conceives of nothingness in its belonging to Being. But is the character of this identity of Being and Nothing the same as in Heidegger?

Besides the section in the *Differenzschrift* in which we found Hegel's critique of the understanding and which was the first text that presented Being and Nothing as identical, the most extensive analysis of the connection of Being and Nothing for Hegel is to be found in the beginning of the *Science of Logic*. Heidegger contended that the identity of Being and Nothing as it is presented here is a merely formal identity lacking the insight into the finitude of Being found in Heidegger's own characterization of that identity. For Heidegger claims that in that text Hegel only speaks of identity of Being and non-Being because each is "pure indeterminateness and emptiness" (*WL*, 66). Now, from Hegel's description of both Being and Nothing, it is clear that such a formal identity does exist. But is this formal identity the only, or true, basis of the connection of Being and Nothing?

"What is the truth is neither Being nor Nothing, but that Being— does not pass over but has passed over—into Nothing and Nothing into Being. But it is equally true that they are not undistinguished from each other, rather that they are not the same, that they are absolutely distinct, yet unseparated and inseparable and that each immediately vanishes in its opposite. Their truth is, therefore, this movement of the immediate vanishing of the one in the other: *Becoming*" (*WL*, 67). The essential dialectical connection of Being and Nothing is not the logical identity of two originally distinct concepts which are subsequently seen to share the same formal properties; it is rather in the always already having gone over into one another that this connection is to be thought, and this having gone over into one another of Being and Nothing Hegel names becoming. Because the truth of this belonging together of Being and Nothing is a perpetual becoming, and since Hegel claims that "there is nothing in heaven or on the earth that does not contain both Being and Nothing" (*WL*, 69), it is quite easy to see why one must not interpret this self-contradictory beginning of the odyssey of the Absolute as a static comparison of the logical structure of two concepts. Rather, this identity of Being and Nothing must be seen as the temporal *occurrence* which, in happening, sets forth the dynamic, dialectically propelled process which the *Science of Logic* describes. Bataille's Hegel-inspired meditation on sacrifice expresses this well: "Time is not the synthesis of being and nothingness.... There is, in fact, neither isolated being nor isolated nothingness; there is time. But to affirm the existence of time is an empty assertion in the sense that it gives less the vague attribute of existence to time than the nature of time to existence; in other words, it empties the notion of existence of its vague and limitless content, and at the same time it infinitely empties it of all content." [36] Every dialectical transition that follows can only be understood as a necessary implication of this dynamic identity of Being and Nothing. That identity, the development of which passes through the experience of anxiety, is another indication that Hegel does not conceive negation as more original than Nothing; rather the converse is true: negation is not the negation of an already disclosed and posited being or Being but is itself disclosed as belonging to the inner, essential, negativity of Being itself. In short, only because Being cannot initially be thought apart from its conceptually radical other, non-Being, does the dialectical spring that is the essence of Being itself spring into action. The dialectic is the development of this contradiction in all of its complexity and consequences up to its disclosure of the Absolute infinity of this identity.

Thus Heidegger's claims to the contrary notwithstanding, such an identity of Being and Nothing appears to draw even closer to the way in which Heidegger characterizes this identity, that is, as the occurrence of nihilation in the essence of Being itself. So the problem arises more sharply: in his effort to justify his abiding claim to have thought the beginning of thought itself more originally than metaphysics, and to have done so by uncovering the unthought identity of Being and Nothing, Heidegger has sought to differentiate himself from Hegel, yet despite Heidegger's assertions of the differences between his own position and Hegel's, the proximity of the two seems more apparent than ever. Despite this proximity, Heidegger claims to have demonstrated that the identity of Being and Nothing means that Being in its essence is *finite* (*WM*, 119), while Hegel contends that the identity of the two dialectically entails the achievement of the *infinite* Absolute. Though both Hegel and Heidegger interpret the original identity of Being and Nothing as an occurrence disclosed in anxiety, each develops the meaning of this identity in quite different ways. For Hegel the identity of Being and non-Being discloses the inner conflict and tension at the heart of the real; for Heidegger it is evidence for the impenetrable darkness and ultimate nonconceptualizability of the real. There is an obvious difference in intent between Hegel and Heidegger, but because the evidence each musters on behalf of his own intentions is so closely related in important ways, the achievements of both are soon to be called into question.

VII

Heidegger still might be able to legitimate his claim that metaphysics is a flight from the finitude of Being, but he can no longer substantiate the means of defending this claim by simply pointing to the failure of metaphysics to confront the original and radically nihilating sense of non-Being belonging to Being itself. When Plato spoke of non-Being as contrary to the logos, he did so to admonish those wishing to follow the path of philosophy not to enter into such a thought. At the other end of the Platonic tradition Hegel agrees that non-Being is contrary to the traditional logical understanding, but this is the reason that the contradictory thought of non-Being dialectically propels thought beyond the limitations of this traditional intellectual understanding to the full knowledge of the Absolute. Heidegger's claim that the very thought of non-Being destroys the foundations of the metaphysical project is no longer as self-evident as he says it is because he ignored the fact that Hegel could invoke the very same thought in his efforts to complete and fulfill the demands of metaphysics. Heidegger's case for having destroyed Hegel as a representative of metaphysics cannot rest on the analysis of anxiety as he has presented it. The full radicality of dialectical negation includes recognition of the experience of anxiety, and that alone undermines Heidegger's second attempt to disentangle his thought from Hegel's. It is not yet clear what this deepening entanglement between Hegel and Heidegger means: whether it indicates a dialectical and idealist residue in Heidegger's ontology of finite Being; whether it points to a concealed insight into the finitude of Being in Hegelian thought; or whether it simultaneously says something about both the project to complete and the project to destroy metaphysics. However, one thing at least is quite clear: Heidegger can no longer afford to avoid a serious confrontation with Hegelian texts and arguments. While he continues to struggle to find a way to define and defend his ontology of finite Being, he can no longer use Hegel as a pretext for his own purposes but must rethink his own claims in the light of Hegel's opposition to them. Thus, Heidegger, who in 1925 made remarks such as the one that described the Hegelian dialectic as at bottom merely sophistry (*L*, 252), in 1935, at the end of "The Origin of the Work of Art," can comment on Hegel's claim that "Art, according to its highest determination, is, for us, something past," by saying that "the decision about Hegel's remark is not yet made" (*H*, 67); and, in a 1934 lecture on Hölderlin, Heidegger is finally compelled to concede that "the infinite thought of Hegel is no contrived formula" (*HH*, 132). Shortly after "What is Metaphysics?" there is a shift in Heidegger's position with regard to Hegel, and not insignificantly this shift corresponds with the celebrated "turn" in Heidegger's own thought. During this formative period, which was tumultuous in Heidegger's life as well as his thought, the tone and substance of references to Hegel gradually change so that they no longer portray him simply as an opponent against whom Heidegger must separate himself. So, for instance, throughout Heidegger's decade-long meditation on Nietzsche, references to Hegel, though infrequent, are generally sympathetic, such as the remark that "The last and greatest aesthetics of the Occident is Hegel's" (*N*, I, 100). Likewise Heidegger's encounter with Hölderlin, which proved to be a lifelong dialogue that presents Hölderlin as Heidegger's true predecessor, is in a significant sense equally an encounter with Hegel, for as Heidegger concedes: "It is no accident that the thinker who put the thought of Heraclitus in the only philosophical system that is thought to its ground and end found in western philosophy, Hegel, was Hölderlin's compatriot in both age and studies. Hegel and Hölderlin grew up in a common spiritual world" (*HH*, 129). In short, following the second effort to separate himself from Hegel, Heidegger increasingly points to Hegel as representing a real riddle for thought, and not its greatest enemy. During the 1930s Heidegger's confrontation with Hegel has less the character of a collision of opposites and

more that of an intimate struggle forcing both Hegel and Heidegger
to reveal the presuppositions and prejudices upon which each bases
his thought.

This discovery of a deeper proximity to Hegel does, however,
present a very real problem for Heidegger, for the final difference
between them still remains: Hegel claims to have thought the ground
of thinking absolutely while Heidegger contends that this is an impossibility. Heidegger's project to destroy metaphysics has met with a
scrious obstacle in the figure of Hegel. Significantly, during the years
of this discovery Heidegger speaks less of the "destruction" of metaphysics and morc frequently of "overcoming" or "coming to terms"
[*Verwindung*] with it. A crucial element in the problem that metaphysics now poses for Heidegger is found in the infinite thought of
Hegel. The need to search for his real differences with Hegel becomes
the occasion for Heidegger's 1930/31 (the hundredth anniversary of
Hegel's death) lecture course on Hegel's *Phenomenology of Spirit*. Thus
only three years after the publication of *Being and Time* in which the
figure of Hegel represents the highpoint of the forgetfulness of Being,
Heidegger devotes an entire lecture course to a careful "explication
de texte" of the first two sections of Hegel's text on the science of
experience as the basis for the absolute thought of infinite Being.[37]

One might expect that this extensive reexamination of Hegel would
explicitly treat the problems that surfaced as a result of Heidegger's
previous criticism of the Hegelian concepts of time and nothingness;
however, such is not the case. In fact, of the two issues on which
Heidegger confronted Hegel, one of them, the notion of nothingness,
is completely omitted from the lecture, and of the other, the concept
of primordial time, Heidegger says very little, only briefly seeking to
reassert his separation from Hegel in the matter. Thus, despite a
growing recognition of his proximity to Hegel, Heidegger still wants
to argue that "If ever the locating of the problematic of *Being and
Time* is thoroughly senseless, then it is so with Hegel" (*HP*, 209).[38] A
real residue of Heidegger's early prejudice against Hegelian thought
still remains even though the purpose of this course is to force Heidegger to take a closer look at Hegelian metaphysics.

Yet one should not hastily conclude from this sort of remark that
Heidegger has not become aware of the significance and complexities
of the confrontation with Hegel. Though most of the text of Heidegger's lecture is in the form of a teaching commentary that does not

try to enter into a real dialogue on those topics central to Heidegger's own thought, there are some sections in which Heidegger does take the opportunity to expose the meaning of a point in Hegel by bringing it closer to the way in which Heidegger himself interprets that point.[39] In other words, at times the commentary takes the form of an unsettled dialogue and confrontation about the same themes. Heidegger now shows that he is willing to learn from Hegel in the way that he has already learned from Kant, for instance. At every previous turn in the destruction of the metaphysics of Being, Heidegger presented Hegel as an apparent, but only apparent, exception to that tradition, and yet, when we push the semblance of an accord more forcefully than Heidegger did, we find that Hegel has indeed frequently used Heidegger's own critical wedge against metaphysics for his own quite different purpose. As their paths continue to cross, the issues at stake become less clear, as does the final point of contention between Hegel and Heidegger. At one point in his lecture course on Hegel Heidegger quite clearly describes what he sees as the significance of his encounter with Hegel: *"Our confrontation is at the crossroad of finitude and infinity, a crossroad, not a mere contraposition of two standpoints"* (*HP*, 92). That Heidegger now names his confrontation with Hegel as a "crossroad" indicates that he realizes that the struggle between them is not one of mere opposition but an intimate struggle of entanglement. That he names the point at issue in the crossroad as the finite and the possibility of its infinite retrieval indicates that he still conceives the struggle as over the metaphysical denial of the full force of the finite. In an essential sense the core of the ontology of finite Being and the subsequent destruction of a metaphysic of Being intersects the Hegelian effort to reconstruct the Absolute for thought. The perplexities and puzzles that this injects into what it means to speak of finite as well as infinite Being cast serious doubt upon the self-presentation of each ontology. Yet, despite the inherent hostility of results, both rest upon a similar set of defenses and evidence that is quite unique in the history of philosophy. Up to this point, Heidegger's critique of Hegel consisted primarily in Heidegger's appeal to elemental experiences and insights he contended were absent in the Hegelian system—insights such as those Heidegger claimed into the essence of time and the identity of Being and Nothing. Now, however, Heidegger's critique undergoes a shift in its basic strategy, and so he focuses increasingly on the different development that Hegel finds in such original experiences. The claim now is that Hegel never fully understood the entitlements granted by those original experiences. Heidegger now might be willing to concede that Hegel at least touched upon the fundamental phenomena that circumscribe Heidegger's own concerns, but that Hegel has mistaken the real results and consequences of those original experiences. Heidegger wants to argue that the nature of these experiences *as original* and so *as the starting point* for philosophical reflection, not simply *as such*, opens up a finite horizon for reflection and so cannot lead to the Hegelian concept of the infinity of reflection. Thus when he says that "*The end (for Hegel) is only the beginning which has become other and returned to itself*" (*HP*, 52), he is arguing that Hegel misunderstood something essential about the nature of such a beginning. Now Heidegger indicates that the divergence of outcomes is to be located in the way each characterizes the philosophic beginning itself. Both begin their ontology with similar "contents" and topics (time, history, Being, Nothing), but it is now no longer the content but the structure and logic of beginning as such that moves to the forefront of Heidegger's concerns. After this lecture course on Hegel, and in many ways a result of it, Heidegger's purpose is to describe the ontological consequences to which the logic of beginning with such primordial phenomena commits us. In the years immediately following this rereading of Hegel, the themes of beginning, origin, and the hermeneutic circle increasingly come to the center of Heidegger's concerns. With these themes Heidegger now intends to demonstrate that the original tentativeness, incipience, and concealedness of the beginning of a philosophical reflection that follows the path of such elemental phenomena cannot be surmounted but is only deepened, the deeper thought penetrates their essence and meaning.

3

Beginnings, Origins, Circles, and Spirals

What we call the beginning is often the end. And to make an end is to make a beginning. The end is where we start from.
— *T. S. Eliot*

It is well known, but insufficiently remembered, that asking the question of where and how one must begin in order to arrive at an ontology that does not distort and close off access to those questions that call for an ontology involves more than procedural concerns, for one can only answer this unavoidable question as a matter of principle. No matter how one answers the question of the beginning, the answer always contains an anticipation of that which reaches far beyond the simple starting point for reflection. The first or principal decision that constitutes the beginning is that related to possible ends: its where, character, and content. One faces the problem of beginning not merely chronologically, but ontologically. This conflation of the ontological with the chronological gives a special sharpness to the paradox of beginning: in order to have begun properly we must have already faced the question of the beginning philosophically, yet in order to have done this we must have already begun. The question of the beginning, while inescapable, is thus both circular and inconsistent at once. As such, the question of the beginning is like the topic of non-Being in that it is hostile to the laws of the logical understanding, but unlike the idea of non-Being, which falls into neglect throughout the history of philosophy, the riddle posed by the beginning is ineluctable and so among the most ancient of philosophic concerns.

Many of the most significant transformations and ruptures in the history of philosophy are important by virtue of the new answer offered to this question of the philosophic beginning. Thus from Socrates, through Augustine and Descartes, Hume and Kant, to Marx and Husserl new traditions have been founded by some sort of redefinition of the nature and place of the philosophic starting point. Certainly much of what we find in antiquity is guided by this concern. When the mythopoeic speculations on the genesis and principles of the intelligible world began to fracture, philosophy rushed in to pick up the same concerns. The first philosophers were the thinkers who gave reasons for a first principle starting from which nature could be explained and ending with which thought could retrieve itself. Much of what we find so obscure about Heraclitus and Parmenides is best understood as a meditation on the place and nature of the philosophic beginning, and most of the differences between them is a result of the way each responds to the "with what" and "how" of this riddle. Aristotle's discussion of the various senses of "beginning"—a discussion that takes its own beginning in an analysis of Aristotle's own predecessors—and of the link between what is referred to by the "beginning" and by "cause" (*Metaphysics*, 1012b–1013a) is a key text in the eventual self-understanding of metaphysics as a search for first causes. From the outset the metaphysical way of posing the question of the philosophic beginning has been linked to the question of first causes. Even the celebrated "quarrelle des anciennes et modernes" can be interpreted in terms of the modern introduction of the search for a radically new beginning. Modernity comes into being not only as a repudiation of its past but also as a passionate attachment to the idea of a new beginning purified of the uncertainties and ambiguities of what went before it. Goethe's remark sums up this sensibility well: "From here and today a new epoch in history begins." Descartes' attempt to wipe the slate clean in the second *Meditation*, unleashing hyperbolic doubt as a destructive force in service of a new and secure beginning, is a paradigm but not isolated example of vigorous repudiation of the past that ushers in the modern age. This syndrome of the new beginning and of its methodological safekeeping is an element in modern thought unknown in antiquity, for there we cannot find the metaphysical equivalent of the "big bang" such as we find in the Cartesian cogito, Leibnizian monad, or Spinozist God. Even while closing the door on the modern period, Hegel and Heidegger succumb to a species of this prejudice of modernity insofar as each speaks of the end of philosophy as it once was; however, both escape the full implications of the metaphysics of modernity by the search for a new beginning that is not ahistorical and "shot from a pistol," but that is able to give an account of both its past and possible future beginnings. At least that is their shared intention.

So when Heidegger moves to address the riddle of the philosophic beginning, he is making yet another effort to plunge directly into the essential and unthought core of metaphysics in order to separate himself from that tradition. As Heidegger raises it, the question of the beginning not only concerns the content, the given, which belongs to the beginning, but more importantly concerns the nature of the beginning *as such*. Heidegger's effort to confront and overcome the metaphysical conception of the philosophic beginning is directed especially toward the modern conception that the beginning represents a clean break, or rupture, with previous conditions that holds out the promise of the eventual achievement of unconditioned and infinite knowing such as outlined in the Hegelian notion of Absolute Spirit. Once again, the Hegelian results come forward as the extreme case of a "position" Heidegger wants to overcome; and yet once again Hegel will step forward as having what Heidegger grants as at least an apparent accord with Heidegger's own position, since both find a special and similar significance in the riddles posed by the question of the philosophic beginning. But while Hegel finds the inner contradiction and circularity of the beginning as further testimony for the dialectical path to the Absolute, Heidegger finds this inner and unreconcilable ambiguity of the question to be evidence for the ineradicability of the ontological difference that is the basic trademark of finite Being.

I

From the outset of Heidegger's efforts to destroy metaphysics as a theory of Being, the question of the philosophic beginning has played an important role. Yet hitherto this has been a rather concealed role, for the topic of the beginning had been addressed only obliquely in Heidegger's discussions of primordiality and originary phenomena. But there is a difference between the structural question of the beginning and those early treatments of the primordial phenomena, fundamental dispositions, and original time as disclosed by the analysis of the facticity of Dasein: the question of the beginning is not primarily a question of how to interpret a primordial phenomenon but a question about one of the guiding logical presumptions inherent in the traditional conception of philosophy. At this point in the project to overcome metaphysics, it is the very idea of philosophy as such that gets called into question. It is also at this point that Heidegger finally abandons his own efforts to outline a universal fundamental ontology and begins to speak in terms of turning to the broader concerns of the "task of thinking." During this period of the "turn," Heidegger's efforts to overcome metaphysics as a way of thinking Being no longer rests primarily upon attempts to disclose some essential and "primordial" evidence, such as Heidegger had claimed was found in his notions of temporality, anxiety, or Nothing, that can be contrasted with its "vulgar," metaphysical counterpart. Instead, Heidegger now tends to legitimate his critique of the metaphysical attempt to achieve the decisive and absolute ground of Being upon the failure of such attempts. Henceforth, it is the question of the entitlements of thought that describes itself as philosophic, that is, the scope of philosophy itself, that moves to the center of Heidegger's concerns. What Heidegger later describes as the "step back" and the "way back into the ground of metaphysics" is not so much designed as an "alternative philosophy" to metaphysics but as a new attitude of thinking. Calling philosophy as such into question is the first stage in the effort to break down the disciplinary separation of philosophy from other ways of speaking and thinking the finite: at this point poetry and art first appear as other modes of discourse and ways in which the truth of Being is made manifest. They become other ways of beginning and being en route to the task of thinking. Raising the question of the nature of the philosophic beginning is the way in which Heidegger is able to deepen and broaden his critique of the history of Being as metaphysics. It is not until the 1935 text on "The Origin of the Work of Art" that Heidegger explicitly turns to the question of the logic of the beginning as such, but once this question surfaces it becomes a leading theme of Heidegger's thought, receiving intensive attention during the following decade in the Nietzsche volumes,[40] the essays and lectures on Hölderlin,[41] and the Schelling book.[42] In every case the effort is to indicate ways in which metaphysics has neglected the essential ontological commitments to be found in the very idea of the philosophic beginning.

Throughout each of these discussions Heidegger makes a very clear distinction between two types of beginning: between the beginning taken as a starting point and as an origin. " 'Start'—that is something other than 'beginning'.... The start is that whereby something commences, the beginning is that from out of which something springs.... The start is left behind, it vanishes in the advance of events. The beginning, the origin, on the other hand, first shows itself in events and is fully there first at the end. One who starts much never arrives at the beginning. Obviously, we humans can never begin with the beginning—only a God can do that—rather we must start, i.e., commence, with that which first leads to the origin or points to it" (*HH*, 3–4). Such a distinction between the two senses of "beginning" should come as no surprise, for we have already seen a foreshadowing of it in the earlier distinction between the ontic and ontological, as well as in Heidegger's analysis of the concept of time, which not only disclosed two senses of time—one original, the other derivative—but analyzed the derivative notion of time as a succession of now "points" from which time ceaselessly took its start. Heidegger frequently goes to great lengths to demonstrate that the traditional metaphysical conception of an issue is a derivation and leveling down of the fullness of the phenomenon at stake. The same approach is made when Heidegger turns his attention to the theme of the beginning. Here his claim is not that the tradition has failed to understand the paradox of the beginning as violating the laws of logic prohibiting circularity and self-contradiction but that it has failed to recognize the anticipatory and staying power of the beginning. From the logical point of view, the beginning is something to be gotten beyond; it cannot hold simply because of its inherent illogicality, and as such it is understood as a starting point to be left behind in the course of further understanding. A classic example of such a philosophical starting point is to be found in the ambiguities pertaining between the Cartesian beginning in the cogito and its starting point with radical epistemological doubt: the *Meditations* start with the destructive work of doubt but do not begin until doubt stops. Unlike Heidegger's early analysis of anxiety as underpinning and informing the basic and enduring traits of factically existing Dasein, Cartesian doubt is vanquished and brought to an abrupt halt by the real beginning found in the cogito sum. Doubt gives no hint of functioning as a kind of epistemic anxiety. Likewise the comparison points out the ways in which anxiety exceeds doubt in its lasting power. But the point to be made is that while Descartes wants to begin with the security of the cogito, the cogito itself relies upon the earlier starting point in doubt. There is then a certain ambiguity and duplicity in the Cartesian philosophical beginning—one that Descartes neglects—and this ambiguity is, Heidegger argues, a hidden yet essential characteristic of any philosophical beginning whatsoever. Furthermore, Heidegger argues that metaphysics has always been blind to this original yet enduring differential element of the philosophic beginning, for to recognize it is to recognize the fundamentality of what Heidegger calls the "ontological difference." But what this means, and how Heidegger arrives at this thought, first becomes clear in a closer look at the character of the beginning as Heidegger presents it.

The most extensive meditation of this period on the complexities of the philosophic beginning is in "The Origin of the Work of Art." Though the title of the essay might lead one to suppose that the principal topic of the text is art and hence constitutes Heidegger's contribution to a theory of aesthetics, such is not the best description of that essay. In fact, we soon come to recognize that the genitive "of" in the title is—as is typical for Heidegger—both subjective and objective at once. This ambiguity in the title of the text indicates that it will treat of the origin of the work of art (objective genitive) as well as that which the work of art is originating (subjective genitive). The meditation on the work of art is inseparable from the meditation on the nature and role of the origin. Indeed, the first words of the text speak not of art but of the meaning of "origin": "The origin is that from which and through which a matter is what it is and how it is. That, which something is, we name its essence. The origin of something is the source of its essence" (UK, 7). It is immediately announced that the task of the essay is to make visible the source of the essence of art, its origin, yet from the title and the first two paragraphs of the text, we find that this task soon reveals itself to be a treatment of the theme of the origin as such, for "all art is essentially an origin and nothing else" (UK, 65).

At the outset of the essay Heidegger anticipates the result: art is original in the dual sense of being a new beginning and of being inimitable. The true work of art will show itself as founding and setting up a world (as, for instance, Homer can be said to have contributed to the founding of the self-understanding of the

Greek world), and as such it is essentially productive and thus not *re*producible. What is just as important as what Heidegger says about art is the way in which he goes about making his argument, for from the start the structure of the text itself is a mirror of its topic. The first page of the essay immediately gets entangled in the circular argument that the origin of the work of art can only be made apparent in understanding the originality of that which has already come to be as a work of art. The essence and origin of the work of art is found in the very creative act that happens in the work; it bears its own origin within itself and opens up its own conditions. Hence Heidegger's remark that "everyone easily notes that we are moving in a circle. The usual understanding demands that this circle be avoided because it violates the laws of logic" (*UK*, 8). This remark must not be taken as an excuse for an awkward or misfired beginning to the text but as a comment on the character of the beginning as such—a character that this essay wants to wear on its sleeve. This then is the first trait of the primordial sense of beginning for Heidegger: it involves us in a circle. One place that we find the meaning of this circularity of the beginning most clearly evident is in the experience of the work of art. Unlike the traditional metaphysical admiration for the syllogistic line of argumentation of mathematics as embodying the basic features that philosophy would like to make its own (calculability, reproducibility, the possibility of certainty), Heidegger finds the circularity of the work of art and the nonobjectifiability of aesthetic experience a better place to turn for phenomenology's efforts to find models for its own self-understanding.[43]

It should be noted that, despite Heidegger's argument that metaphysics abhors circles and loves syllogistic straight lines, the image of the circle does play a prominent, almost archetypal, role in Greek philosophy and literature. Hesiod makes much of the cyclical motion of the heavens and the seasons as the sign of their immutability. Parmenides speaks of the "unshaken heart of well-circled truth" disclosed by doors that open on a "revolving axis" (DK B 1.7–8, 17–20). Plato describes the soul as a permeable sphere engendered by a complex series of rotating circles (*Phdr.* 251d), and the cosmology of the *Timaeus* describes the cosmos as a perfection of circles upon circles. In Hippocrates we read that disease is an instability and disruption of the circles of the soul. And in Aristotle's *Physics* we learn that the things in nature that move eternally in a circle are the best things in nature (261b 27f).[44] Augustine's description of God's nature as like a circle whose center is everywhere and its circumference nowhere stands at the end of the Greek relation to the image of the circle. But by and large the image of the circle in antiquity (after Aristotle and until Hegel it disappears as a dominant image or metaphor in philosophy) is traditionally an image of reconciliation, unity, infinity, wholeness, perfection, or what might best be described as a "homecoming." It becomes, in Emerson's words, a "primary figure . . . repeated without end . . . the highest emblem in the cipher of the world." [45] Clearly Heidegger's discussion of the circularity of the philosophic beginning and of the complex circularity of the originality of the work of art moves in precisely the opposite direction of such reconciliation and homecoming: for Heidegger, the image of the circle serves not to represent the infinity of the unity of thought and Being but the ineradicable finitude and insurmountable original-ity of the ontological difference. The circularity of the ontological difference, which was once analyzed in the "circular Being of Dasein" (*SZ*, 315) as its special existential fore-structure, is an expression of the finitude of Being itself. In speaking about circles and origins we are not speaking logically, formally, or chronologically, but onto-logically and temporally. According to Heidegger's remarks at the outset of "The Origin of the Work of Art," the question of the philosophic beginning and the image of the circle belong together most clearly in the experience of the work of art.

But the circularity of the primordial beginning is not only manifest in the image of the work of art, for the logic of the circularity of the beginning is so fundamental for Heidegger that it must necessarily be a central element of every experience of Being and so of every key Heideggerian argument. Experiences such as translation, the disclosure of nature, others, and history all come to the fore in later works as exhibiting this original circularity. But even if we neglect the brief discussion of the hermeneutic circle found in *Being and Time* and restrict ourselves instead to the two topics we have considered thus far, the concepts of time and non-Being, we find the notion of circularity present in both. Besides the few, but important, direct references to the hermeneutic circle in *Being and Time*, Heidegger's concept of primordial temporality as a futural-past-presentness is easily recognized as outlining a circular structure, and though "What is Metaphysics?" makes no explicit reference to the notion of circle, the identity of Being and Nothing developed there immediately involves one in a circular discussion of their mutual belonging together. Despite this, the logic and full import of this circularity and its belonging together with the question of the philosophic beginning largely goes unacknowledged in those texts and so remains unclear.[46] One of the goals of the essay on art is to address the relation of originality, circularity, and truth.

Heidegger begins by noting that the difficulties of speaking of this original and enduring circularity of the true beginning are compounded when we hold fast to those traditional laws of the understanding which regard logic and its laws to be the highest laws of thought. From this vantage point all talk in favor of circularity commits the fallacy of *petitio principii*. Heidegger's reference to this fallacy has a purpose: first, to make clear that he is not advocating that we commit this fallacy but that, by invoking the notion of the circle to characterize the meaning of the origin, he wants to point to something quite distinct from a naive logical error; and second, his purpose is to point out that, in obeying the laws of logic, the traditional understanding is incapable of grasping the true character of the beginning. This second point should already be quite apparent, for the issue of the beginning arose out of the problem of speaking about the nature of the original identity of Being and Nothing, an identity that the traditional logical understanding was incapable of conceiving. Once again another style of thinking is requisite. But with regard to the other purpose of Heidegger's comment we must ask: if the circle to which Heidegger refers is not the circularity warned against in the fallacy of *petitio principii*, and if it is not the infinite circle of homecoming found in Greek philosophy and literature, then what sort of circle is it that characterizes the original circle? Whereas the traditional and logical understanding represents circularity as a movement closed in upon itself in the manner of empty repetition, Heidegger's conception of circularity articulates an essential characteristic of the beginning itself as originating, and as such this circularity describes the entry into the movement of origination. Thus Heidegger contends that if thought is to be true to its task, the circle is not to be avoided but entered into: "(we) must carry out this circular movement" for to do so is "the feast of thought" (*UK*, 8). But why is this the case?

Already in *Being and Time* we find a clear answer to this question:

"This circle ... is not a circle in which an arbitrary way of knowing moves, rather it is the expression of the existential pre-structure of Dasein itself" (SZ, 153). The circle must be entered into because it describes the precondition and character of our very access to the question of the meaning of Being as it is found, "the circular Being of Dasein" (SZ, 315). This circularity of Dasein is a consequence of its way of Being; namely, its way of relating to beings in their Being and reaching an understanding of Being gained through those beings to which it comports itself. The circularity of Dasein is the character of the temporal movement of Dasein as spanning and inhabiting the inseparable difference between Being and beings. In other words, the circle is an expression of the *ontological difference*.

Thus far we have contended that, for Heidegger, the first significant characteristic of the beginning is that it is a circle and that this circle is not to be understood according to the rules of logic, which conceives it as a *vitiosum*, but as an expression of the ontological difference. But in order to become clear about what this means, it is necessary that we remember that this circularity is also a characteristic of Heidegger's concept of primordial time; in other words, primordial time does not begin with an isolated ahistoric starting point but has "always already" begun. Likewise, we may say of Heidegger's notion of the beginning that, as circular, it too has always already begun. Thus, the beginning is never an *a*historic, *pre*suppositionless, *pre*given, situation-*free* starting point; rather, the true beginning is what it is as always already underway and always an anticipation of its possible end. But to acknowledge the circularity of the beginning requires that we recognize that, in some sense at least, the beginning already has a certain anticipatory wholeness to it, but as begun and still underway, it is not yet complete or finished. This tension between the wholeness of the beginning and its being already underway is the mainspring of the movement of origination characterizing the philosophic beginning. The beginning cannot be a static starting point, rather it is temporally ecstatic origination. As such a dynamic process, the beginning originates and opens up the course of that which follows. The development of the beginning is not a leaving behind of the beginning, nor a mere repetition of it, but a deepening and centering into the beginning itself; that is, the beginning "circles in this (original) circle" (UK, 8). Thus, the beginning itself requires a constant relocation of the circle into which it centers. This means that the beginning requires a continual dislocation of itself: "Philosophy (carries out) a continual dislocation of places and levels. That is why one often does not know which way to turn in it" (*FD*, 1). In a significant sense the very idea of the philosophical beginning brings with it an inherent and essential displacement of itself and its topic. Any localization of the beginning is equally a dislocation of the circularity of the original, yet provisional, fullness of that beginning; as such, the philosophic beginning initiates a movement of both disclosure and closure at once.

From this description of Heidegger's notion of the beginning it is not immediately clear why Heidegger describes what "happens" in this circular movement of origination as "a happening of *truth*" (*UK*, 25). If truth is conceived as the fullness of disclosure, then the beginning is anything but the happening of truth for it is both a continual self re- and dis-location. The beginning as Heidegger analyzes it does not open the way to the full disclosure of the given but to the simultaneous alteration of the given as initially disclosed. That is why along with the analysis of the beginning Heidegger says that "truth, in its essence, is un-truth.... The essence of truth is in itself the primordial struggle" (*UK*, 43). Because the happening of truth in this dynamic movement of origination means that each new relocation of the topic and locus of truth, that is, each stage of unconcealedness, is simultaneously the dis-location of the previous locus of truth, i.e., is concealing, it must be the case that there is no unconcealment without concealment. Springing from a circular origin, truth as disclosure not only comes to be along with its other but it also is always part of the history of such occurrences, which are all "pregnant with the force of plurification and dissolution."[47]

When Heidegger speaks of the meaning of truth that happens in origination, he says quite clearly that such a notion of truth is to be thought according to what the Greeks called *aletheia*. Yet, for all the talk of the relation between philosophy and truth, he claims that "The essence of truth as *aletheia* remains unthought in the thought of the Greeks and in all philosophy which follows it" (*UK*, 40). More precisely, what has remained unthought throughout the history of philosophy's account of the nature of truth is the insurmountable concealedness belonging to the essence of truth. This concealedness is not to be equated with *pseudos*. That is, concealedness is not some absolute other antagonistic to truth but is the inevitable and enduring dislocation of any philosophic beginning, which is an essential element of truth itself. Heidegger is not arguing that falsity understood as incorrectness accompanies all truth or that the full disclosure of truth of Being is possible but is simply outside of the realm of human possibility; rather, he is arguing that the essential nature of truth is inseparable from untruth. The best way to measure and speak of truth is not in terms of rightness, correctness, correspondence or coherence but rather in terms of the scope, depth, and originality of disclosure. Truth is always best spoken of as disclosive and interesting, and its best "measure" is the vitality of the effect of its occurrence. Error, conceived not as a mistake but as a straying away from the origin, is the price of disclosure.[48] From its first appearance, the original sense of the truth of Being is at once already a dislocation or debasing of the locus of that very truth. But it is important not to mistake the nature of this essential untruth. The concealedness that describes the untruth belonging to the essence of truth is not to be thought as the falseness of incorrectness or inadequacy; rather, this concealedness that is the ineradicable counterpart of unconcealedness is to be thought as *lethe*. This means that the original and circular struggle that marks the happening of truth is the struggle of unconcealedness and forgetfulness.

When Heidegger speaks of metaphysics as "the forgetfulness of Being," he is not simply saying that metaphysics is a willful error on the part of a long line of thinkers but that it rests upon an essential risk found in the truth of Being itself. Yet, strangely and significantly, metaphysics is not aware of itself resting upon this risk inherent in philosophically asking and beginning the question of Being. Saying that the forgetfulness of Being belongs to its truth means of course that the history of metaphysics as the history of this forgetfulness is not a monolithic or massive historical error, but that it conceals within itself, even against itself, an inseverable relation to the truth of Being that Heidegger himself wants to describe. Not surprisingly then, at about this point Heidegger's project to "destroy" metaphysics begins to manifest an evident change in tone: Heidegger increasingly regards his predecessors as partners in a dialogue, rather than as enemies of thinking. Not every predecessor comes to be regarded as Heidegger's companion—Plato and Descartes still stand out as two important figures to whom Heidegger's resistance has not abated—but those who do—Heraclitus, Aristotle, Kant, Hegel, and

Nietzsche dominate this group—come to be regarded as Heidegger's true contemporaries in the "thinking and speaking of Being" (which might explain the almost complete absence of any reference in his work to Heidegger's own twentieth-century contemporaries). In view of what he says about the possible essence of truth opened up by the philosophical beginning, Heidegger must mitigate, if not abandon, his own insistence upon a clear and distinct separation of his own approach to Being from the metaphysical approach. Hitherto Hegel has served Heidegger as a foil in his project to destroy metaphysics, and in large measure it has been his failure to disentangle himself from Hegel that has led Heidegger to this reassessment and turn in his own thinking. Now however, if Heidegger is to draw the full consequences of this essential ineradicable errancy that belongs to truth itself, he must be willing to recognize that his own project to overcome metaphysics is not exempt from such entanglement in errancy, just as metaphysics must not be conceived as the absolute other to truth. The already disclosed proximity between Hegel and Heidegger is one reflection of that entanglement. Yet the thorniness of this proximity to Hegel becomes all the more sharp because Hegel could not endorse a remark such as the one Heidegger now makes that "The essence of truth, i.e., unconcealedness, is governed by a refusal" (*UK*, 43). The proximity only highlights the differences between them.

As opposed to Hegel's absolute unconcealment of the truth of Spirit, the special mark of Heidegger's concept of truth is that concealment belongs to the very process of unconcealment itself. This is why for instance Heidegger says of the original identity of Being and Nothing that it discloses Being as essentially finite. The struggle of Being and Nothing, like that of unconcealedness and concealedness, as the fundamental issue of the philosophic beginning is intrinsically insurmountable: Being is never able to extend its truth over that of the unthinkability of non-Being. This struggle "can not be shoved aside nor merely subdued, rather from it matters open up" (*UK*, 51). As describing the logic of the philosophic beginning, this struggle that happens as the movement of origination is "the founding of truth" (*UK*, 62); as such, it is the institution or foundation of unconcealedness struggling with forgetfulness. This inaugurating and founding struggle can take place in several arenas—Heidegger refers to the founding of a state and the asking of questions as examples—but what is important is that the struggle of origination, because of the nature of every origin, cannot be finished once and for all. Heidegger's fondness for certain Heraclitean fragments can be appreciated once one realizes the way in which Heraclitus too is a thinker of such an inextinguishable struggle.[49] Anaximander is another—by definition nonmetaphysical thinker—who has given voice to this process; for him, temporal process is the heart of the coming-into-being and passing-away of truth. But it is important to remember that this struggle of unconcealedness against forgetfulness means as well that forgetfulness struggles against unconcealedness; in other words, this struggle that originates is circular and does not open a path to the full unconcealedness of the truth of Being. Yet this circularity is not the movement of empty repetition, for such would be the finish of the beginning as founding struggle, and this would leave philosophy condemned to a perpetual deadlock of opposing opinions. To say this would leave thought powerless in the face of the new and unable to account for its own efficacy and history; rather, it is this very same circularity that founds the movement of history as a dynamic process. Thus, "whenever there is a beginning a thrust enters history, history either begins or begins again. History does not mean the sequence in time of events of whatever sort, however important. History is the transporting of a people into its appointed task as entrance into that people's endowment" (*UK*, 64). Authentic beginnings, by virtue of their very circularity, set free the essential living historicity of an appearance of Being. The true beginning spins new possibilities into the present, shifting the locus of that present. The circles it discloses are thus not concentric but heterocentric circles.

This is what distinguishes the beginning as origin from the beginning as starting point: the beginning as origin is historical, whereas the starting point is not. The starting point in initiating newness may begin a sequence of events which follows this newness, but the introduction of mere newness is not the institution of history, for history has a more original meaning than that of the mere sequence of events. The historicity of history lies not in its character as a sequence but in opening up a future.[50] The mere newness of the starting point and the futurality of the origin are different in this regard: the merely new fades in its newness to become the mere past, whereas the original, in founding futurality, lasts in always arriving out of the future. The

American philosopher, Justus Buchler, has made a similar point, but a point that in some ways surpasses Heidegger's in that it makes an effort to link the questions of originality and value: "The qualification 'inventive' is necessary.... The rational spiral, in which communication generates judgments that promote communication, goes upward, not downward. The rational man welcomes the extension of his proceptive boundaries in the direction of invention. He is not just a seeker of 'new experiences' ... but of experience which enriches query.... The rational man is willing to undergo the labor of assimilation, since he implicitly perceives that the incompletion within life is perpetual and that the denial of query is stagnation and ruin. Reason cannot be a worship of the new; every moment bears newness, and mere persistence in time is no rational value." [51] Buchler's sense of "invention" bears a striking resemblance to Heidegger's sense of the origin; for both, it is distinguished from sheer "newness" by its disclosive force. This is the reason Heidegger speaks of the origin as an occurrence of truth: the origin lasts and does so as historical. It is in this sense the principle (*arche*) which guides history—at least for a "while." Thus, when Heidegger says "the beginning already concealedly contains the end" (*UK*, 63), he does not mean that the end is there as a *telos* lying in some future or as a point which the beginning is an effort to attain. He does mean that the end is there in principle. The movement of history is archaeological, but not always, or principally, teleological. But what is the difference between the end as *telos* and end as *arche*?

Attaining the end as *telos* would require that the beginning finish, or complete, itself as the movement of origination; that is, that it heal the incompleteness of the beginning as unfulfilled *telos*. The image of the circle in antiquity as standing for a kind of homecoming conceives the end to which the beginning points as just such a *telos* disclosed by the promises of the beginning. But in order to understand how the end as *arche* differs from this, we must recall that the essential principle of the beginning for Heidegger is that it is a continual re- and dis-location of both itself and what lies beyond it. This means that the beginning is authentic only so long as this dislocating movement of origination continually opens itself up. The genuine beginning always originates more than itself: "The beginning always contains the undeveloped fullness of the unfamiliar, i.e., the struggle

with the familiar" (*UK*, 63). The promises opened up by the beginning are not always disclosed in the beginning. The more authentic
the beginning, the more it discloses promises and possibilities that
reach beyond or even overcome the horizon of that beginning taken
as a starting point (we will return to this topic of the promises of the
origin in the discussion of history and the "not yet" in chapter 6).
Thanks to its own nature, that which is genuinely original cannot
complete itself nor be brought to completion, for to do so would be
to locate it finally so that it ceased to be itself. To attempt to bring
to a halt the dis-locating, self-opening process of the origin is to forget
the essential and radical untruth belonging to the idea of the origin
as such. Thus when Heidegger says that the beginning contains the
end (as *arche*), he means that the beginning has already determined
itself as always unhealable; that is, as always a dislocation. Original
thought, a thinking that stays with the promises of the beginning,
does not come "home" to itself in the end but discovers its own
essential homelessness. The location of this end is not therefore the
completion of the beginning but the discovery of the beginning as, in
principle, enduring origination. It is the discovery that the circularity of the struggle of origination implies a wholeness which dislocates
itself in the very process of being located. This discovery is an end
insofar as the beginning is now uncovered *as* beginning. It is, in a
sense, not so much an end as another beginning. This is the meaning
of Heidegger's celebrated notion of two beginnings:[52] the new beginning is the uncovering of this movement of origination, that is, this
movement of unconcealing, as originally self-concealing. The new
beginning is the discovery of concealment as belonging to the possibility of unconcealing; it is the turn into the first beginning not in
the manner of empty repetition but as an "infinite task" because
concealment will always continue to conceal itself most of all.

II

At this point it is proper to recall that the discussion of Heidegger's
notion of the beginning was originally undertaken as a result of
Heidegger's claim that the source of his quarrel with Hegel over the
possibility of thought thinking itself absolutely, that is, Hegel's claim
to have achieved the end of philosophy (cf. *PG*, 12), was to be located

in the different ways in which each characterized the beginning. By and large, both Hegel and Heidegger were in agreement that the beginning of thought was to be located in the occurrence of an original identity of Being and Nothing, yet they disagreed fundamentally on the outcome of this identity. In order to locate the source of this difference we inquired more precisely into the nature of this identity in its role as origin.

Thus we found that, for Heidegger, the beginning

1. is not to be characterized as an isolated, or absolute, starting point, but

2. is always already underway prior to the establishment of any particular starting point; it is thus,

3. circular in its attempt to re-capture itself. But this very effort of the beginning to re-capture, assemble, and uncover itself shifts the original locus of the beginning; that is, it re-leases, dis-sembles, and conceals the very locus which it seeks. This struggle of assembling-dissembling that the beginning opens up founds

4. the principle of history, and, as such,

5. is in the end a return to itself as what it is in principle.

Given these attributes of the beginning for Heidegger, we must now inquire into the nature and role of the beginning for Hegel, and we must ask specifically:

1. Does Hegel characterize the beginning as an isolated starting point, or as a circle?

2. Does the beginning open up the struggle of assembling-dissembling?

3. Does the beginning recede into the past, or does it last as a historical principle?

4. What is the nature of the end of the beginning?

Despite the new status accorded Hegel as a dialogue partner in the thinking and speaking of Being, Heidegger still must find a way to separate himself from Hegel on the matter of those commitments found in the philosophic beginning. During the period of his "turn" Heidegger realizes that if he is to overcome metaphysics, then he must overcome the metaphysical prejudice concerning the illimitable entitlements of thought. At this point in his confrontation with Hegel the focus is upon ways in which Heidegger might demonstrate the excesses of Hegelian thought.

III

As was the case with Heidegger, the theme of the beginning is a pervasive one for Hegel, and, as was the case with Heidegger, both issues which we have previously considered, time and Nothing, occur within the context of the discussion of the beginning: the discussion of time, which was found in Hegel's notion of Desire, clearly moved within the circular movement of the *an sich* and *für sich*, and the meaning of the notion of Nothing was found in the context of Hegel's discussion of the origin and need of philosophy. Yet, the most extensive treatment of the role and nature of the beginning for Hegel is to be found in the section of the *Science of Logic* entitled "With what must science begin?". This brief text forms the beginning of the first book of the *Logic* entitled "The Doctrine of Being." As a prelude—conspicuously outside of the argument—Hegel discusses the character of the philosophic beginning in light of the special problems of the beginning as such. In the case of philosophy, "the beginning of philosophy must be either mediated or immediate, and it is easy to demonstrate that it can be neither the one nor the other; thereby each manner of beginning finds its refutation" (*WL*, 51). Saying this is simply the Hegelian way of expressing the ancient paradox of the beginning: to begin one always needs some principle to follow, but to arrive at such a principle one must have already begun. The question of the beginning, says Hegel, can be resolved only in recognizing that "the principle of a philosophy also expresses a beginning.... Thus the principle should be the beginning and that— and this is the first order for thought—which is first in the order of thought" (*WL*, 51–2). Like Heidegger, Hegel finds the riddle of the beginning as such a topic not to be avoided, as is demanded by the logical understanding. And also like Heidegger, he points to the very idea of the philosophic beginning itself as harboring an essential principle guiding the course of what follows. But unlike Heidegger, Hegel finds this principle for thought inherent in the beginning qua philosophic. In the resolve to think philosophically there is simultaneously the discovery of the principle of philosophy. Beginning to philosophize carries with it a host of ontological commitments and consequences.

"The beginning is logical insofar as it is made in the element of freely self-existing thought, i.e., in pure knowing" (*WL*, 53). The Hegelian requirement for understanding the beginning is quite simple: "Only the resolve, which one can also regard as arbitrary, need be present, namely that one wishes to regard thought as such" (*WL*, 54). The overcoming of the antinomy and vicious circularity of the beginning is made only in the resolute entry into the self-conflicting element of the beginning itself as both mediate and immediate at once. But this entry into the beginning is accomplished only once one has grasped the principle and task of philosophy itself, and this, for Hegel, is found in the project of thought to become pure wisdom: "that philosophy approaches the form of science,—to the goal to lay aside its name as *love* of *wisdom* and to be *real wisdom*,—it is this which I set out for myself" (*PG*, 12). Indeed, the principle of philosophy is this effort to become the pure wisdom of knowing Being absolutely, i.e., in *every* respect and absolved from all that is nonessential with respect to Being. In order to make clear what this means, Hegel remarks briefly that, insofar as the beginning is made from a particular, determinate content, the goal of philosophy is infected by the subjectivity and contingency of the choice of the beginning. Thus, Hegel contends that, if we are to satisfy the principle of philosophy, that is to achieve absolute wisdom, then the beginning of philosophy must be made absolutely, and so "the beginning is thus pure Being" (*WL*, 54). In other words, the guiding principle of philosophy itself for Hegel, to grasp pure Being, requires that the beginning be made with pure Being. The task of philosophy determines its first true topic.

Clearly, however, this characterization of the requirements of the philosophic beginning makes it imperative that one who is to be in the position to complete the task of philosophy already have at least some vague knowledge of the end after which the beginning strives. In short, the idea of the philosophic beginning itself requires that we have already begun, for the beginning is nothing other than "the unity into which pure knowing returns" (*WL*, 57). Hegel is not unaware of the contradictions inherent in saying this; in fact, from this necessary circularity of the form of the philosophic beginning he concludes that "essential for science is not so much that the beginning be a pure immediacy, but rather that the whole itself be a *circulation in itself* wherein the first becomes also the last and the last also the first" (*WL*, 56). The beginning of philosophy has revealed itself to be "a circle which returns into itself, which does not have a beginning in the same sense as other sciences, such that the beginning only has a relation to the subject which has resolved to philosophize, not however to the science as such" (*Enz.*, sec. 17). Thus, the beginning is only a starting point for a particular subject who decides to enter into the beginning which is already underway prior to any particular point of entry. Insofar as one is unable to see beyond the beginning as this isolated point of entry, one is unable to overcome the subjectivity of one's own standpoint, for the true beginning is not a starting point but a *circle*, and once one realizes that, one discovers that the particularities of one's own idiosyncratic starting point are immediately surpassed in their particularity. Thought requires a surrender to its topic, so that when we actively engage in philosophizing—in following the identity of thought and Being—it is meaningless to speak of particularity or standpoints. It is only after we have abandoned, or before we have made, the resolve to enter fully into this identity that the search for the legacy of particularity comes to be asked. In true knowing the individuality of the knower recedes, and the knower and the known meet in an identity. My own individual start in philosophizing is inconsequential, for once philosophizing begins, the task it opens up reveals a topic that has already taken that individuality up into itself. Thought and its topic always form a whole. Thus Hegel writes that "every part of philosophy is a philosophic whole, a circle which closes in upon itself . . . the solitary circle breaks through . . . and founds a further sphere; the whole presents itself therefore as a circle of circles of which each is a necessary moment, so that the system of its proper elements constitutes the whole Idea which equally appears in every particular" (*Enz.*, par. 15). The task of philosophy demands that it enter into and carry out this circularity that is the principle of the philosophic beginning. But this, Hegel reminds us, is incomprehensible to the linear and logical understanding. Like every genuinely dialectical thinker, Hegel finds that "real thought never takes a straight course, rigid and unchanged . . . thought that seeks a straight course . . . cannot comprehend what is living and on the terrain of transformation." [53]

The circle that characterizes the beginning for Hegel is obviously not the static circle of empty repetition conceived by logic as a fallacy.

Rather, the circularity of the beginning, as already underway, is always underway. The beginning is always a becoming: "It is becoming itself, the circle which presupposes its end as its purpose and has its end for its beginning; it becomes actual only through being carried out and by the end it involves" (PG, 20). The beginning is already the movement, of process, of becoming, and indeed it is, already in its initial moment, the process of becoming itself: "The advance from what is the beginning is only to be regarded as a further determination of the beginning, so that the beginning lies at the base of all that follows and does not vanish from it" (WL, 56). The beginning, which is this movement of becoming, is not left behind in the course of this movement but remains to determine and guide it. As such, it is the principle of this movement. With this we are returned to Hegel's original contention that the principle of a philosophy, a principle that surmounts the limitations of the subjective starting point, expresses the authentic philosophical beginning. For Hegel, this principle is the principle of the beginning itself as the movement of becoming. Discovery of the authentic beginning, a discovery that is given with the recognition of the task of philosophizing, is simultaneously the discovery of the end of philosophy toward which thought is propelled by the beginning.[54]

Thus even a cursory analysis of the role of the beginning for Hegel enables us to answer some of the questions about which the confrontation of Hegel and Heidegger on the notion of the beginning centered. To the first question: yes, like Heidegger, Hegel does conceive of the beginning as a circle which is already underway, rather than a starting point. To the third question: yes, Hegel does conceive of the beginning as founding a process of becoming and thus as the lasting principle of this process. To the fourth question: again yes, Hegel does conceive of the end as the return into the beginning which already anticipated that end. Clearly, Heidegger did not give Hegel his due when he said that "[for Hegel] the end is only the beginning which has become other and returned to itself" (HP, 52). The beginning for Hegel is richer and far fuller with possibilities than Heidegger indicates. Yet, perhaps the most distinctive trait of the beginning for Heidegger is that it constantly re- and dis-locates itself; that is, that it is the process of dis-semblance as well as assembly and, as such, discloses the belonging together of truth and untruth. Since this is an attribute of the beginning, we must once again ask: does Hegel conceive the circularity of the beginning as the struggle of assembling and dissembling, and how does he interpret this? Is there a complexity and circularity inherent in the authentic idea of the philosophic beginning that endures in that which comes from that beginning? In what sense can Hegel claim to have achieved the promises of the beginning by bringing them to an end? All of these questions ask about the logic of the circle as Hegel conceives it.

IV

The theme of the circle is a persistent one in Hegel, but this comes as no surprise, for the odyssey of Spirit as that which philosophy thinks is the movement of Spirit coming to know itself; that is, it is the circular movement of *self-return*. In this regard Hegel invokes the image of the circle in the quite traditional way as standing for a kind of homecoming and healing of the diremption between thought and its topic. Despite this traditional representation of the circle as describing a wholeness, the path outlined by the circle traces a route marked by struggle just as it does for Heidegger. Hegel gives clear indication of this when he says that "Spirit is opposed to itself in itself . . . it is a hard, infinite fight against itself" (*VPG*, 77). The dialectically mediated homecoming of Spirit, described by the "long labor of the concept," is a complex course, hard and even violent. Indeed, Hegel contends that times of general happiness are the "blank pages of world-history" and that "history is the slaughter bench of the happiness of peoples and states" (*VPG*, 35). The concretization of Spirit as a fight against itself displays the real patterns and plans at work in history; patterns and plans that point in the direction of a reconciliation of Spirit with itself. The reconciliation is equally the recovery of, and return to, the full promise given in the beginning. But although it is clear that the movement of Spirit is a circular one, and that it happens as the struggle of Spirit against itself, the question remains: is this struggle the consequence of the intrinsic self-dislocation of the beginning? Does Hegel, like Heidegger, find something about the philosophic beginning that sets philosophy into conflict with itself as a matter of principle? To what extent does Spirit remain at war with itself even at the stage of its own reconciliation?

In order to answer these questions we need to return once again to the key Hegelian concepts "Being-in-itself" and "Being-for-itself," since the dialectic and history of Spirit can only be understood as the interplay of these two concepts. They are the legacy of the beginning to what follows. Yet the difficulty in interpreting these concepts is that, despite their centrality to the structure of the movement of the dialectic, Hegel never explicitly analyzes them as such; rather, their meaning is only to be found in the operative role that they play in understanding this dialectical movement of Spirit.

The idea expressed by the phrase "Being-in-itself" is made most visible in its meaning in everyday speech in which it speaks about the simple thereness and being-at-handness of something. The preliminary thought which "Being-in-itself" expresses is simply that things are insofar as they hold their Being to themselves. Normally one would say of this table in the study, that tree in the field, and the rock nearby that, though they are different types of beings, they clearly display themselves as in themselves. In saying this, one merely tries to express that these things "are" in their immediacy, that is, they rest in themselves. Thus, ordinarily the words "in itself" name that which has a relatively stable lasting identity with itself and which thus rests essentially undivided within itself. While that which is "in itself" might be complex, its complexity does not reach out beyond itself affecting and being affected by its context, rather even its complexity and potentialities for consequences rests in itself. But Hegel does not merely adopt this ordinary conception of this phrase "in itself," though it does provide a preliminary understanding of Hegel's own use of it. An echo of the everyday sense of the phrase is found in the *Phenomenology*. Hegel's first characterization of the "in itself" is as "the unity with itself ... which does not take seriously Being-other and estrangement ... " (*PG*, 20). This "first" component of the circularity of Spirit has a rather unhistorical, nonrelational, and static character about it.

But it does not require any great insight to realize that the popular notion of "in itself" is insufficient to explain the meaning of what is, namely, that it provides an inadequate means of interpreting Being. Even the crassest mode of the logical understanding recognizes that the world does not quietly rest in such a repose of identity and isolation. Though it may appear that objects such as stones and desks and trees have the way of Being which the notion of "in itself" names, it is quite clear that there is a disruption of this reposing immediacy insofar as there is appearance of human Being, that being whose way of being we have already characterized as Desire. Though human beings do appear in the world and of course are able to be revealed and regarded as simple and inert Being-in-itself, this is not possible insofar as they are revealed as human beings rather than things. Everyone recognizes that the horizon of the "Being in itself" does not extend into the way of being of Desire. Human beings cannot be explained in the same way a thing can be explained. Whether successful or not, human beings live always in the process of self-realization and self-determination. As desiring, human beings are never merely "in" themselves, because they always are living in the manner of having to be. We define ourselves as interacting with the world and others, and we suffer from "identity crises" because for us this interaction always has a disruptive and mediating impact. Thus, even from the perspective of the intellectual understanding, human beings are always "for themselves" even while potentially appearing in the mode of restful identity for others. The living person is always a self-relatedness that continually determines itself anew. Such a conception of the words "for itself" indicates that it is a dynamic concept implying a certain incompleteness and differentiation in that which is able to be described as "for itself." On the basis of this simple and evident differentiation of things that appear into those which appear only as "in" themselves and those that appear "for" themselves, the traditional, that is the nondialectical, understanding divides the world of appearances up into objects and subjects.

Hegel does not deny the correctness of the ordinary conception of the "in itself" and "for itself"; he does, however, deny that this conception of them as separate modes of Being is adequate to explain the full Being of the world of appearances. The problem with this way of conceiving what is, is that it would lead one to conceive the world as divided into two regions that merely occurred alongside one another, and in so doing it would invite the postulation of the duality of a "subject" lying at the base of Being-for-itself and an "object" lying at the base of Being-in-itself. In other words, such a conception of the "in itself" and "for itself" as ways of interpreting Being is incapable of satisfying the goal of philosophy which is to conceive Being absolutely and in its wholeness so as to grasp the unifying thread of what is. A world understood as bifurcated into separate regions of such subjects and objects, a world in which the subject nevertheless has to know and makes its place in a world of both subjects and objects, is not yet the conception of the world that philosophy needs to fulfill its task. Hegel's special discovery with regard to these concepts, and his way of surpassing the traditional subject-object conception of the world of appearances, is to show that nothing has the way of Being of only the "in itself," or only the "for itself," but that all that is, is only to be comprehended as the ceaseless interplay and struggle of these concepts.

The way in which Hegel demonstrates and explains this struggle of the in itself and for itself is by showing that there is no reposeful, simple identity that is not in its very own nature infected by the dynamic of self-differentiation, nor is there dynamic differentiation that is apart from static self-identification. More precisely, the in itself and for itself do not stand in the relationship of two already existing independent concepts, rather they are internally related to one another, each dependent upon the other for its own meaning. The struggle between the in itself and for itself is not one of external opposition but of inner tension. Hegel justifies this claim by demonstrating that the identity which is the character of the in itself is gained only relative to a differentiation against what does not belong to this identity, that is, by being for itself. Likewise, the differentiation which is essential to the movement of the for itself is gained only insofar as it identifies itself as different, that is, by being in itself. This means that, rather than characterizing two separate and distinct dimensions of what is, the notions of in itself and for itself must be seen as analytic distinctions of the larger whole found in the internal relation that unites them in one. Though the dynamism of the for itself and the stasis of the in itself are opposite movements, each is possible as itself only by way of its relation to its opposite. This necessary opposition of in itself and for itself outlines the structure of the contradiction at the heart of the circular movement of dialectic. The inextinguishability of their opposition gives rise to the inexhaustible life of the dialectic.

Thus, we can easily see why Hegel insists that dialectic is not our arbitrary method or merely the "best" method among many, but that it is the only way adequate to speak of Being, for as he describes it dialectic is the name for the structure of Being itself and the native style of its appearance. To say that Being is dialectical is to say that it is a complex and conflict that is originary and circular. In other words, Being is neither in itself nor for itself, nor the sum of the two, but is rather this absolute, inseverable internal relation, division, and unity of the two out of which all that is comes to be. This inner relation of the in itself and for itself, this Being-in-and-for-itself, is the character of that wholeness which draws the movement toward itself as the end of dialectic. This end is absolute insofar as it has absolved itself from the duality of the in itself and for itself that have not yet been recognized in their identity. It is not absolute in the sense that this identity itself has been absolved from the struggle of the two. This is quite impossible, for the identity is only in and through this struggle. The war of Spirit with itself cannot cease, even in the stage of its own reconciliation. The homecoming of Spirit is not its abolition but rather the moment in which the full potential of Spirit as dialectical is unrestrained. The path of the dialectic, contained in principle in the idea of the philosophic beginning as such, does not lead away from or outside of the circling in upon itself of the dialectic. The Absolute and end is not some other to the dialectic of the beginning; it is rather the arrival at the center of that beginning itself.

Such a description of dialectic as the circular interplay of the identity of the in itself and the differentiation of the for itself echoes the famous statement in one of Hegel's earliest works, the "System-fragment" (1800), where he says, "Life is the union of union and non-union" (*FS*, 422). It would not be arbitrary to interpret (or even translate) this description of the dialectic which lies at the essence of life by calling it the assembling of assembling and dissembling. Thus one can find ground to interpret Hegel's analysis of the struggle of the in itself and for itself as showing how the in itself, in being assembled in an identity, necessarily dissembles itself in differentiating itself against what it is not, while the for itself, in being before itself, necessarily assembles itself in an identity. Like Heidegger, Hegel can point to antecedents in Heraclitus' understanding of conflictual unity: "Graspings: whole and not wholes, convergent divergent, consonant dissonant, from all things one and from one all" (*DK*, Fr. 10). To make manifest, to assemble this inner relation of the struggle of assembling and dissembling is the task of philosophy. For Hegel this inner circular struggle is itself ultimately an assembling, but the circle that is brought back to itself is not an empty repetition of a starting point in a simple in itself opposed to a for itself. Rather, this absolute relation that issues out of the true philosophical beginning is an assembling process that has overcome the level of opposition between the two elements each of which independently appeared as a satisfactory key by which the logical understanding may think Being. The recognition of inner unity and wholeness of what at first appears to be a duality is the recognition of the original circularity and necessary return of the struggle of the in itself and for itself. Thus, the achievement of the *end* of dialectic is a return to the promise and truth of the *beginning*.

Thus, to answer our second question with regard to Hegel's characterization of the beginning, we must say yes, Hegel does conceive of the beginning as the circular struggle of assembling-dissembling, but we must add that, for Hegel, this struggle is itself ultimately assembled into a wholeness absolved from an externality in the relation of the in itself and for itself, namely, that it is resolved into a circle which does not dislocate itself. In other words, the beginning, for Hegel, originates a movement of progression toward a *telos* which is already present in potency in the nature of the beginning itself.

V

Both Hegel and Heidegger contend that the very idea of a philosophic beginning outlines the eventual scope of the ends made possible by that beginning. In short, both argue that in reflecting upon the nature of the beginning and upon the idea of that primordiality which it is the task of philosophy to disclose we find the essential possibilities of the end of that beginning. Furthermore, both agree that the idea of a philosophic beginning involves thought in a circularity: for Heidegger this circle is a reflection of the hermeneutically circular Being of Dasein; for Hegel it is an expression and moment of the dialectical circularity of the concrete and universal. For Heidegger, this circle is the emblem of the aporia of finitude; for Hegel, it is the true image of truth's unconditioned wholeness. Both Hegel and Heidegger characterize the logic of beginning in largely the same way, yet Hegel asserts that it is possible for thought, from this beginning, to assemble itself absolutely, while Heidegger asserts that the beginning, in being the movement of origination, always dislocates the very possibility of any final gathering of itself into wholeness. Hegel claims to have uncovered the principle leading to the absolute ground of what is, while Heidegger claims to have demonstrated the very groundlessness of any such ground. Despite the very real similarities of their respective analyses of what each describes as an essential and unthought commitment latent in the task of philosophy itself, the final differences between Hegel and Heidegger still cannot be mitigated. Nevertheless, there have already been too many points of contact on a quite eclectic set of philosophic points to ignore the complexities raised by these differences. Heidegger himself recognizes that this proximity runs deep into the special excellences of both Hegelian dialectic and Heideggerian phenomenology, and far beyond the level of the superficial appearance of an accord as he described it in *Being and Time*. The challenge to Heidegger is to find a way to legitimate his own efforts to outline an ontology of the finitude of Being in the face of the proximity of his own "arguments" and those offered by Hegel in the name of what can only seem most alien to finite Being—the Absolute.

The simplest way to characterize the basis of this opposition is that it is rooted in Hegel's claim that the Absolute is latently present in the beginning. The end of philosophizing is to recover this beginning with a concreteness and complexity not yet given in the beginning, but without which this task of philosophy could never be fulfilled. From the beginning to the end of his career Hegel abides by the strong conviction—morally based for the most part—that fulfillment of this task, and the redemption of its ancient promises, is possible. But Heidegger disputes this: "Is the Absolute really real in the *Phenomenology of Spirit*? If yes, then it must be this before the beginning of the work itself. The right of the beginning cannot be demonstrated through the end, because the end is itself only the beginning. Does only a leap into the wholeness of the Absolute remain?" (*HP*, 215). Only because Hegel finds the Absolute already there in the beginning is the circular struggle of the dialectic of Spirit able to spiral forward, ultimately to return to itself, so that truth for Hegel, like Parmenides, is able to be a "well-rounded circle." The apparent closure and hermetic quality of this self-return of Spirit is not troubling to Hegel because Spirit is Absolute from the outset. Because it is absolute as having no other, the spiral outlined by the circularity of the dialectic of Spirit does not represent a closure but a disclosure of the full presence of the beginning. If on the other hand it were the case that the wholeness of the Absolute was not latent in the beginning—if indeed it could make sense to speak like Hegel, if that were the case—then, in the Hegelian framework, thought would be condemned to wander endlessly. But that is simply too antithetical to his own vision and purposes to be entertained as a real possibility, for his conception of the task of philosophy is that it must ask how we can look at the world such that we can witness the harmony of its parts and may think coincidence of thought and Being in it.

The problem that Heidegger now faces is that of demonstrating that the Absolute is not present in the original identity which calls for and founds thought. Though Heidegger's analysis of the principle and logic of the beginning had presented its circularity as hermeneutic and so inherently finite, at the end of the lecture on Hegel he hints that he might locate the impossibility of attaining an Absolute in the finitude of the human way of Being: "What should man do as an existing being? Where does he stand such that he can leap or not leap and so become an other? Can, and should, man leap away from himself as a transition in order to leave himself behind as finite, or is his essence not rather this departure itself in which he takes into possession what is his?" (*HP*, 215–216). The question Heidegger must ask is how Hegel can defend the claim of the original and fundamental presence of the Absolute for us. Can the thinker as existing, finite Being ever legitimately begin with the Absolute?

The point at which Hegel and Heidegger cross paths is thus over the decision as to the presence or impossibility of the Absolute for thought. It is, therefore, not surprising that Heidegger's next substantive encounter with Hegel begins with an analysis of the *parousia* of the Absolute in Hegel's concept of experience.

4

The Question of the Absolute

Perfection of practice, like completeness of opinion, is always approaching, never arrived; Truth, in the words of Schiller, *immer wird, nie ist.*
—*Carlyle*

The more attentive thought becomes, the more it homes in on itself. It is this homing instinct that has long served as the basic instinct of the philosopher who, dedicated to speaking and thinking about the strangest and most baffling elements of the world, has found thought itself most worthy of thought. Nothing is more fundamental for understanding the world than the capacity for thought and speech both of and about the world. And nothing is more surprising. Yet it is equally true that nothing is more difficult to disentangle from its precedent and subsequent conditions and present involvements so that it presents itself as itself in its own brand of clarity. When the Greeks discovered the powerful possibilities of conceptual language there quickly arose a fixation upon the power of thought to form concepts. Intoxicated by its own capacity to find sense in its world, thought sought itself conceptually, and so on its own terms. The seeds for the Kantian discovery of the intelligible preconditions of experience were shown in the earliest and most basic attachments of the Western metaphysical tradition: Heraclitus' "I went in search of myself," and the Platonic dictum "Know thyself," while not cognitively targeted nor existential imperatives, are expressions of this effort of thought to think itself freed from the shadows of any unthought thought. So long as thought leaves itself unthought it remains at least potentially bound to the limiting conditions of particularity and subjectivity. Frequently even those, like Kant, who speak most eloquently on behalf of the limits of thought in the face of its self-appointed task are compelled to leave open a door for the means to overcome the dilemmas of such subjectivity. So what Kant forbids in the first *Critique*, he readmitted in the name of God in the second. That is why, despite its diversity on the matter, metaphysics has been characterized as a longing for the unconditioned as that absolved of the restrictions of the given immediacy. Hegel's presentation of the mediated immediacy of the identity of thought and Being belongs to this tradition as its highpoint.

Heidegger, on the other hand, claims to "have put the presumption of all unconditionedness behind us" (*VA*, 179). Against the claim of the Hegelian Absolute to have no other to it which provides conditions for it, Heidegger argues not on behalf of a relativity of thought as conditioned but simply that he has abandoned this presumption of the idea represented by the unconditioned. It is in this sense that Heidegger's efforts to overcome metaphysics and to outline an ontology of finite Being take the form of a renunciation of the will to an absolute ground. But he contends that the metaphysical self-understanding is so profoundly determined by this presumption of the idea of the unconditioned that it cannot conceive of any other way to fully recover the fundamental experience of Being and thinking in the world than in terms of a "will to the ground." Even in the case of one, like Kant, who recognizes that the limits of our knowledge offer no legitimate path to the unconditioned, there is nevertheless no talk of dispensing with the idea of the unconditioned as that which "forces us to transcend the limits of experience and of all appearance" (*KRV*, B xx) and is "demanded by reason" for judgment. So Heidegger's efforts to "step back" and release his own questioning from the forces and demands of the unconditioned, as an inappropriate assumption about the relation between Being and thinking, is the effort to release himself into another, nonmetaphysical way of thinking. Heidegger's attempt is not to abandon the homing instinct of the philosopher but to own up to the essential homelessness of all thought and to live up to the insight of his contemporary, Bloch, who knew that "home is a place we have not yet been." [55]

Since Hegel understands his own philosophical system as analytically and synthetically reconstructing the dialectic progress from experience to Absolute knowing, he becomes in Heidegger's view the extreme case of this commitment to the unconditioned. As such Hegel remains the focus of Heidegger's efforts to escape metaphysics. To that end, Heidegger now turns to Hegel to ask (now fully aware of the complexities of asking about Hegel) first his reasons for this enthusiasm for the Absolute. When Hegel speaks of the Absolute, by what evidence or authority does he do so? How can he present the Absolute as present in a way that allows him to speak of knowing the Absolute? In what sense is Hegel's achievement in the history of philosophy a fulfillment and perfection of that history as having returned to its original promises? But despite the new, probing attitude toward Hegel expressed by such questions, Heidegger remains dedicated to driving home the same concern expressed earlier: "Hegel saw everything that is possible. But the real question is whether he saw it from the radical center of philosophy, whether he exhausted all the possibilities of the beginning so that he could say that he is at the end" (GP, 400). Like Hegel, Heidegger wants to say that he is at the end of philosophy, but the senses of end which each claims and of the historical juncture represented by that end are quite different: for Heidegger it entails the renunciation of the metaphysical will to a ground, while for Hegel it requires the resolute determination to will to the ground. Heidegger's sense of the renunciation of the will to the ground means that the present moment must be defined by its break with the tradition that it inherits, so that the contemporary historical situation requires that we continue to turn a critical eye to the past as a prelude to moving forward. For Hegel, the achievement of history in his day frees us from such retrospective work carried out by Hegel himself and so liberates us to move forward freed from the partialities of thought developing itself in alienated forms.

The differences between these assessments of the legacy of a tradition that has come to an end are clear. Their respective reasons for these differences are equally clear: while both find the special meaning of the end of philosophy tied to the character of the philosophic beginning as such (and as it happened in Western philosophy), their analyses of the nature of the beginning result in a clear difference between them. Hegel finds the Absolute already present in the beginning; Heidegger finds the beginning always only tentative and provisional. The circularity of the beginning understood as the first appearance of the Absolute leads to an end that is the true homecoming of Spirit. On the other hand, the circularity of the beginning

understood as finite is the basis for Heidegger's claim that if we are
to follow the path of the essential homelessness of thought, then we
must release ourselves from this, the will to an unconditioned ground.
Heidegger does not break away from philosophy as the effort of
thought to find itself, but he does break with the prejudice characteristic of metaphysics: namely, that thought can only find itself once it
finds itself to be unconditioned. Once again the decisive issue concerns
the nature and entitlements of the philosophic beginning; however,
it is no longer simply the structure and logic of beginning that is in
contention, but rather the content of the philosophic beginning.

This question concerning what is "given" with any philosophical
beginning forms the topic of Heidegger's next extended involvement
with specifically Hegelian language, texts, and themes in the long
essay/commentary entitled *Hegel's Concept of Experience*. As the title
indicates the topic to be examined is Hegel's notion of experience as
the site of the full original presence of Spirit and as harboring the
route to the unconditioned ground of thought. But the purpose of
this essay is not simply to clarify a problem in Hegel, for it also
provides the occasion for Heidegger to formulate his objections to the
unconditioned out of (rather than against) Hegel's own defense of it.
Again, the confrontation with Hegel is the occasion for Heidegger
to attempt to characterize and overcome the presumptions of metaphysics. Hegel has become more of a vehicle than an obstacle to
Heidegger's own purposes. That is what he means when he says that
"The language of thought which has grown out of its destiny calls
thought of another kind into the clarity of its own thinking, in order
to set that other thinking free into its own essence" (*HBE*, 143). In
order to develop a dialogue with Hegel over the question of the
Absolute, Heidegger's commentary on Hegel's text on the "Science
of Experience" is guided by three strategies:

1. characterizing the Hegelian concept of the Absolute;

2. presenting Hegel's justification for the presence of the Absolute;

3. outlining the basis of Heidegger's objection to Hegel's position
   with regard to the Absolute.

I

The text of *Hegel's Concept of Experience* was developed out of a 1942/43
seminar that Heidegger gave on Hegel's *Phenomenology* and Aristotle's

Metaphysics, and the effort to draw a long and largely continuous line running between Hegel and Aristotle builds the opening comment of the first section of the text. Heidegger remarks that when Hegel names the task of philosophy as coming to the actual knowledge of what truly is, he echoes Aristotle's definition of metaphysics as the contemplation of what is present in its presence. However, Heidegger notes that between Aristotle and Hegel the determination of "what truly is" has turned out to be Spirit, the essence of which is self-consciousness. This new dimension of self-consciousness, which was first opened up by Descartes, is, according to Hegel's metaphor in the *Lectures on the History of Philosophy*, the land which proves to be the true ground of thought itself. Hegel sees his task, says Heidegger, as to survey this ground and take full and complete possession of it. This is done only insofar as thought achieves "the unconditioned [Absolute] self-certainty of knowing" (*HBE*, 118). So already in the basis of the Hegelian conception of the principle and goal of philosophy as metaphysics Heidegger discovers the first determination of the Hegelian concept of the unconditioned. As Absolute, the topic of thought can only be "Spirit: that which is present and by itself in the certainty of unconditional self-knowledge" (*HBE*, 118). In other words, the unconditioned Absolute, as the complete and transparent return to itself, is the circle of return which no longer dissembles itself, and, as such, it brings to an end the dissemblance of the first appearance of Spirit.

Heidegger's approach to Hegel in the text begins by placing Hegel firmly within the tradition of metaphysics established by Aristotle and advanced by Descartes. He does this in order to bestow a unity upon his predecessors up to and including Hegel, so that he can more clearly define the break represented by his own place in the tradition. He also does this in order to ask how it is that Hegel can claim to have brought the dissemblances of that tradition to an end. But to answer this question Heidegger realizes that the line he has drawn needs defense since the idea of locating Hegel as a successor to Descartes needs to be qualified, for Hegel was not simply a successor, but was equally an opponent of the Cartesian conception of the unconditioned. For Descartes, knowledge is conceived as a means to grasp and know 'what truly is," and so knowledge is regarded as other to Being. This distinction between knowing and what is known is the reason why Descartes conceives of truth as a matter of the conformity of knowing to the known. Hegel on the other hand makes clear that any separation between knowing and that which is known, namely, Absolute Spirit, would conceive that Absolute in a non-Absolute manner, that is, as having an *other*. Therefore, truth for Hegel is conceived as "knowing the self-certainty of self-consciousness in its unconditional essence and thoroughly to be in this knowledge as knowledge" (*HBE*, 121). Truth is a matter of self-validating of certainty.

Once truth is conceived of as the absolute self-certainty of knowing, the locus of truth is moved out of the realm of correspondence between knowing and objects, and into the realm of knowing itself. In this way we see that true knowing must absolve itself from dependence upon its objects. Kant's transcendental turn whereby objects are seen in their dependence upon the knower is a first step in this direction. But Kant, who arrived at the antinomies of reason, did not go far enough, since for Hegel the process by which knowing comes to be liberated (absolved) from dependence upon objects that are other to it is the process resulting in the absolute and unconditioned character of knowing knowing itself. It is this very process, in its respective stages beginning with the futile certainty of sensuousness and passing through sense perception to understanding into the unconditioned self-knowing of reason, that the *Phenomenology of Spirit* retraces. Since Hegel speaks of this process as experience, we can understand why the title of Heidegger's essay indicates that its purpose is to examine Hegel's concept of the dialectical process of the coming to be of Absolute, unconditioned knowing. Foremost in this process is Hegel's claim that if the Absolute is to be allowed to come to be, then it must be present from the beginning since, as he demonstrated at the beginning of the *Logic*, to begin with any partial determination of what is would require that the Absolute be assembled and this would require conceiving knowing as the means of assembling the Absolute—a position which Hegel has already criticized in Descartes. Any beginning which does not begin with the Absolute, that is, any beginning which is partial with respect to the task of thought to think itself absolutely, is a beginning which is untrue, since, for Hegel, "truth is the whole" (*PG*, 21). Heidegger recognizes that this is so for Hegel and thus says: "The Absolute is already [from the beginning onward] in and for itself with us of its own accord. This Being-with-us (*parousia*) is in itself already the way in which the light of truth, the Absolute, casts its light upon us" (*HBE*, 120). To be *parousia* thus belongs to the nature of the Absolute, and as such it constitutes the ultimately inalienable element and true beginning of thought itself. But how are we to understand what this means? And how does this fit together with the other traits of the Absolute to build the meaning of the Absolute as unconditioned?

Thus far Heidegger has determined the Hegelian concept of the Absolute as being that self-certain knowing which comes into the fullness of its original possibilities through the process of absolving itself from any dependence upon anything that is other to it. It appears, in Heidegger's words, as *parousia*; that is, as *ousia* which is "by us" (*par-*). This last characteristic of the Absolute means that the coming into full possession of itself of the Absolute occurs in and through "us," human beings: "This 'with us' has disclosed itself as the 'not without us'" (*HBE*, 188). Thus, Heidegger says, "The presentation is an essential way of presence (*parousia*). As such, i.e., as being present [*Anwesen*], it is the Being of beings that are as *subjects*. . . . The subjectness [*Subjektität*] of the subject is the Being of the subject [*Subjektsein des Subjekts*], that is the subject-object relation" (*HBE*, 122). Thinking the *parousia* of the Absolute is to think the subjectness of the subject, and that entails the disappearance of the contingent subjectivity of the subject. It is important to clarify the meaning of the subject through which the Absolute comes to presence, and to note that it is not the subject as ego such as it is conceived in Fichte's position. The identity of the subject and the Absolute does not entail an absolute subjectivism. The subjectness of the subject for Hegel is not to be opposed to the world of its objects, rather "The subject has its Being in the *representing* relation to the object" (*HBE*, 121). This means that the coming to appearance of the Absolute as unconditioned is to be understood as founded in representation: "All the moments of Absoluteness have the character of representation. In them is the essence of the *parousia* of the Absolute" (*HBE*, 125). The self-certainty of the unconditioned for Hegel is thus grounded in the Being of the experiencing subject's representing relation to its objects.

The structure of representation as the path to the Absolute can be explained as follows: insofar as the relation between the subject and object renders the object present this rendering present is a presentation of the object, but in rendering the object present as present to a subject it is re-presentation. To that extent the structure of representation resembles Kant's notion of transcendental apperception, but the Kantian "I think" is always nonrepresentable to itself as itself by virtue of the conditions of representation. But the Hegelian representing subject, as Spirit, is not other to the conditions of its own dialectical representation, and as such is able to rethink itself. In re-presentation the subject returns to itself and becomes aware of itself as essential to the possibility of the presentation of any object whatsoever. This self-discovery which representation reveals shows the essential relation between the subject and object as a *subjectness*. Thus Heidegger's characterization of the presence of the Absolute as *parousia*, and his claim that subjectness is the essential character of the re-presentation of the Absolute, together form an interpretation of the famous Hegelian notion that "substance is subject" (*VGP*, 19). The *par-ousia* of the Absolute must be seen as an expression of the subjectness of the subject, and this subjectness is the substance which itself underlies all that is. It is in this sense that subjectness is the fundamentum, the land or ground, of philosophy itself.

In naming subjectness as the domain of the presence of the Absolute, Heidegger is not accusing Hegel of a naive subjectivism that, in the words of William James, finds "the trail of the human serpent over everything." [56] Heidegger is quite aware that it is in this very concept of subjectness that Hegel finds the real and true ground of Being itself. Accordingly, Hegel does not find subjectness as identifiable with the individual ego, but rather uncovers subjectness as the universal and common ground which is ontologically prior to any individual subject; that is, subjectness is the structural meaning of Spirit itself. Because individual subjects belong to subjectness, Hegel may claim that Spirit is knowable in its concrete shape, and because Spirit has its "subjects" in the form of world historical individuals, it is always at work universally. Thus it is never merely an abstract universal but is always at work as the concrete universal.

If it is the case that the *parousia* of the Absolute implies that the domain of the Absolute is Spirit, then a further characteristic of the Absolute becomes visible. In naming the domain of the Absolute "Spirit," Hegel wanted to capture the all-pervasive and unifying power of the Absolute; that is, the inability of all otherness to resist the march of Spirit. This means that the Absolute is to be conceived as "the toil of enduring disunity [*Zerrissenheit*]" (*HBE*, 127). In other words, the Absolute is absolute as this final healing, or in Hegelian terms *Aufhebung*, of all external differences. The Absolute has its unifying power in being the identity from out of which, and back into which, all that truly is can be said to be. It is in this sense that the Absolute is the unconditioned home of thought itself, and it is the task of philosophy to reconstruct the process by which thought locates itself therein.

II

Heidegger's analysis of Hegel's concept of experience is an attempt to characterize the Hegelian concept of the Absolute as unconditioned and to link both the Absolute and its sense of unconditionality to a long tradition of philosophical presumptions. The results of that analysis yield a portrait of the Absolute that can be characterized as:

1. the *circle* of return to its own beginning which is complete, i.e., which no longer dissembles itself;
2. as such, it is the *self-certainty* of *self-knowledge*.
3. As this discovery of the return to itself, it occurs in the manner of *re-presentation*;
4. this means that it happens as the domain of *subjectness*, and this in turn implies that
5. the Absolute, though always present, requires human beings to actualize it, i.e., it is present as *par-ousia*.
6. As such, the Absolute is the *universal and common* ground of what truly is;
7. it is this by virtue of being *the unifying power of identity*, *Geist*, which *reconciles all difference* such that nothing stands opposed to it.
8. These traits of the Absolute when taken together reveal it as the *home of thought* to which it is the task of philosophy to return knowingly.

Together these traits of the Absolute build the domain within which and as which the Absolute presences and makes itself known. In whatever way Hegel characterizes this domain, whether it be as Spirit, Idea, or Reason, its essential character must always be the inescapability of this domain and the essential knowability of this domain. Insofar as we are able to find ourselves within this domain of the Absolute, insofar as the Absolute is the true element and home of thought itself, we must recognize it as the true land of philosophy that Aristotle named as the task of philosophy to contemplate and which Descartes first pointed to in a way that Aristotle had not known. For Hegel, the history of thought represents the progressive dialectical disclosure of the ineluctable necessity of the Absolute for thought. The end of the history of thought is nothing other than the disclosure of its own element and possibility. In every region of human affairs and knowledge one finds only further evidence for the unconditioned and, more precisely, the full concretization of the unconditioned as Absolute Spirit.

In saying this, the question of how Heidegger presents Hegel's justification of the *parousia* of the Absolute is answered. If the task of philosophy as Hegel inherits it from Aristotle is ever to be fulfilled, then the Absolute, the home of thought that it is the task of philosophy to think if it is to be absolute, can never be assembled from a nonabsolute position but need always be already present. The very idea and possibility of philosophy itself contains the only possible (or necessary) justification for the *parousia* of Absolute Spirit as unconditioned. But of course to make sense of this one need remember that for Hegel, as for Heidegger, philosophizing in the broadest sense is not an occasional preoccupation but is the fundamental principle of the human way of Being as always transcending the given particular in order to understand that immediacy in the larger, mediated context of generality, time, and history. For Heidegger such transcendence is always finite as are its achievements; for Hegel, on the other hand, transcendence is a recovery of itself and is therefore unbounded and unconditioned. The history of thought, viewed through a Hegelian lens, is the working out and sublation of all the illusory alienations of thought. At the end of that history we discover what made it possible at all and what gave it its unity and end: the Absolute, which as Spirit and subjectness is the inalienable element and principle of thought and history. Thus the idea of the Absolute itself is its own demonstration and justification. To give any justification for the Absolute other than the Absolute itself is, moreover, impossible, for to do so would require that there be an other to the Absolute.

III

This self-validating *parousia* of the Absolute as unconditioned is the sine qua non of the Hegelian system. It is also the element of Hegelian thought that Heidegger finds most objectionable, for he claims that it is the extreme case of the metaphysical will to overcome the essential happening of truth as the circular concealing and unconcealing determined in the principle of the philosophic beginning. As the presumption of the full and unconditioned disclosure of the real, Absolute Spirit is an expression of the forgetfulness of Being insofar as it is the will to conceal the essential ambiguity of unconcealing and concealing characteristic of the truth of finite Being. In other words, Heidegger's objection to the idea of the Absolute is that it not only overlooks, but is the highest concealment of what he calls the ontological difference.

The notion of the ontological difference is the key concept lasting throughout Heidegger's career; we find reference to it as early as the lectures of the 1920's and as late as the last seminars of the 1970's. Despite the centrality of this notion, it remains one of the most difficult Heideggerian concepts to grasp. In *Hegel's Concept of Experience* the idea of the ontological difference is first announced as naming the concealed ground of the essence of metaphysics. In other words, it is introduced as the as yet un-thought ground of that which the Hegelian concept of the Absolute presents as already grasped in thought. Heidegger thus intends to un-ground, or under-cut, the idea of the Absolute by attempting to demonstrate that there is indeed a ground, or prior possibility, for the presence of the Absolute, and that this prior possibility is indeed other than that which eventually leads Hegel to the unconditioned as Absolute Spirit. Furthermore, Heidegger contends that this blindness to the ontological difference is not simply a matter of a deficiency in the specifically Hegelian position, but that it "has its concealed ground in the essence of metaphysics" (*HBE*, 161). Hegel's errancy lies in the task to which he sets himself: the metaphysical task of thinking the unconditioned. The effort to decisively grasp the fullness of Being, the metaphysical presumption to which Hegel subscribes, commits Hegel to a set of assumptions that blind him to the true finitude of Being. Hegel's concept of experience is distorted into the *parousia* of the Absolute by the very idea of philosophy that he has uncritically inherited. Even in the course of his dialogue with Hegel, Heidegger has once again conceived his quarrel with Hegel as being paradigmatic of his effort to distance himself from a metaphysical way of thinking.

In order to understand the way in which the ontological difference names the unthought ground of metaphysics, it is necessary to recall the definition of the task of metaphysics as introduced by Aristotle: metaphysics is to inquire into beings as beings, *theorei to on he on* (*Met*, Z, 1003a 21). This interrogation of beings involves a going beyond beings to that which lets them be what they are; it is a transcendence to the basis of their being-ness, a basis which the Greeks named *ousia*. Thus, in its effort to think beings freed from the limitations and partiality of conditions, metaphysics becomes the effort to intelligibly gather beings together into an unconditioned and grounded whole. But otherwise, metaphysics, as the effort to find the *logos* of *onta*, is determined as essentially ontology. As the will to a ground, this in turn requires the gathering together of the beingness of beings, so that metaphysical ontology is essentially ousiology. The course of the history of metaphysics reveals a multiplicity of determinations of ousia, and with regard to this, Heidegger's effort to separate himself from this ousiological tradition must not be seen as merely the attempt to rename or redefine ousia and thereby surpass previous metaphysics, but as the effort to challenge the persistent metaphysical prejudice that there is a substance either beyond beings as the first and highest being (*theion*) or as the common denominator of all beings. In other words, Heidegger is attempting to distance himself from the *onto-theo-logical* way of conceiving what is, and he does this because it conceals what he sees as the true issue for thought, i.e., the ontological difference.

There are three essential characteristics of the ontological difference[57] that can clarify its meaning. First, it names the "difference between Being and being" (*WG*, 132). Second, it is the as yet unthought origin of metaphysics, for "already in the essential beginning of metaphysics the difference that prevails in the ambiguity of the *on* remains unthought, so that this 'thoughtlessness' constitutes the essence of metaphysics" (*HBE*, 163). Third, it is to be explained as an expression of the ambiguity of the word *on* which, according to Aristotle, names the first topic philosophy must think: "The ambiguity of the *on* names both what is present as well as presence itself"

(*HBE*, 162). This last trait of the ontological difference provides an easy access to understanding the other two.

Heidegger's attempts to find or impose a unity upon philosophy as metaphysics always point to the idea that philosophy was determined by Aristotle to be the contemplation of the *on he on*, and though there have been modifications of this Aristotelian definition, the fundamental issue of philosophy has remained *to on*. Furthermore, Heidegger contends that in this conception of the issue of thought there hides an ambiguity that gives rise to metaphysics as onto-theology, and that onto-theology, as the effort to think the ground of what is unambiguously, is itself founded upon this un-thought ambiguity of "what is." Heidegger explains this first by noting that the grammatical form of the word *on* indicates that it is a participle, and as such may be taken in either a nominative, substantive sense, or in a verbal, active sense.[58] The word itself rests upon both a temporal and substantive sense, and this linguistic ambiguity, Heidegger argues, reflects an essential and deeper ambiguity characteristic of that which first beckons thought. But it is precisely this characteristic that is covered over by the legacy of the Aristotelian conception of first philosophy as directed toward the beingness (ousia), rather than the coming-to-be, of beings (*onta*). This unthought ambiguity and concealed circularity in the definition of that which metaphysics interrogates is not peculiar to Aristotle, nor is it a deficiency to be found in some metaphysicians; rather, it belongs to the essence of metaphysics itself, and indeed this ambiguity is even to be found in those early Greek thinkers who prepare the way for metaphysics. Thus, "if we think, as will be necessary for thought, the essence of metaphysics in terms of the emergence of the duality of what is present and presence from out of the self-concealing ambiguity of the *on*, then the beginning of metaphysics coincides with the beginning of Western thought" (*HBE*, 162). In other words, when the realm of Western thinking was opened up by Anaximander, Heraclitus, and Parmenides, they experienced this ambiguity in that which is to be thought, but they did not name it *as* this ambiguity; and by the time Aristotle formulates the task of thought, the language of metaphysics has begun to take root, and this twofold nature of the matter of thought has been largely forgotten.

This forgottenness of the inner circular differentiation, or ambiguity, of that which is to be thought is not inconsequential but shapes the fundamental destiny of philosophy as metaphysics. On the basis of this hidden ontological difference Heidegger declares that the history of metaphysics has been the forgetfulness of Being, for "the forgetfulness of Being is the forgetfulness of the difference of Being and beings" (*SA*, 336), that is, the difference between the coming-to-be and the beingness of beings. This means that Heidegger's career-long attempt to separate himself from metaphysics as a way of conceiving what is, is at the same time the effort to think what Heidegger claims is the unthought ontological difference of Being and beings.

The meaning of this difference becomes clearer still once we recall that Heidegger's presentation of the identity of Being and Nothing revealed that the way of conceiving nothingness to which Heidegger opposes himself is one which conceives nothingness as negation. The limit of this conception of non-Being is that it poses all questions about Being along the model of questions about things. That is why Heidegger claims that the traditional way of thinking nothingness is incapable of thinking it as what it is in truth, for it can only think Nothing as the negation of a something. This critique of the way of conceiving nothingness according to the model of thingliness is, by virtue of the identity of Being and Nothing, at the same time a critique of the way of conceiving Being according to the model of beingness, i.e., as ousia. Hence Heidegger's critique of metaphysics, of which his critique of Hegel is once again an instance, is that the difference between Being and beings is forgotten and that this occurs as the identification of the two in the notion of ousia. And thus Heidegger's objection to the Hegelian claim of the par-ousia of the Absolute is not that the Absolute requires us to reveal itself, but simply that the Absolute is conceived as ousia, which Heidegger contends conceals the original inner duplicity and ultimate opacity of that which it is the task of thought to think. Only by concealing the ontological difference that is the original topic of thought could Hegel conceive the outcome of thought as the Absolute and unconditioned identity of Spirit's return to itself. Hegel's claim that the Absolute is the healing of all diremption in the identity that is the home of thought is, for Heidegger, the forgetfulness of the primordial difference which needs to be thought. For Heidegger on the other hand, thought knows itself as at home only in this insurmountable homelessness of an oscillation between Being and beings. The circle that thought follows in following the topic of thought is not the circle of the ubiquitous

Absolute immune against conditionedness, but is the hermeneutic circle outlining the inescapable closure and disclosure of conditions and their other.

IV

The question of the *parousia* of the Absolute first arose out of Heidegger's challenge to the Hegelian conception of the beginning of thought. Both Hegel and Heidegger fundamentally agree on the structure of the beginning as the inner dynamism that sets in motion and determines the resulting circular struggle to recapture itself. However, Hegel makes the claim that this movement of origination occurs as the first appearance of the Absolute Spirit, and on the basis of this, the ultimate outcome of the beginning must be recognized as the liberation of thought from all otherness, i.e., that the outcome is an unconditioned and absolute knowing. In opposition to the Hegelian concept of the Absolute, Heidegger names the ontological difference as the essential character of the circularity of the origin, and against Hegel, his purpose is to show how the characteristics of the Absolute only serve to conceal this true task of thought. Thus Hegel finds that experience itself, as happening within the domain of Spirit, provides the grounds for the completion of the task of philosophy; namely, the discovery that thought makes that it comes into its own only when it thinks itself rather than a foreign content. Heidegger, on the other hand, finds that the fundamental difference between Being and beings, a difference the span of which underpins and provides the horizon for experience, is ultimately an irreconcilable difference. So while Hegel is drawn by the necessity of the Absolute as unconditioned, Heidegger is driven ever more deeply into the insurmountability of the conditions that provide the environment for thought.

It seems that Heidegger has finally succeeded in drawing the line between his own project to overcome metaphysics and Hegel's claim to have completed the metaphysical project. Ironically, Heidegger did this in the first encounter with Hegel that approached Hegel as a dialogue partner rather than as an opponent. But before we accept Heidegger's own account of the line between them, we should be sufficiently critical of Heidegger's interpretation of Hegel to take another look at his characterization of the Hegelian achievement in the history of thought. To this end, three questions need to be addressed to Heidegger's reading of Hegel:

1. Is Heidegger's presentation of the concept of the Absolute just?
2. Does Hegel add anything to the justification of what Heidegger has termed the "*parousia*" of the Absolute?
3. Is there present in Hegel's thought the recognition of that which Heidegger has named the ontological difference? If not, then what would Hegel find objectionable about the ontological difference?

The bottom line of course is once again found in Heidegger's claim to be the only thinker of the history of thought who has understood the fundamentality of the ontological difference and the way in which this ungrounds the very will to a ground that has driven the history of metaphysics.

V

Since most of the traits of the Hegelian concept of the Absolute were developed out of Heidegger's careful exegesis of Hegelian texts, and since most of the ways Heidegger characterizes the Absolute as unconditioned are explicitly described as such by Hegel himself, we would not expect there to be much dispute over them. Indeed, such is the case, for of the eight general characteristics of the Absolute that can be teased out of Heidegger's analysis only two, that the Absolute occurs in the manner of representation and therefore in the domain of subjectness, are disputable by virtue of being couched in un-Hegelian ways and so worth a second look.

Hegel's critique of representation is quite well known, and, to be sure, we have already witnessed evidence of this in his critique of logical understanding, which was presented as incapable of conceiving the original identity of Being and Nothing because it is unable to overcome a thinking predicated according to the model of beings, i.e., representational thinking. For Hegel, representational thinking is trapped on the level of opposition, or finitude improperly conceived, and so it is precisely this idea of one-sided representation which Hegel attempts to overcome with the notion of the wholeness of the Absolute. Both Hegel and Heidegger would agree that representational thinking proceeds according to the way of conceiving the presentation of beings to a subject. Both describe representational thinking as a mode of thinking that conceives of Being as a highest, supreme being. But, Heidegger's claim to the contrary, Hegel asserts that, whereas the structure of representation necessarily conceives Being according to the model of beings and so remains on the level of "external identity" (*PR*, 144), this only provides further testimony for need of the Absolute understood as the self-transparent grasping of the absolute inner identity of the manifold of beings. This inner identity, or *logos*, which is that which absolute knowing knows as the Absolute, is not a highest being, but is qualitatively different from beings without on that account being other to them. There is a real, one might say ontological, difference between beings and Being for Hegel, and more importantly, the mode of thought requisite to Being is quite different from the representational understanding adequate to the level of determinate beings. The Absolute is unconditioned and complex in its internal structure in a way that no representation of the Absolute can grasp. To fully grasp the domain of Absolute Spirit thought must first recognize the fundamental place that it already has in it. Hegel bases his contention that the Absolute is the overcoming of the representational attachment to beings on the claim that the true must be conceived "not as *substance*, but just as much as *subject*" (*PG*, 19), and that the thinking subject is not to be conceived as another being, but as "pure, *simple negativity*" (*PG*, 20). If substance becomes subject, then it is equally true that the subject cannot be accounted for in any way that treats the subject in the first instance as an individual being. So a full analysis of Hegel's own demonstration that the Absolute is not to be conceived as representational delivers us over to the second questionable Heideggerian charge against the Absolute, namely, that it occurs as the domain of subjectness.

Hegel's critique of a philosophy of subjectivity is a lifelong one, appearing as early as *Faith and Knowledge* (1803) where, in his analysis of Fichte's position, he says that "subjectivity . . . which is opposed to objectivity is in absolute opposition and simply not able to fulfill the task of identity" (*GW*, 415), and the same fundamental critique appears in Hegel's work as late as the *Encyclopedia* (1830) where the critique of subjectivity occupies the first division of the third part of the "Philosophy of Spirit." Throughout his career Hegel attempted to demonstrate the inadequacy of any philosophical position that does not overcome the narrowness of any framework that conceives the isolated subject as the locus of philosophical truth. But this criticism of any turn to the subject seems to stand in blatant contradiction to Hegel's own claim that the Absolute must be viewed not merely as substance but as subject as well. However, we can resolve this apparent contradiction in Hegel once we recognize that there are two senses in which Hegel speaks of "subject." The sense of "subject" which Hegel criticizes is that of the subject as isolated ego; in other words, the largely discrete subject that stands opposed to its objects. The other sense of the "subject," the one by which Hegel attempts to overcome the one-sidedness of a representational subject, is the subject conceived as a negation. Such a conception of the subject is not bound by existing determinations, or negations, in the manifold of things; rather, this "subject" as negation has the function of negating all determinations, and so this subject is what it is as the overcoming (negating) of all differentiating determinations—a process that results in the manifestation of their true inner identity. Furthermore, the subject as negation is only this activity of negation, for insofar as it is a determinate being it must negate itself. This nonisolated sense of "subject" as that which unifies in the negation of all negation, that is, as that which unifies dialectically, is what Hegel names Spirit. It is only on the basis of the subject conceived as Spirit that Hegel is able to escape the one-sidedness of the subject conceived of as opposed to, and so conditioned by, its objects. The true subject/substance, Spirit, is the sublation of both subject and substance taken as something other than either thought or its topic. The finite subject, while not being dissolved, is thus disclosed as in truth the subject of infinite Spirit.

The explanation for this capacity of Spirit to take the subject into itself as Hegel conceives it is quite simple: Spirit, which always has its subject, is "there" prior to any particular, isolated subject or object, for Spirit is the universal and common ground upon which and out of which all further determinations gain any significance whatsoever. This prior presence of Spirit does not, however, mean that Spirit exists independent of the manifold of what is. If that were the case, then Spirit would merely be a transcendent supersubject, or an enlargement of the individual subject. Instead, Spirit requires the active history of individual subjects without which it would be "the lifeless solitary" (*PG*, 564). In short, Spirit is the Hegelian name for the *parousia* of the Absolute, and this then means that the dispute over Heidegger's characterization of the Absolute as representation and as remaining within the domain of the subjectness returns us full circle to the unresolved quarrel over the legitimacy of what Heidegger has called the *parousia* of the Absolute and of what Hegel describes as the ineluctable domain of Spirit. By way of attempting to resolve this quarrel we must recall that Heidegger had objected to the notion of the Absolute because it concealed the ontological difference, which he described as the true, and yet most neglected, issue of thought. Heidegger's claim is that Hegel's conception of the Absolute represses the full scope and meaning of the concretization and differentiation of Being. The charge is not simply that beings are more manifold and radically plural than Hegel recognizes, but also that Being is to be thought in its final difference from beings. In short, Heidegger argues once again that Hegel has concealed the finitude of Being as it is witnessed in the ontological difference. But we must now ask how Hegel would reply to this Heideggerian objection to the notion of the Absolute.

VI

There is one topic in relation to which Hegel addresses all three of Heidegger's objections to the concept of the Absolute—the issue of tragedy.[59] In his analysis of tragedy, Hegel not only attempts to demonstrate the inadequacies of a position founded in the narrow sense of subjectivity and representation, but he also attempts to demonstrate how Spirit inevitably overcomes such inadequacies by sublating its finitely conceived finite forms. In Hegel's discussion of tragedy we find the cornerstone of his presentation of the necessity of the reconciliation and unification of differences in an absolute identity freed from all submission to external conditions. In this respect it is important to note that a theory of tragedy is no mere adjunct to the Hegelian achievement, but that it provides Hegel's reply to Heidegger's claim that the thought of the ontological difference, which testifies to the insurmountability of unthought conditions, is more original than the thought of the unconditioned yet agonistic Absolute.

There are four significant and extended examinations of the notion of tragedy in Hegel: two are to be found in the *Phenomenology*, one is to be found in the *Lectures on Aesthetics*, and one in the essay *Natural Law*.[60] All four of these analyses have one fundamental trait in common: each appears as the transition to a higher level of unification; that is, each introduces the movement of the reconciliation of the conflict of differences in a higher identity. In short, the idea of tragedy, which for Hegel is a necessary moment in the dialectical development of human consciousness and history, represents the high point of thought in conflict with itself; it also demonstrates in a compelling way the intolerability of this inner conflict. Thought cannot remain at odds with itself anymore than the tragic situation can endure. Just as the confrontation that defines tragedy cannot hold fast, so too must thought in conflict with itself, by virtue of resting upon incompatible conditions, sublate itself into an unconditioned unity with itself. So most interesting in the idea of tragedy is its ultimate untenability in the face of the same demands that it establishes.

In the *Aesthetics* we find that there are three essential moments of this movement which lead tragedy to this point: "first, [the appearance of] multiple ends ... second, the collision [of these multiple ends] ... third, the tragic reconciliation" (*VA*, III, 563). Together these three moments present tragedy as the gathering together of disparate and conflicting elements into an inner tension that reveals the higher identity that unifies these elements into a whole, and that of course is their truth. The precondition for this movement of tragedy is the appearance of a multiplicity of conflicting ends each of which is the result of special conditions that present themselves as true, i.e., as the universal end. But such a multiplicity of ends standing in opposition to one another is merely the conflict of apparently unrelated opposites until the conflict is recognized in its truth, i.e., not merely as the conflict of opposites external to one another, but as the inevitable collision which results from an inner division in an inseverable whole. Thus the tragic conflict is the "inner diremption (*Zwiespalt*) in itself ... the being torn of the one and the same" (*VA*, III, 570). The tragic situation is one that could not be otherwise, since the clashing elements must face one another as elements of the same whole. Both Creon and Antigone, national and familial law, are nourished by and directed toward the same human space that was ancient Thebes.[61] This tearing asunder, which is the root of the tragic collision of opposites, produces the need for a reconciliation, for as Hegel notes in another context, "to grasp the absolute connection of these opposites is the deepest task of metaphysics" (*VPG*, 41). More precisely, Hegel's contention is that unless this inner diremption is healed, subjectivity, representation, and the concomitant domination, i.e., the one-sidedness of the logical understanding, remains. In order to recognize how this division is overcome, its source must be recognized.

Tragedy only gains its true meaning and intensity in the ineluctability of its source. This is why the Greek notion of *moira* is the leading notion in understanding the meaning of tragedy. The destiny, or fate, which produces this collision and which *moira* names, is inescapable because it is rooted in what is unthinkable as escapable, i.e., in life itself. From the time of his first published work, Hegel insists that "one factor of life is the necessary diremption (*Entzweiung*) which eternally reconstructs itself against itself" (*D*, 21). The source of this diremption is thus to be understood as arising out of the philosophical key to comprehending life; namely, the *parousia* of Spirit in all of its concrete and diverse expressions. Spirit is not an abstract other-worldly notion, but is only as manifested in the full diversity and complexity of life, and as such it includes the inevitability of conflict with itself. Because Spirit is the real expression of the original identity of Being and non-Being, it harbors within itself an essential conflict and negativity. In the end, the inevitability of the tragic collision is to be accounted for in the work of the negativity of the subject which produces the struggle against itself that characterizes Spirit. Thus, in *Antigone* for example, which for Hegel is the paradigm of Greek tragedy,[62] we find that Spirit has objectified itself in the two extreme forms of the family and the state, which differ in their mutually incompatible ends and which necessarily collide, since they are part of the same ethical realm. This is the difficulty that gives rise to the tragedy "that the Absolute eternally plays with itself,—that is, that it eternally gives birth to itself in objectivity" (*NR*, 495). In *Antigone* we find Spirit torn asunder and objectified into the two extreme powers that, though opposed and in conflict, cannot exist separately from one another, for the state only exists through the continuation of the family, which in turn requires the state in order to be preserved and sustained. The essence of tragedy consists in this circular conflict born of the interdependence of fragments of a larger whole that have objectified themselves in an opposition to one another. But, as Hegel notes, this circular conflict, or inner diremption, which is the essential trait of tragedy, is not the full significance of tragedy. Rather, tragedy gains its true philosophical import in the way in which it points to its own completion, and in this resolution of the conflict we find the unconditioned, the reconciliation of the circular struggle.

We have already analyzed the resolution of this circular struggle in our consideration of Hegel's notion of the movement of origination. There we saw how the inner tension of the struggle of the "in itself" and "for itself" was resolved in the recognition that there is an interdependence of these two apparently opposite notions and that this internal relation uniting them circumscribes the larger whole within which these two apparently separate powers are dialectically unified harmoniously. So it comes as no surprise to find the same struggle in the reconciliation of the tragic conflict.

What is lacking in the situation of the tragic collision is a consciousness of the whole. Conflict is the dominant character of the relation between the different ends only insofar as the division between the relation is held to be absolute. But once this division is recognized as a derivative abstraction of an original whole, we realize that "the differences ... are not accidental characteristics. Rather, because of the unity [of the difference] from which alone discordance might have come there are articulated groups of the unity permeated by its own life, unsundered spirits transparent to themselves ... that preserve, amidst their differences, the untarnished innocence and concord of their essential nature" (*PG*, 311). In other words, the reconciliation of the tragic conflict first appears in the recognition of the essential inner structure which holds these conflicting opposites together in tension. Creon and Antigone, for example, belong together and find their respective identities and differences only within the same ethical realm. This essential sameness or inner unity is, however, that which originally destined the tragic collision in its inescapability, but the dialectical transition and sublation sets to work once it is revealed as the basis for the very synthesis of the opposites into a *harmony*. So the key insight that tragedy discloses shows the transformation of this inner structure from its original role as the source of tension and diremption into its role as the source of harmony and reconciliation.

The full account of this transition from tragedy to its higher unity is found in a rather surprising passage in the *Phenomenology*: "The reconciliation of the opposition with itself is the *Lethe* of the nether world in the form of death,—or, the *Lethe* of the upper world in the form of absolution ... from the transgression.... Both are *forgetfulness*, the disappearance of the actuality and action of the powers of substance, of their component individualities, and of the power of the abstract thought of good and evil; for none of them for itself is the essence, rather this is *the tranquillity of the whole in itself* " (*PG*, 516). What is so startling about this description of the path of reconciliation is that it is characterized as a forgetting and overcoming in the form of either death or absolution. The reference to death as a possible outcome of the conflict of wills reminds one of the risk of death; that is the decisive question faced by the wills that confront one another in what develops into the dialectic of the master and slave. That dialectic is the struggle for freedom and autonomy; the later dialectic that is developed in tragedy is subsequent to the first stage of freedom. Both of the wills in the tragic conflict are more highly developed and freer (though still not yet the freest wills). Whereas the avoidance of death is the turning point of the master-slave dialectic, the unavoidability of death (or an absolution that is so complete as to represent a dissolution and kind of death) is the truth of the dialectic of tragic conflict. Both death and absolution are presented as modes of forgetting because their results are a kind of dissolution and abolition of the fixity of opposition hardened into the tragic situation. Both are ways in which the opposition is surmounted; furthermore both indicate that the inner tension of the tragic conflict cannot be surmounted or assimilated so long as the opponents of the conflict stubbornly hold on to the mutually incompatible claim to be the universal, and recognizing this is the recognition of the futility of the attempt to escape the conflict or to overcome it by vanquishing one side of the conflict. The discovery of this futility can be disclosed by death, as was the case with Hamlet for whom "in the background lay death ... from the beginning" (*VA*, III, 574), or by absolution, but in either case the result is that each of the opponents lets go of, is deprived of, or forgets its claim to be the universal. The inner tension and mutual interdependence of the two sides remain, but this tension is now free to establish itself as the common ground of the opponents and as such it is established as the higher identity which grounds the apparent differences. The reconciliation of the tragic conflict thus requires a radicalization of the difference, or the struggle, which is the very source of tragedy. Following his analysis of *Antigone*, Hegel gives this higher identity of reconciliation a name: Spirit (cf. *PG*, 313), and it is in this notion of Spirit that Hegel claims to have demonstrated the path which overcomes the one-sided opposition which characterizes the narrow sense of subjectivity and representation.

It is important to remember that the reconciliation of the tragic collision does not entail the complete escape or abolition of the inner difference of the conflict. In an essential sense both sides involved in the tragic conflict are defeated—neither Creon nor Antigone is victorious, for Antigone's defeat is equally the defeat of Creon's purpose—and the tragedy discloses what will remain intolerable as an aporia only so long as the way to the higher unity of Absolute Spirit is not opened up. Any attempt to escape or abolish that tragic aporia merely signifies a return to the earlier level of abstract identity and the domination of one claim over the other, a return that the power of the negative eventually will once again tear asunder. Rather, the resolution of the tragic conflict must sublate this aporia by preserving the inner difference of these conditioned claims, because this difference is itself the source of the resultant harmony. Working through tragic difference is the passage to the higher order of the reconciliation of such difference, and this reconciliation alters the very conditions which made the tragedy possible in the first place. By passing through to this new level of reconciliation, the realm within which the differences opposed one another is opened up in a way that reveals their opposition as illusory. In the case of *Antigone* this means that the ethical and political realms both of Thebes and of familial life are expanded and freed from their respective contingencies. Conceptually, this means that the concept of tragedy reveals Spirit as this higher process of preserving a conflictual unity. Thus to fail to recognize Spirit is merely to fail to radicalize, or think deeply, the inner difference, or conflict, which lies at the root of this conflictual unity.

Tragedy alone does not lead to the final appearance of the Absolute; however, it discloses the need for the radicalization of the thought of conflictual difference that first points the way to the appearance of the Absolute in its truth as an absolute and unconditioned identity.

VII

The parting of the paths of Hegel and Heidegger over the question of the Absolute and unconditioned as a possibility for thought is quite evident. Heidegger's challenge to thought is to release thought from its ancient relation to the will to an unconditioned ground. Interestingly, he does not find Hegel the highest expression of submission to this will; it is rather Nietzsche, whose attachment to this willing ground led to the nihilism of the pure will to power willing itself uninhibitedly and unconditionally, who represents the extreme commitment to this metaphysical ideal. Hegel, on the other hand, finds the satisfaction of this will in its linkage to thought, Being, and ground in the domain of Absolute Spirit. In this he represents the triumph of the metaphysical way of interpreting thought's urge to think itself freed from foreign content. Thus Hegel can say that "the real is the rational, and the rational is real" (*PR*, 24), by which he does not mean that everything is reasonable but that all that is reasonable will be able to be preserved.

Heidegger does not deny, nor want to destroy, the task of thinking thought. The end of philosophy for Heidegger does not herald a release from thought's recognition of its own role in the constitution of a world. It only signals a release from the metaphysical prejudice that such a recognition necessarily implies the search for an unconditioned and absolute ground. The notion of the ontological difference, as naming a radical, yet insurmountable ambiguity in and for thought, is a bid to destabilize and render untenable any ultimate and unconditioned identity. It is, Heidegger argues, this original ambiguity that always calls for thought, and any effort to sublate or obliterate it is a forgetting of Being. The import of the ontological difference is that the thought of this inner, primary, rift reveals the need to preserve the difference as difference, and this means that the circularity which characterizes the thought of what is, because of this ambiguity, must necessarily be a constant movement of re- and dis-location. The truth of what is, which thought seeks in seeking itself, is therefore the struggle of both revealing and concealing at once; indeed, only insofar as this struggle is preserved does truth "happen." Thus Heidegger claims to overcome the one-sidedness of a metaphysics of subjectivity and representation by having thought the origin of the thought of what is more radically than it had yet been thought.

For Hegel too there is an inner tension or difference which is a necessary moment of that which it is the task of thought to think. But, for Hegel, the import of this original diremption is that in it thought discovers the need to overcome the difference as unassimilable through the radicalization of the thought of the difference itself in the more primordial identity. This means that the circularity, which Hegel along with Heidegger agrees to be the structure of the thought of what is, must necessarily be a return to its beginning. But, for Hegel, the truth of the thought of what is, is therefore the transparency of self-certainty in which Spirit, "what truly is," *reveals* itself; indeed, only insofar as this struggle is reconciled does the whole, that is truth, appear. Only thus, Hegel claims, is the one-sidedness of a metaphysics of subjectivity and representation overcome. It seems then that Hegel does recognize something like an ontological difference in the inescapable diremption of the negative power of Spirit. But Hegel does not recognize this diremption as insurmountable, for the true matter of thought is the identity, the *logos*, which the more radical thought of this diremption reveals.

The real difference between Hegel and Heidegger on this question of the Absolute is most evident in the relation which each has to the previous history of thought. Hegel sees always and everywhere only predecessors en route to the full disclosure that he is the first to make. According to his own self-understanding he brings metaphysics to an end, and as he understands this end, it entails some release from it to a fully dialectical form of thinking. A style of thinking that does not shy away from, but embraces, contradiction, conflict, and aporia. Hegel does not make the naive claim occasionally ascribed to him that history and thought come to a halt in the Hegelian system. History and thought are too dynamically conceived and rich in the myriad forms of their concretization for Hegel to ever even entertain such a thought. Instead Hegel looks to the history of thought recollectively: history of every species takes place, he says, in the "temple of Mnemnosyne" (*VGP*, 19), and this means in it all that is essential in conflict and contradiction is preserved while the accidental and contingent is negated. Foremost among the essential structures of any historicizing is the openness to a future and its as yet undecided aporias, and this is always preserved in Hegel. What is not so clearly preserved is an openness to the past. Thus when Hegel turns to his predecessors he sees them only as predecessors, never as contemporaries or as spokespersons of epochs alien to his own. For him, the conflicts and aporias of that past have been resolved into their higher forms.

Heidegger's purpose, on the other hand, is to deconstruct this Hegelian reconstruction of the past. Like Hegel, Heidegger wants to preserve thought's essential openness to its future(s), but, unlike Hegel, Heidegger also finds the past of thought as yet undetermined in an essential sense. The inner circular difference and ambiguity in the historical topic of thought lies concealed at the core of the history of thought. That is why Heidegger says that the end of philosophy as metaphysics speaks of the need to take a "step back" into the history of thought. Both Hegel and Heidegger describe their relations to the past of thought as *Erinnerung*, but while for Hegel this means a recollection and reconstruction of the past for the present, for Heidegger it refers to the need to retrieve the forgotten origin of both history and thought—an origin which once recollected destabilizes and debases the traditional grounds of philosophy as metaphysics. In both cases we arrive at a position that can only be described as an end and new beginning.

Thus the confrontation between Hegel and Heidegger now centers about the question of the meaning of this difference, or diremption, and the extent of its presence in the real content and future direction of thought. The struggle between Hegel and Heidegger is now revealed to be the struggle to demonstrate and justify the claim that each makes to have thought the meaning of this inner difference more originally. For Heidegger this claim is the basis of his deconstruction and overcoming of metaphysics. For Hegel this claim is the basis of his construction of the concept of the Absolute and thus the completion of metaphysics. The proximity of Hegel and Heidegger is now quite clear, and it is out of this nearness that each must struggle to demonstrate to have thought "what truly is" more originally and more radically than the other. From this center of the proximity of Hegel and Heidegger, their paths part, and so it is necessary to attend closely to the reasons and justifications that each offers for moving away from this center in the direction that each claims is the more original, and inescapable, one for thought.

5
The Claims of Radical Difference

The simulacrum is never that which conceals the truth—it is the truth which conceals that there is none. The simulacrum is true.
—*Ecclesiastes* as quoted by Baudrillard

Since Parmenides outlined the identity of thought and Being requisite for the "Way of Truth," the logic and demands of identity have traditionally come to overrule and subdue the idea of difference. Any gap or rupture between thought and its topic, any residue of an ontological difference, is regarded as a flaw to be overcome if thought is to live up to the demands of the unconditioned. Even Kant, who makes an uneasy peace with the ineradicable antinomies of thought, speaks of the tug of identity in terms of an inner need: "For what necessarily forces us to transcend the limits of experience and of all appearances is the *unconditioned*, which reason, by necessity and right, demands in things in themselves, as required to complete the series of conditions" (*KRV*, B xx). Only as resting in the fullness of identity does thought lay claim to such hallmarks of metaphysical truth as wholeness, unity, completeness and noncontradiction. That is why both Hegel and Heidegger say that metaphysics has traditionally been a philosophy of some species of identity, so that in a significant respect the logic of philosophy itself can be witnessed in the working out of this relation between identity and difference.

The analysis of this relation has been largely the province of logic itself. From Aristotle to Quine the riddles of this relation by and large have been addressed as relations of the structure of language, and more often than not this is taken as a matter primarily concerning predication. Transferred to logic and linguistics this core issue of metaphysics is reduced to an important, yet subordinate problem of a philosophic field adjacent to metaphysics proper. So, for instance, Kant's only explicit treatment of the relation of identity and difference is as a topic in the "Transcendental Dialectic" concerning the "Concepts of Reflection," that is, as "relations in which concepts in a state of mind can stand to one another" (*KRV*, B 317). For the most part, the complexities and nuances of this relation between thought and its topic remain unexamined in speculative metaphysics itself. An exception to this is inevitably found in any dialectically based metaphysics, for the contradictions of the concepts of identity and difference are quite naturally amenable to a dialectical analysis. Not surprisingly then Hegel's account of the logic of his system and of the Absolute that, as *parousia*, guides it is frequently expressed in terms of the relation between identity and difference. More precisely, the Absolute in Hegel's words is "the identity of identity and difference," that is, the culmination and achievement of self-identity of Spirit coming to terms with its own manifold differentiation. If Hegel's Absolute can be said to bring metaphysics to an end, then it is by having satisfied the full complexities of a philosophy that is able to give an account of the world as an identity differentiated in itself. That which Spinoza called "maximal richness," that is, the diversity of the world as finite, is, Hegel maintains, only preserved and appreciated in the fullness of this identity.

The paths of Hegel and Heidegger part on this point: the way to the Absolute and the way to the ontological difference lead away from each other on the question of this relation of identity and difference. Both argue that thought is beckoned by an original diremption in Being itself, and that this original ontological bifurcation shows up as a rupture between thought and Being. For both thought is at its best when it is responsive to the fundamental discord between itself and its topic: the difference between the thought of things and the Being of things, the relation between thought and Being, is the first and foremost theme of philosophical reflection. But for Hegel, the more original and radical thought is, the deeper it reflects upon this difference, the more it draws near to the identity which reconciles this duality. For Heidegger, on the other hand, the more thoughtful thinking is, the more persuasively it leads one to the recognition of the need to preserve the opening provided by this difference as difference and to the recognition that something essential about both thought and Being is concealed in this difference. Heidegger's purpose is to challenge Hegel's contention that the finite is first given its due only once it is seen as belonging to the matrix of infinite inner relations constituting Spirit as an absolute identity of identity *and* difference. Against Hegel, Heidegger argues that the finite has an integrity all its own that prohibits the presumptions of any philosophy of identity.

Given the centrality of this issue for Heidegger's confrontation with Hegel, it is no surprise that Heidegger's next extensive dialogue with Hegel is to be found in a book entitled *Identity and Difference*. Significantly the only other thinker considered in this short but important text is Parmenides, one of the original thinkers of Western thought and the godparent of every metaphysics of identity. In his effort to demonstrate the priority of the ontological difference over the self-identity of Spirit as Absolute, i.e., in attempting to justify his claim to have thought the enduring origins of thought more radically, Heidegger increasingly turns his attention to the original thinkers in the history of Western thought in order to disclose the veiled ambivalence of thought's initial commitment to such later unqualified metaphysical presumptions as the requirement of identity for the task of thought. His intention is twofold: first, to point to the recognition of this ontological difference as a condition for the genesis of philosophy as found in early Greek thought, and to show how the subsequent development of philosophy as metaphysics rests on a repudiation, or at least forgetfulness, of this condition. In this way, the interpretation of the real historical origins of thought gains a significance for Heidegger matched in that history only by Hegel. For Hegel too, history becomes the principal evidence which he offers in defense of his claim that the Absolute is the outcome of the most radical thought of what is. For both, thought is understood as destined by virtue of the nature of its beginning: Hegel finds the true destiny of thought in the coming-into-full-appearance of the Absolute; Heidegger finds it in the ever-disruptive recollection of the ineradicable finitude of the ontological difference.

I

The text of *Identity and Difference* consists of two short essays written during the same year, 1957. The first essay, which was occasioned by a seminar on Hegel's *Science of Logic*, deals with "The Principle of Identity," while the second considers "The Onto-theo-logical Constitution of Metaphysics." Taken together these essays link three of the central points of contention in Heidegger's challenge to metaphysics: the dominance of the principle of identity as containing and concealing the original ontological difference; the essentially onto-theological prejudice which underpins the metaphysical attachment to omnipresence; and Hegelian metaphysics as exemplary of the metaphysical need to tacitly, yet unknowingly, give due to the onto-logical difference as indispensable even for its own obliteration. In this last point, Heidegger begins to emphasize a point that he has made since the first attempts to destroy philosophy as metaphysics, but that he has perhaps not taken fully into account; namely, that metaphysics contains the seeds of its own dissolution. At this point in his career Heidegger has come to discover both that the "forgetfulness of Being" is an element in the "destiny" of thought, and that the effort to impose a unity upon the tradition(s) of thought from Parmenides to Hegel, while still requisite for coming to terms with the contemporary task of thinking, is nevertheless an effort to impose a unity on a tradition that is always already dissolving itself as such a unity.

In order to fully understand this highly condensed and often confusing text, it is necessary to read it along with two other texts from roughly the same years: *Der Satz vom Grund* and *Grundsätze des Denkens*. These three texts collectively build the basis of Heidegger's efforts to think through fundamental metaphysical concepts to the finite structure of Being itself. These fundamental concepts, or *Grundworte*, are fundamental in that they name what Heidegger sees as the fundament, or ground, sustaining and leading metaphysics itself. Heidegger's intention in these texts is not to "improve" upon these metaphysical concepts but to examine them in order to disclose the still hidden essence of metaphysics itself and to overcome that habit of thought by going back into the ground of metaphysics. The analysis of these *Grundworte* thus serves to open up what Heidegger contends is the unthought yet decisive element in the history of metaphysics as a way of speaking of Being. Curiously, and against the expectations raised by the title, Heidegger's analysis of these *Grundworte* of metaphysics quickly opens up onto two themes that have become the hallmark of Heidegger's later work: technology and language. Most surprising is the claim that the unthought essence and destiny of metaphysics has something to do with modern technology. Stranger still is the corresponding claim that thinking about modern technology will tell us something about metaphysics which has been neglected by the metaphysical tradition even in the age of technology. The link that Heidegger draws between modern technology and metaphysics is the key to interpreting and overcoming each of those relations to Being: according to Heidegger, technology, which operates on a premise that takes things of nature as calculative objects, is the full and final calcification of Being corresponding to the paralysis of thought typifying metaphysics. Drawing this conceptual link between the essence of technology and the essence of metaphysics permits Heidegger to escalate and expand the challenge he makes to metaphysics. Turning the tables on metaphysics as working on the assumption that the finite needs to be overcome, he now argues that not only is there no absolute captivity to the finite, but that the extreme captivity of thought is to be found in the metaphysical attachment to the infinite. The early philosophically tentative and ambiguous intimations that the infinite represents the freedom of thought is finally betrayed by the real and unambiguous outcome of the history of philosophy as metaphysics. Technology, which Heidegger regards as the true constellation of man and Being in the contemporary world and as the metaphysics of the historical present, provides a vivid testimony for the captivity, paralysis, and unfreedom of thought that has attached itself to the infinite and left no room for the finite. This is Heidegger's strongest argument against metaphysics; it is also his most complex. It begins by reexamining the role of the principle of identity in the formation of metaphysics and in contemporary technological rationality.

The essay "The Principle of Identity" opens by taking a careful look at the traditional formulation of the principle of identity. The usual formula is presented in logic in the form of an equation, $A = A$. But, as Heidegger notes, the idea of an equation is that it expresses the equality of at least two elements. This means that the formula really states that one A is equal to another A; however, this means that "the usual formula for the principle of identity conceals precisely that which the principle intends to express: A is A, i.e., that A is itself the same" (*ID*, 10). The logical expression of identity does not say anything about the nature of this self-sameness of a thing with itself. *Equality* is not the same as the sameness of *identity*, yet it is the identity of thought and Being that is at stake in metaphysics. Surely the principle of identity does not prove that thought and Being are equal. By explaining identity merely in terms of equality, logic offers nothing to the need that metaphysics has to articulate the meaning of identity. If the identity of thought and Being is conceived simply as an equality, then the side-by-sideness of the two falls far short of the real wedding of the two demanded by the idea of the unconditioned. Logic, at least as it has been traditionally conceived, quickly shows itself as inadequate to the needs of metaphysics as having to wrestle with, and go beyond, the original difference between thought and Being. There is a need to rethink the essential sense of the principle of identity, moving away from this equality of an equation to an understanding of how it is an expression of self-sameness. This transformation of the formula $A = A$ to A is A is, Heidegger admits, inspired by Hegel:

Hegel shows that this law of thought says more and something other than that which the customary representation of it immediately imparts. This usual representation finds nothing to it. Thus the formula for the principle of identity is conceived by the representing intellect as an empty principle. Hegel shows however that this principle, $A = A$, could not say what it says if it had not already broken through the empty sameness of the A with itself.... This principle could not even be a principle, i.e., an enduring context, if it did not first abandon that which it presumes to say, namely A as the completely empty sameness of something with itself which is thus unable to be developed any further: A as abstract identity.... In his *Logic*, Hegel not only made the richer truth of this law of thought visible in its fundament, but at the same time he demonstrated in an irrefutable manner that our usual thinking not only does not follow this law of thought precisely when it offers this law as correct, but that it contradicts it (*GD*, 36).[63]

By taking this clue from Hegel and reformulating the principle of identity we can, if we listen carefully to its fundamental sense (*Grundton*), learn something of the presuppositions and essence of identity and the way in which it resonates in the ground of metaphysics itself. Once we do this Heidegger contends that we realize that "the principle of identity speaks of the Being of beings ... To every being as such belongs identity, unity with itself" (*ID*, 12). Heidegger continues by explaining what this statement means: "What the principle of identity, heard in its fundamental key, states is exactly what the whole of Western European thinking has in mind, namely: the unity of identity forms a basic characteristic in the Being of beings"

(*ID*, 13). Nevertheless, the traditional conception of the principle of identity does not reflect this fundamental key but displaces that sense by conceiving identity as an equality, and this reflects the metaphysical prejudice that Being must be objectified as a static and omnipresent component in an equation with thought. It is this prejudice that Heidegger intends to investigate further and undermine. He does this by searching for the historical and conceptual foundations of this prejudice in the sayings of one of the original and decisive thinkers in the western tradition—Parmenides.

The Greek word for identity is *to auto*, and the first significant appearance of this word in the philosophic tradition is to be found in Parmenides' famous fragment *to gar auto noein estin te kai einai*. After introducing this fragment, Heidegger remarks that what is said in this sentence is quite different from that which is expressed in the doctrines of subsequent metaphysical thinkers, which say that "identity belongs to Being. Parmenides says: Being belongs in an identity. . . . In the earliest period of thought, long before thought arrived at a principle of identity, identity itself speaks out in a pronouncement which rules as follows: Thought and Being belong together in the Same and by virtue of this Same" (*ID*, 14). Heidegger does not argue that Being belongs in an identity, but he does say that the issue here is how one is to interpret the meaning of this identity that Parmenides describes as *to auto*. Heidegger's first remark in this direction, that "we interpret Sameness to mean a belonging together" (*ID*, 14), certainly does not represent a radical challenge to the logical-metaphysical conception of identity. This conception of identity as a belonging together is by itself insufficiently unique, for it could be interpreted in ways quite agreeable with the traditional metaphysical conception of identity as a relation of equality pertaining to relata. However, Heidegger notes that metaphysics emphasizes the idea that is expressed by the word *together*, and consequently metaphysics conceives this belonging together as a being placed into an order, i.e., into the unity of a manifold in a system which is mediated through a unifying synthesis. In short, Heidegger's objection to the traditional conception of identity goes beyond the difficulties that he finds in the logical conception of identity as an equality to include an objection against the speculative-metaphysical enthusiasm for the real *synthesis* of differences. This is the novel dimension of Heidegger's critique of the concept of identity: he concedes that

Hegel before him had recognized the real limitations of the logical sense of identity as an equation, but beyond Hegel—and of course against him—Heidegger argues that even the synthetic achievement of a full togetherness of original differences fails to express the original sense of identity that belongs to Being and is expressed by Parmenides' word *to auto*.

The fragment of Parmenides which forms the background of Heidegger's meditation on the principle of identity, *to gar auto noein estin te kai einai*, does not speak of any identity whatsoever, but specifically speaks of the special belonging together of thinking and Being. But Heidegger points out that since thinking is the distinctive characteristic of man, what is at stake in how this issue of identity is resolved concerns the relation between man and Being. Thus Heidegger says, "Man and Being are appropriate to each other. They belong to each other. From this belonging to each other, which has not been thought out more closely, man and Being first have those essential determinations by which man and Being are grasped metaphysically in philosophy. We stubbornly misunderstand this prevailing *belonging together* of man and Being so long as we represent everything only in categories and mediations, be it with or without dialectic" (*ID*, 19). The question raised by the principle of identity concerns the real shape of the "identity" of man and Being. Though it is not immediately clear why or how, Heidegger wants to argue that something essential about the self-understanding of man's epochal Being-in-the-world is expressed in precisely how the identity that thought seeks with Being is conceived. Yet Heidegger claims that this very issue of the appropriateness of the identity of man and Being remains unthought in the history of metaphysics which has "stubbornly misunderstood the prevailing belonging together of man and Being" by representing it in categorical terms and as a matter of mediation between man the subject and the objectivity of Being. Continuing with this charge, Heidegger contends that metaphysics has traditionally represented this togetherness as some unity of a manifold of subject(s) and object(s) and so as the systematic order achieved by means of the mediating power of synthesis. Yet Heidegger wants to argue that the very idea of an order, which is either founded in, or the outcome of, a conception of Being as grounded in a static identity or equality, is misleading.

In order to avoid being misled and in order to enter into the proper thinking of this belonging together, one must move away from the attitude of representational thinking. Once again Heidegger charges Hegel, the thinker of absolute identity, with being a representational thinker. Heidegger has tried elsewhere and earlier to make this label stick to Hegelian thought, but unlike the previous passages in which this charge was made, this time Heidegger attempts to redefine the essential character of representational thought by saying that it applies to any thinking that conceives Being as the *ground* upon which beings as beings rest. This means then that the move away from representational thinking and the traditional conception of the principle of identity associated with it is the spring away from the search for Being conceived as ground. But where does this spring away from the ground spring to? "There, where we are already admitted: in the belonging to Being" (*ID*, 20). Such a statement might strike one as strange, or perhaps mere wordplay, but Heidegger asserts its utter importance when he says that "the entry into the realm of this mutual belonging together determines and defines the experience of thinking" (*ID*, 21). Thus, Heidegger claims that the true experience of thought, which ultimately remains unthought in the history of metaphysics, discloses this mutual appropriation of man and Being and that this appropriation, while not functioning as a ground, nevertheless provides the possibilities and legitimation of authentic philosophical discourse.

Heidegger claims that such a mutual appropriation always shows itself in the real constellation of Being and man in the world and that today this constellation prevails as the world of technology. Heidegger is not alone in identifying technology as the special and dominant feature of contemporary life—sociologists, political theorists, environmental groups, and other philosophers have made the same point even before Heidegger—but Heidegger's remarks about technology are unique in that he draws a real connection between technology and metaphysics, and in that he argues that the analysis of the values and imperatives of technological thinking tells us something about the errancy of metaphysics. More precisely, it tells us that metaphysics rather than fulfilling its claim to release us from the captivity of the finite has delivered us over to a different form of captivity, one that is felt in the uneasiness that has grown in the face of growing technological "advances." But this needs explanation. What does the growing technological ordering of our world have to do with the thought of the ontological difference and with Heidegger's effort to demonstrate the destruction of metaphysics by having thought more radically than is possible in metaphysics? How does the challenge of technology point to that experience of thought which has remained as yet unthought in the history of metaphysics? This issue of technology clearly has little or nothing to do with Heidegger's challenge to metaphysics if we conceive technology one-sidedly as a matter of man's doing and making, i.e., if we conceive technology strictly from a subjective viewpoint. To understand what technology has to do with the mutual appropriation of man and Being, and with the ontological difference, it is necessary to unpack the essence of technology in a phenomenological way.

Technology, we are told in Heidegger's essay devoted to this question, is not simply a matter of the workings of machines or tools that are designed to "ameliorate" the human condition but is a way in which "what is" reveals itself to us and a decision that we make about the essence of what reveals itself to us. Furthermore, Heidegger claims that technology is a manifestation of the dominant character of the contemporary constellation of Being and man. What makes this so troubling is that reflection upon the essence of technology indicates that rather than being a way of disclosing the Being of nature as itself, "The disclosing which rules in modern technology is a challenging which demands that nature produce energy" (*TK*, 14). Thus, technology is a way of revealing, or disclosing, what is by challenging, and this challenging is ultimately a way of distorting Being. In clarifying the nature of this disclosing of what is by challenging, Heidegger introduces the crucial yet perplexing notion of the *Ge-Stell*.

Though the word *Gestell* exists in everyday German, Heidegger uses the word in a rather unconventional manner. Normally the word means "frame" or "stand," as in *Bettgestell* (bed frame) or *Buchgestell* (book case). It is also closely related to the word *Gestellung*, which is a military term meaning "reporting for duty." Yet, to fully appreciate the word as Heidegger presents it, one must hear the two components of the word: the prefix, *Ge-*; and the verbal root, *stellen*. The prefix indicates a placing together, a gathering, or grouping (e.g., *Ge-birge*: a "mountain chain"). The verb *stellen* means to place, to put, to posit; moreover, it is the verbal root of the word *Vor-stellen* ("representing"), a word which both Hegel and Heidegger find

significant as indicating a mode of thought that is inadequate to the
topic of thought. Once we take together all of these senses and uses
of the word *Gestell*, we can see why Heidegger uses this word to name
the condition of being placed together into an order that is at our
disposal and ready for use. The customary English translation, "en-
framing," carries with it the sense that it designates a way of thinking
that operates within frameworks; however, it does not carry with it
the clear etymological connection to representation. Heidegger uses
the word *Gestell* to point to that way of disclosing that is primarily a
subjective making available within a framework, and this he contends
is the palpable metaphysics of the present. "Here *Gestell* means the
way of disclosure which rules in the essence of modern technology
and which itself is not technological" (*TK*, 20). This means that "the
question of technology is the question of the constellation . . . *in which
the essence of truth itself happens*" (*TK*, 33). The discussion of the essence
of technology is revealed as a question concerning the essence of
truth, and it is this conception of the essence of technology as a way
in which truth happens that builds the bridge between the question
of technology and Heidegger's efforts to overcome metaphysics. It is
Heidegger's contention that technology, as a deficient way of disclosing what is, is the inescapable consequence of the metaphysical
insistence on the fundamentality of the principle of identity, and that
this is further proof of the errancy of metaphysics itself.

But, since Heidegger has already indicated that there are many
ways that truth happens, and since he has yet to claim any sort of
normative sense of how truth best happens, one might object that he
has already necessarily conceded that technology can be a way in
which truth happens. What then is Heidegger's objection to technology, and how does this point to a more original and radical
thought of what is than is possible in the metaphysical quest for a
stable and secure ground governed by the principle of identity? In
other words, why is the spring away from the ground necessary?

II

The analysis of the essence of technology and of the notion of *Gestell*
was occasioned by a meditation on the principle of identity, and in
particular by the sigificance of this principle for the way in which it
conceives of the relation of Being and man. According to Heidegger,

the contemporary manifestation of this relation is found in the technological structure of the present world. Heidegger claims that there is an essential connection between the present technological constellation of Being and man and the metaphysical principle of identity. More specifically, this connection is first gleaned in the notion of *ground*, for both the essence of technology as *Gestell* and the traditional conception of the principle of identity conceive what is as necessarily ordered, unified, and mediated in a synthesis which serves as the basis for all that follows. In short, both the technological rationality and the logic of identity conceive what is as necessarily grounded. The famous Leibnizian formula "Nihil est sine ratione" reflects this as far as metaphysics is concerned, and that the same is also the case for technology is quite evident in the inability of technology to tolerate accidents and the unexpected (the necessity of "safety features" testifies to this). That which lies outside of the rational horizon of the secure ground of identity has no Being; conversely, all Being has its reasons.

Heidegger examines this principle that "nothing is without reason" [64] in a lecture course published under the title *Der Satz vom Grund*, and here the connection of metaphysics and technology is made more apparent when he says: "Modern technology pushes toward the highest possible technology. Perfectability rests upon the thorough countability of objects. The countability of objects presupposes the unlimited validity of the principle of reason. In this way the principle of reason can be said to dominate the essence of the modern age of technology" (*SG*, 198). The quest for an independent and secure ground leads to a subordination of Being to the ground. Making the principle of groundedness the highest principle for the disclosure of truth is simultaneously a restriction of the conditions for the appearance of Being; Being is disclosed only insofar as it fits the ground. In the technological framework within which man and nature are disclosed, this ground is determined in terms of calculability. In the end, calculability must be recognized as the new standard of objectivity. Only that which is available for calculation can count as real, and the standards of calculation no longer rely solely upon material objectivity. Thus "the presence of nature in the thematic horizon of nuclear physics remains unthinkable so long as it is represented as a matter of objectivity instead of availability" (*ZF*, 12). Technology belongs to the destiny of Being as metaphysics insofar as it represents an objectification of the real; it is a transformation in that destiny insofar as it brings with it the dissolution of the traditional standards of the objectivity of the object. That which is outside of the horizon of perfection, calculation, objectivity, and repeatability is denied any place for appearance. That which is without purpose or reason—the accidental and purposelessness such as is found in play and art—has no room as itself within the technological framework, nor can it be explained upon the grounds of metaphysics. But in this way the independence and integrity of both man and world are leveled down and fixed. This is also the reason why Heidegger says that technology discloses what is by forcing it; it approaches that which is solely as a means to further the end of gathering all that is into a ready and reliable complex of materials. Things of nature and man are both ossified into separate natures and come thereby to be regarded in terms of their instrumentality and calculability rather than their full, living phenomenality and presence.[65] Under the dominion of technology "presence does not rule, rather assault dominates" (ZW, 100). Indeed, Heidegger charges that the attitude of domination and attack is not only characteristic of the modern technological rationality but is equally appropriate as a way of characterizing any manner of conceiving Being on the basis of a ground conceived as identity, order, and unity. Against this attitude and horizon for thinking Being, Heidegger asks if there is a more original way to conceive what is and a more original determination of the essence of man than the traditional conception of him as the rational animal capable of grasping the principle of ground as reason.

Paradoxically, it is technology itself that points the way to this more original determination of man and Being. Already in the essay on art, written some twenty years before Heidegger's intense concern with technology as the metaphysics of the present, he made a remark that indicated the positive lesson of technology: "The earth shatters every penetration in it. It converts every merely calculative importunity upon it into a destruction. This destruction may herald itself under the appearance of mastery and of progress in the form of the technical-scientific objectification of nature, but this mastery nevertheless remains an *impotence of the will*" (*UK*, 36). So it is in the *failure of the subjective will to order* that technology points to this more original determination of what is. It is in the inabilities of the technological rationality to satisfy its own demands of perfectibility and calculability that that which exceeds what can appear in the technological-conceptual matrix reasserts itself. The accelerating dissatisfaction with the technologically ordered environment, the alienation from nature conceived as a "stockpile of resources," and the limits of technology's own ability to fulfill its promises all point to the need for thought to look outside of that way of thinking Being that is characterized by its approach to Being along the model provided by technique. But this failure of the will to order is slow to happen, and Heidegger admits that, even in the failure of the will to order, the will still presents the appearance of its domination and progress. There is no denial on Heidegger's part that modern technology is quite dazzling in its abilities, but this, he says, does not in the least mitigate the fact that the technological paradigms for thought—paradigms such as utility and calculability—are deficient approaches to Being and so are destined to fail according to their own standards. This certainty of the failure of the will is one way in which Heidegger argues for the need for the spring away from the idea of the ground, from what he terms "calculative thought," into the attitude of "meditative thought" (SG, 199) and its peculiar groundlessness. Being does not appear on demand, nor can it be expected to appear only within our preconceived framework which only anticipates or provides for what can be calculated. The conceptual frame of technology is not inclined to open itself to the unexpected and noncalculable, and as such cannot succeed in its effort to conceive the totality of beings within its own horizons. But this is not the only justification that Heidegger offers for his claim that the analysis of the essence of technology points to a more radical thought than the thinking founded on the identity and order of ground.

One year after the publication of *Identity and Difference* Heidegger writes that "The calculative and ordering demand of all that is, and can be, displaces the infinite relation. Even more: the demand which rules in the domination of the essence of modern technology holds this essence into the unexperiencable from which the power of this demand receives its destiny. What is this? It is the middle of the whole infinite relation. It is pure destiny itself" (HEH, 178). Heidegger's claim is that there is a special displacement of the essential infinite relation between man and Being in the technological world, but that this effort to relocate both man and Being fails because it is incapable of displacing the very possibility, belonging to the original circular relation of man and Being, of surprise, novelty, and displacement itself. Modern technology cannot, Heidegger contends, displace the nontechnological essence of technology itself, and yet in the displacement which is effected by modern technology, that which is displaced, "the illimitable relation," becomes all the more present in its absence. In *Identity and Difference* Heidegger calls this illimitable relation *Ereignis*, "the photographic negative" of the *Gestell* (*VS*, 104), and it is in this notion that Heidegger contends that one finds the authentic outcome of the most radical and original thinking of Being.

Given the themes through which Heidegger has previously attempted his deconstruction of metaphysics, it comes as no surprise that Heidegger characterizes this crucial notion of *Ereignis* as an original temporal event that opens up the circularity of the mutual belonging together of Being and man. It is, according to Heidegger's claims, "that realm, vibrating within itself, through which man and Being reach each other in their essence, achieve their essence by losing those qualities with which metaphysics has endowed them" (*ID*, 26). In other words, Heidegger's contention is that prior to anything like the thought of ground, the conception of man as a rational animal, or of Being as an infinite and omnipresent object, there occurs an event which makes the thought of ground, man, and Being, however they are ultimately construed, possible. This event of the appropriation of man and Being is not the union or encounter of two already existing opposites subsequently joined synthetically together, for to conceive it as such would merely be to posit them as something like a subject and object as already existing. Nor can this event be construed as a complete a priori and independent unity out of which opposites first are articulated, for to conceive it as such would be to invoke something like Hegel's notion of the original *parousia* of the Absolute, and this is a notion already called into question by Heidegger. Rather, this original event is that out of which and in which anything like a subject or object could be said to be at all, and yet according to Heidegger, because this event is not prior to any articulation of opposites and because it does not function as a fundamentum, it does not have the determinate character of the Absolute. Thus, "the grounds which essentially determine historical man stem from the essence of grounds. That is why these grounds are unfathomable" (*SG*, 71). The notion of *Ereignis* is not, therefore, to be understood as the ground of all grounds, for it is precisely the fundamentality of the concept of ground which needs to be overcome. It does not provide a basis for understanding man and Being, for it equally opens up the possibility of debasing every such basis. Instead, the notion of *Ereignis* is presented in order to remember the hidden and unthought source which is the self-withdrawing opening (where "opening" is to be understood in the verbal sense) and precondition for the self-identity of beings at all. In other words, every identity and union of thought and its topic, or man and Being, no matter how it is determined, owes its being what it is to a hidden union with what it is not; namely, an indeterminate openness. This hidden union of the event of appropriation is a further determination of the ontological difference that we had earlier characterized as the nonhealable circular struggle of the movement of origination. In the notion of *Ereignis*, Heidegger deepens his presentation of what he characterized as the "groundless ground" in *Being and Time*. There this groundless ground was conceived as "founded" in the temporality of Dasein, but here, in order to avoid the liabilities of a possible subjectivism latent in that earlier presentation, it is presented as an "eventful mirror play" (*VA*, 172) to which we belong only "insofar as our language is appropriate to it" (*ID*, 26). The critical shift in the later presentation of the ontological difference is that here it is said that we witness the happening of this event of mutual appropriation of man and Being, which is "the relation of all relations" (*US*, 267), only insofar as it is manifested as language (cf. *US*, 215).

The strength of this remark comes as somewhat of a surprise despite the well-kown centrality of language in the ontology of the later Heidegger. His claim is not simply that language plays an indispensable role in the event of the appropriation between man and Being, but that *only insofar as* our language is the language of Being are we able to witness and participate in this event appropriately. The character of one's discourse provides the horizon for the possibilities of one's understanding of Being, because the contextual place opened up and articulated by the event of appropriation is a languaged place. The possibilities of language, of what can and cannot be said, its syntax, malleability, and relation to other languages fundamentally determine the history and shape of the place that comes to be out of the appropriation between man and Being. The language and expressions of metaphysics, logic, and technology— operating according to principles of identity, groundness, reason, and categories, and nominatively inclined—displaces and shuts out the full finite and self-concealing temporal character of this event of the mutual appropriation of man and Being. As this insistence upon a conceptual language inappropriate to this original clearing of Being, metaphysics and technology alienate themselves from their own source. The "forgetfulness of Being" shows itself as an inability and unwillingness to hear the claims and call of language itself. When language is heard, then it is the limits and failures of language itself that come forward along with that which it illuminates. This deafness to the "peal" of the event of appropriation is not the result of some willful error of man but seems rather to belong to the essence of language itself, for although "the Saying which happens in the event is, as showing, the ownmost way of this event" (*US*, 266), it must also be said that in naming beings, pointing out things that are, language points away from itself as disclosing Being: "... [when] we speak a language the language itself never comes to word" (*US*, 161). Indeed, it is precisely because language, wherein we witness the happening of the origination of that which it is the task of thought to think, is poorest at pointing to and speaking out itself that this event has gone unthought in the history of thought, even though it is precisely this languaged event which first lets there be a history of thought whatsoever. This is the reason that Heidegger finds poets who have given themselves over to listening to the claims and possibilities of language to be closer to the call of the event of appropriation to Being than philosophers who have insisted upon the language of rigorous categories and of logic. The original identity to which both man and Being belong is found in the way in which each belongs to language in this special sense of opening.

Out of this identity both man and Being come to be what and how they are. This, in part, is the sense of Gadamer's remark that "Being that can be understood is language." [66] It is also the reason that Heidegger can quote George and say that "where word breaks off, no thing may be" (*US*, 163). The final outcome of Heidegger's analysis of the traditional principle of identity is thus the following: "The doctrine of metaphysics represents identity as a fundamental trait of Being. Now it is shown: Being belongs in an identity with thought, the essence of which stems from this letting-belong-together which we name *Ereignis*. The essence of identity is a trait of the *Er-eignis*" (*ID*, 27). In short, insofar as the traditional sense of identity as a static equality of relata is conceived as a fundamental trait of Being, i.e., insofar as Being is conceived ousiologically and man is conceived subjectively, thought forgets that more original dynamic identity of language as disclosing the belonging together of man and Being, which lets Being be revealed in the first place. This more original identity, which is the mutual event of appropriation named by the notion of *Ereignis*, is an identity which exists only as identity conceived as the belonging-together of what remains different. Man and Being remain marked by a final difference, but equally each is itself only as belonging to the other in the identity of this mutual event of appropriation. This more original identity is itself nothing apart from man and Being; it is rather the event which happens only insofar as the difference which lies at the origin of that which is to be thought remains *as* difference. The integrities of both man and Being arise in and out of this relation of their belonging together that outlines their difference. Only insofar as man and Being are released into their own is the richness of their identity and "illimitable relation" disclosed. To forget this original ontological difference is simultaneously to conceal this original identity. To synthetically surmount this original difference into a higher identity, and so argue for the essential oneness of man and Being, is to conceal the true essence of this more original identity which is only as contemporaneous[67] with difference. To forget, or to conceal, this original event of identity-and-difference is to forget the true context, or place, within which Being may first appear at all, and without which thought could not attempt to ground itself at all. *Ereignis* is therefore the opening up to a more original thinking of the constellation of Being and man than is found in technological-metaphysical *Gestell* of the modern world, and as the ineluctable element of what comes into presence for a while, it is the true task of thought to think this clearing. Self-withdrawing and silent about itself, this clearing discloses the true finitude of both man and Being both as belonging together and as fundamentally different in light of their identity.

But now it is necessary to ask how Heidegger applies this to his critique of Hegel, for once again Heidegger takes Hegel as illustrative of the neglect of what he regards as his own radical and novel insight. How for instance does Heidegger differentiate his notion of the contemporaneity of identity-and-difference from Hegel's presentation of the Absolute as a conflictual unity? The answer to this question is found in the second of the two essays in *Identity and Difference*, "The Onto-theo-logical Constitution of Metaphysics."

III

In "The Onto-theo-logical Constitution of Metaphysics," it is quite clear that in contrast to Heidegger's usual treatment of Hegel, he is not so much attempting a critique of Hegel as he is attempting to enter into a real dialogue with Hegel, and this is done out of a growing recognition of a proximity of the way in which each sees the issue of thought as tied to the question of identity and difference. Heidegger acknowledges this proximity when he says: "Hegel rigorously thinks about the matter of his thinking in the context of a conversation with the previous history of thinking. Hegel is the first thinker who can and must think in this way" (*ID*, 33). Heidegger recognizes that for Hegel, as well as for himself, the issue of the identity of thought and Being can only be thought in the context of a dialogue with the history of that relation. This is not due to any arbitrary effort on the part of Hegel or Heidegger to merge history and philosophy, rather such is the case because, for both, the issue of thought is in itself dynamic and so historical, and consequently the historical appreciation of philosophy is itself essentially philosophical. Since neither finds a ground for this relation outside or beyond it, both must look to its history in order to understand the coming-to-be of their own place in that relation. For Heidegger, the way in which thought and Being have appropriated each other in the language and self-understanding of epochs is simultaneously the history of the withdrawal of the clearing of Being and testimony to its finite presence. Thought is only what it can be as having belonged to this still unfinished dialogue with Being. For Hegel, the achievement of Absolute Spirit, the real identity of thought and Being, is the outcome of the history of their mediating relation in the language and culture of historical peoples. With the recognition of this proximity, Heidegger once again acknowledges that he still has not yet won the right to his claim to have overcome the history of metaphysics despite Hegel's claims to have already overcome metaphysics as its completer in the self-identity of Absolute Spirit. But now Heidegger has introduced a new dimension into the quarrel with Hegel; namely, this new determination of the issue of thought conceived in terms of the ever incomplete and historical event whereby man and Being appropriate each other. Thus, although both Hegel and Heidegger recognize the essential inner history of thought's relation to Being, the way in which each characterizes the element or framework of that history differs. That is why Heidegger says: "For Hegel, the matter of thinking is Being with respect to beings having been thought in absolute thinking, and as absolute thinking. For us, the matter of thinking is the Same, and this is Being—but Being with respect to its difference from beings. More precisely: for Hegel, the matter of thinking is the idea as absolute concept. For us, formulated in a preliminary way, the matter of thinking is the difference *as* difference" (*ID*, 36–7). In other words, the dispute is over the final identity or difference characterizing the relation of thinking and Being.

The differing decisions that Hegel and Heidegger make about the character of this difference, which both recognize as the inescapable element thought must think in its effort to think what is, have the consequence of introducing a basic difference in the way in which each carries on the conversation with the history of thought. For Hegel the original ontological diremption between thought and Being discloses itself as always having been possible only by virtue of the prior community of the identity that is their difference. The history of thought's agonistic relation to Being, the struggle of identity and difference, a relation that constitutes the essential history of philosophy, ultimately arrives at the point where thought knows itself as in this identity with Being. For Heidegger, on the other hand, this original ontological scission is the rupture that arises from the mutual self-scission of both thought and Being as each establishes its own integrity out of the identity in which they belong together. For Hegel, this conversation means entering into the power and domain of *that which has been thought*; in Hegelian terms, *Absolute Spirit*. For Heidegger, this conversation means entering into the power and domain of *that which has gone unthought*, but from which that which was thought first becomes possible; in Heidegger's language, the *ontological difference*.

This is the latest incarnation of the long-standing conflict that has characterized the mutually hostile claims that Hegel and Heidegger make with regard to the question of the Absolute. However, Heidegger now approaches this dispute by noting that, though he agrees with Hegel in finding the issue of thought to be intrinsically historical and destined by virtue of its origin, he disagrees with Hegel about the implications of history for that destiny. This dispute is apparent in the way each characterizes the movement and direction of the history of philosophy. For Hegel, the history of thought moves teleologically as an overcoming of what previously had been thought into the gathering together and grounding of all the essential possibilities of thought. For Heidegger, the history of thought moves not as an advance, but as the step back into a region that was forgotten in the history of metaphysics. This step back, as Heidegger presents it, is a questioning path back into and behind the source of the basic character of metaphysics, i.e., into the essence of the onto-theo-logical constitution of metaphysics. Thus the first task for Heidegger is to defend the priority of the step back as a way of following the primordial movement of the history of thought, and to do so by making evident the still concealed essence of philosophy's own origin.

Heidegger is unambiguous on this point: "The onto-theo-logical character of metaphysics became questionable for thought not on the basis of any atheism, but from out of the experience of a thinking which pointed to the yet *unthought* unity of the essence of the onto-theology of metaphysics" (*ID*, 45). It is not by virtue of an encounter with atheism or nihilism that the necessity of the step back from the teleological forwardness of metaphysics becomes evident. It is not Nietzsche, but Hegel, and the experience of thinking along with Hegel, that points the way to the as yet unthought unity of the essence of metaphysics. What is even more astounding is that Heidegger contends that Hegel is quite unaware of this as the most original truth disclosed by his thought. The obvious question with regard to this is: what in Hegel's thought points to this unthought essence of metaphysics?

Heidegger does not answer this question as directly as one might wish; however, we find a clue to a possible reply when Heidegger says: "The essential constitution of metaphysics is based on the unity of beings as such in the universal and that which is highest" (*ID*, 52). To have achieved such a unity is Hegel's self-asserted claim in the history of thought. And, to an extent, that is the case, for in the *Science of Logic* Hegel develops the inner unity of ontology and theology, not as two separate parts of the system but as together in the very logic, the *logos*, of that system which grounds the Being of beings. Furthermore, it is clear that the Hegelian notion of the Absolute must be conceived both as the most universal, i.e., the *logos*, and as the highest, i.e., the *theos*, appearance of what is. But where in the Hegelian concept of the Absolute does Heidegger find that the Absolute points to this unthought essence of metaphysics, an essence that Heidegger had thus far characterized in his notion of the ontological difference and *Ereignis*?

Despite the ultimate identity and absolute unity that characterizes the Absolute, there still remains the necessity of recognizing the inner conflict requisite to the true life of the Absolute. Thus, the Absolute is absolute unity, but only as the unity of *conflict*; it is absolute identity, but this identity is only as identity and *difference*. In short, even in the completion of metaphysics as it is found in the notion of the Absolute, which is finally presented in Hegel's *Logic*, we find the inescapability of witnessing the work of this original difference, which belongs to that which is to be thought. "Only this much is clear, that when we deal with the Being of beings and with the beings of Being, we deal in each case with a difference" (*ID*, 53). Although Hegel understood the fundamentality of the role that this inner conflictual difference plays in the Absolute, he did not, Heidegger claims, grasp the true significance of it. Heidegger offers no explanation for this other than in saying that "we encounter this, which is called difference, everywhere and always in the matter of thinking, in beings as such, and we encounter it so unquestionably that we do not even notice this encounter. Nor does anything compel us to notice it" (*ID*, 55). But what does one discover once this hidden source of the essence of metaphysics is attended to and recognized for what it is? How does the more radical thinking of the original ontological difference disrupt and render untenable the metaphysical response to this same difference?

In responding to these questions Heidegger offers his most extensive presentation of the notion of *Ereignis*: "While we are facing the difference, . . . we can say: the Being of beings means: Being, which is beings. . . . Being here becomes present in the manner of a transition to beings. . . . Being transits (that), comes unconcealingly over (that) which arrives as something of itself unconcealed only by that coming over. Arrival means: to keep concealed in unconcealedness—to abide present in this keeping—to be a being. Being shows itself as the unconcealing overwhelming. Beings as such appear in the manner of the arrival that keeps itself concealed in unconcealedness" (*ID*, 56). This play of Being as self-withdrawing revealing and beings that arrive in the unconcealedness of this place is the play which happens as "the difference of Being and beings, and as the differentiation of overwhelming and arrival, is the perdurance of the two in *unconcealing concealment*" (*ID*, 57). This means that Being can no longer be represented as a higher universal for beings, for the two happen only in the event of this intro-play which is "a circle, an encircling of Being and beings" (*ID*, 62). Being, while having an integrity all its own, has no independence from beings. Its integrity, its self-identity, has only been partially made evident and discussed in the history of philosophy. But its identity *as* difference, that is, the full sense of Being as belonging in an identity with its other, has been suppressed in the resulting metaphysical determinations of the truth of Being. And so all of the metaphysical conceptions of Being as a unique ground hypostatized as independent of beings—*physis, logos, hen, idea, energeia,* substantiality, objectivity, subjectivity, will, the will to power, and the will to will—all are only different static determinations and restrictive identifications of this same ecstatic event of identity-and-difference. The recognition of this original event does not appear as the outcome of a long dialectical process of overcoming previous positions, rather we approach "the nearness of the historical . . . only through the sudden moment of recollection" (*ID*, 59). In the end, one can only point from out of what has been thought to that which lies hidden as the unthought. It is not by an act of the intellect, but by what Heidegger describes as a releasement or step back that the true nature of this ontological event and difference is recalled. The cognitive activity that has traditionally been at work in metaphysical thought, that is, the logical and representing intellect, is incapable of recollecting the full insurmountable force of the original ontological difference. One can offer no final reason or ground why this is so. This is, however, why Heidegger spent his entire career in an unprecedented dialogue with previous philosophers: "Only when we thoughtfully turn to what has already been thought do we ready ourselves for that which is to be thought" (*ID*, 30). The ontological difference, though forgotten in metaphysics, is not completely absent from it. Metaphysics is not the unadulterated oblivion to Being but has always retained the mark of Being as finite. Recovering this mark however requires the full deconstruction of what has been thought, and this in turn requires—initially at least—the effort to see the history of thought as a unity.

IV

Clearly, Heidegger's critique of Hegel must be seen within the context of Heidegger's lifelong effort at overcoming what he has called the representative way of conceiving what is, a way of thinking which Heidegger believes fairly characterizes an enduring element of the entire history of metaphysics. Now, however, Heidegger has expanded this effort to include interpretation of the contemporary technological constellation of Being and man as evidence that the entire metaphysical quest for a ground, which is mirrored in the essence of technology, is doomed to an inescapable subjectivism and so is incapable of overcoming the problem of the dualism of a subject-object conception of the constellation of Being and man. To explicate this expansion of his critique of metaphysics is one of the primary tasks of the famous "Letter on Humanism," for the humanism spoken of is the final outcome of the subjectivism of metaphysics.

In that essay, Heidegger makes a remark about Hegel which makes apparent how he believes the critique of metaphysics and technology could be approached in Hegel: "The modern metaphysical essence of labor is anticipated in Hegel's *Phenomenology* as the self-asserting priority of unconditional production which is the objectification of the actual through man experienced as subjectivity" (*BH*, 337). Given this remark it is clear that Hegel's reply to Heidegger's critique of Hegel's conception of the ontological difference must respond to the following question: How does Hegel conceive of the concept of work, and in particular, does he claim that this concept of work overcomes the problem of the objectification of the real, and, if so, how? In other words, do Hegelian reflections on labor and human subjectivity manifest the same, essentially technological, trademarks that Heidegger says underpin modern metaphysics?

Since it is not insignificant that Hegel's concept of work often appears alongside an elucidation of the meaning and role of language, which was also central to Heidegger's discussion of the ontological difference, we must also ask: how does Hegel conceive of language?

Finally, we must once again ask: how would Hegel reply to Heidegger's claim that in the Hegelian conception of the Absolute as a conflictual unity one witnesses evidence for the inescapability of the thought of the ontological difference?

V

Besides the treatment of the concept of work in the *Phenomenology* to which Heidegger refers, there are two other texts in which we find significant treatments of this concept by Hegel: in the *System of Ethical Life*, composed less than five years before the publication of the *Phenomenology*, and in the *Philosophy of Right*, written nine years later.

The treatment of work in the *Phenomenology* occurs in the context of the master-slave dialectic, where we find the significance of work (the slave) opposed to nonwork (the master). The outcome of this dialectic of work and nonwork is, as is well known, the elevation of the level of existence of the one who partakes of work above that of the one who desires and consumes without working. What is most interesting in this presentation of the concept of work is how, according to Hegel, it overcomes the framework of subjectivity within which Heidegger claims that it operates. Since Heidegger characterized Hegel's concept of work as the objectification of the real through man experienced as subjectivity, we must ask whether work, for Hegel, does in fact entail an objectification of the real, and whether it must be conceived as the result of the subjective action of man.

In describing the situation of the slave as opposed to the master, Hegel draws a sharp distinction between desire and work.[68] Whereas the master lives in a state of perpetual desire and sacrifices himself to his desires, the slave does not idly desire but works. It is in the way that it differs from desire that we most clearly discover the significance of work for Hegel. Desire, a wholly subjective, private, and transitory manner of relating to the world, soon reveals itself in its innermost futility, that is, that desire suspends itself in its self-fulfillment and self-annulment. Desire is a perpetual disappearance and succession of new desires, and the master, by being determined by his desires, is at the mercy of this flux. By themselves, immediate desires, and ultimately that means any desire that another can satisfy for us, are informed only by the whims of the more or less momentary and privative will of the desiring subject. Work, on the other hand, "is desire *restrained* and checked, evanescence delayed; in other words, work shapes and forms" (*PG*, 149). Whereas desire, as the subjective, privative, consuming relation to the world, causes things to be consumed and to disappear, work gives things a form. But the significance of work goes beyond this giving a shape to the world, for in giving shape to his world, the slave not only works free of the domination of the master by learning self-subsistence but also comes to be an object for himself in the products of his work. It is precisely in this moment of work as forming and giving shape to the object of work that the worker begins to become his own self-conscious subject and not merely the subject of the master. Ultimately the slave works to elevate himself to a higher level of freedom than the master who depends upon the slave for the satisfaction of his desires: "In the subject this liberation is hard labor against the pure subjectivity of demeanor, against the immediacy of desire, as well as the empty subjectivity of feeling and the arbitrariness of inclination" (*PR*, #187).

Thus, through work the slave not only transforms the immediate materials of nature and gives them a form, but the slave comes to discover himself as objectified in the world, and this means that the slave transforms himself in transforming the world. But this "self" that is "objectified" is not the private, subjective self which characterizes the master in his desire. To understand why this is so we must remember the original and most basic distinction between the master and the slave: the slave is the one who comes face-to-face with anxiety, whereas the master did not. The two basic traits that characterize the slave, the confrontation with anxiety and the need to work, are not to be viewed as two independent traits but must be recognized in their essential connection. In confronting anxiety, the slave confronts his being as a whole and confronts it as pervaded by nothingness; in other words, the slave is purged of any solid conception of his being, his "self," such as the master retains, for the slave recognizes the final futility of the individual, private self. In this recognition the slave understands the futility of the will to satisfy such subjective desires and so submits to doing work for another. Since an essential element of work is only visible in the confrontation with anxiety, Hegel makes clear that work is not ultimately the expression of the subjective will of the individual, for anxiety is by no means the result of a decision of the will. In anxiety the subjectivity of the individual is transcended by absolute negativity, which, for Hegel, is the Absolute as negative.

In this way, work is not merely the activity of the will of man, but is, ultimately, the work of the Absolute. At first the slave works according to the will of the master, but in the process of giving shape to the world, the slave not only transforms the world but comes to recognize himself as participating in this work of the Absolute. In this case the work of the Absolute is the process of transforming the world and those who live in it into a home. To be sure, the slave does not move from being a slave to this ultimate recognition in one giant unmediated leap; the point is that this recognition is open only to one who works. Long before this ultimate recognition is arrived at, work shows itself simply as the mediation of "the raw material directly supplied by nature ... specifically adapted to numerous ends by all sorts of different processes" (*PR*, #196). But this mediation of nature is the process of the overcoming, or removal, of all that is alien to the slave. At first nature appears as merely other to the slave, but by acting, transforming, and negating (i.e., by working) nature as other, the slave transforms nature as it is given, and in repeating and building upon previous transformations, the slave transforms the very process of work itself (e.g., he works to build machines that do other work).

The real significance of this process is not found in the construction of increasingly sophisticated technology. Rather, what is important in this process of transformation is that work initiates a process of *change*, indeed it originates a process of change as historical *evolution*. This is why work works upon the worker as well as upon the natural world, and this is why it is important to realize that the slave changes himself by transforming the world. It is in this respect that work, for Hegel, is more than the unilateral action of the subjective will of man. Work sets in motion the dynamic and mutually formative process of man and nature transforming one another. The intersection of these two domains, the place where work takes place, is the locus of both human and natural history. To conceive work merely as a subjective action of the will of man would be to conceive the process of history that work initiates as due solely to the will of man, but such, for Hegel, is clearly not the case, for history, according to Hegel, "is the presentation of the divine, absolute process of Spirit" (*VPG*, 73).

The true significance of work as the mediation of nature and the Absolute is thus to be found in work conceived as the formation of culture (*Bildung*). Work, as we have noted, is cultivation in the double sense of forming the world and educating the worker. But, it must be asked whether this notion of cultivation implies both the objectification of the world and a concept of man experienced as subjectivity as Heidegger suggests it does. With regard to the second part of this question, we have already noted that by grounding the concept of work upon the notion of anxiety, Hegel avoids conceiving work fundamentally as the subjective action of man as willing. But in order to answer the first part of Heidegger's charge, that is, that work for Hegel means the objectification of the real, we must deepen the meaning of *Bildung* that work entails.

The transformation that occurs in and through work is a *"practical thinking"* (*PR*, # 197). That this is so should be apparent in the very framework within which Hegel usually treats the concept of work, i.e., as a question to be considered within the context of the formation of the ethical life of a people (*Sittlichkeit*). Indeed, it is in this notion of ethical life that Hegel develops a concept of man as a practical being, and through this he attempts to overcome the dualism of a conception of man as fundamentally other than, or opposed to, the world and fellow men. In his analysis of this practical dimension of the ethical life Hegel attempts to integrate man and his world into a real totality; it is within this totality that the concept of work must be considered. Once the meaning of work is found within this real, practical totality, it is proved to be an "annihilation of the subjective and objective" (*SS*, 11). It is the role of work to nourish this ethical totality, the largest sense of which is found in the state, and its work is to hold this totality together *as* totality; its purpose is not the objectification of nature but the assimilation of nature insofar as it is necessary to sustain the ethical whole. In work then we find the reciprocal formation and cultivation of man and nature. Along with the humanization of nature we find the naturalization of human being.

Hegel might respond to Heidegger's charge by saying that, since it is clear that he does not conceive work merely as the subjective act of man, he can not conceive of work as the objectification of the real. It is clear that from the earliest years of his career Hegel made an effort to preserve the integrity of nature. In his earliest work (1793) Hegel distinguishes between nature and an objectified view of nature: in "the living book of nature the plants, insects, birds and animals are among each other living off of each other, each lives and enjoys, they are mixed together so that one encounters all types together ... [in the objectified view of nature we find that] the insects are dead, the plants dried out, the animals stuffed or preserved and all is arranged together where nature divides" (*FS*, 14). Obviously, this passage was not written with direct regard to the concept of work;

however, it does clearly demonstrate Hegel's strong opposition to any objectification of nature. Thought dialectically, the truth of nature is disclosed as vital and nonobjectifiable. It should be clear why this is so, for a process of objectification would produce an other to the Absolute, and this in turn would mean that the Absolute was non-absolute.

Thus, for Hegel, although the concept of work appears as the moment of the negation of nature as initially an other to the worker, that is, as the formation of the world, it must finally be understood within the larger context within which it is at work. This larger context is the real totality in which the work of the Absolute is found, *the ethical state of a people.* To divorce the concept of work from the practical sphere within which it is at work is to misunderstand the meaning of work for Hegel.[69] Thus, the issue of the concept of work leads to the task of arriving at a more adequate understanding of this practical dimension of Spirit. Such a realm is, to be sure, the realm of the Absolute, but it is now to be manifested in and as the Spirit of a people living harmoniously with each other and their world. By situating work within this larger totality, Hegel wishes to demonstrate that work is not merely a formal relationship of man and world, but that it is to be conceived as a moment of the full conception of what is, and that it plays a real role in the ontological structure of the world. In this way, Hegel attempts to overcome the sort of charges leveled at him by Heidegger, the charges of the objectification of the real and the subjectivization of man; rather than revealing the world as bifurcated into real objects and a fundamentally different human reality, work is the key element in the overcoming of any such bifurcation.

Although this notion of the spirit of a people, which Hegel develops as the system of ethical life, is presented and examined in many respects, it is not insignificant that another problematic central to Heidegger's critique of metaphysics, i.e., language, is one of the most important respects in which one may interpret this larger totality within which work is to be conceived.

VI

The significance of language for Heidegger was that in it one could find testimony for that original and lasting event of appropriation that Heidegger named *Ereignis*. For Heidegger, language is the self-concealing manner in which beings are manifested in, or as, this event, and furthermore that it characterizes the essential element as the mutual belonging together of man and Being. Language is, according to Heidegger's famous formulation, the "house of Being" (*BH*, 311), and the event of the mutual appropriation of man and Being must be thought as a linguistic (or better: languaged) event. The thrust of these remarks on language is always to point to an element of experience, an element outlining the horizons of possible experience, that is historical, in process, and simultaneously revelatory and dissembling. As with each of the other elements of experience and implications of metaphysics that Heidegger analyzes, he wants to lay claim to a unique sense of the phenomenon under analysis. The question is whether or not Hegel's sense of language as an essential element in the formation of culture that is achieved by work and as articulating the ethical Spirit of a people, bears sufficient and significant resemblance to the role and sense of language in Heidegger to warrant yet another attempt by Heidegger to point to that element of experience that resists the sort of metaphysical schematization that Heidegger claims characterizes Hegelian thought.

Like the concept of work, so the concept and role of language, according to Hegel, is to be conceived in conjunction with the idea of the formation of culture. But whereas work was revealed to be formative on the level of the particular (i.e., either the particular worker or particular object) situated within the larger totality of the practical realm, language, on the other hand, reveals itself as constituting this larger totality within which work is at work, i.e., as constituting the meaning of culture on the level of generality. This does not, however, mean that the roles of work and of language are at all separable, or that one works only on the level of particularity while the other is restricted to the domain of universality. It means rather that work works upon language just as language shapes work; it means that language, for Hegel, has the principal task of articulating the larger context, or element, which, as the spirit of a people, is fundamental in forming the ontological structure within which work, as the relationship of man and world, gains its true significance. That is why language has a role in the formation of the element of that which it is the task of thought to think, i.e., Spirit. Language is the shape of a culture as an historical and ethical cultivation of Spirit, and as such it articulates the practical realm within which the work of a people takes place.

Hegel often situates language not as a moment of this larger totality but within the context of the psychology of the individual (cf. for instance, *Enz.* #459), and this frequently has the tendency to obscure the larger place of language in Hegelian thought. It is, of course, true that such is the case, for Hegel speaks about the meaning of language as it is disclosed in the psychology of the individual; it is not, however, true that this is the full meaning and significance of language for Hegel. There is a function of language that, for the most part, remains nonthematized in Hegel, and it is precisely this role of language in the cultivation of the spirit of a people. Thus, we hear Hegel say that "language is only as the language of a people ... only as the work of a people is language the ideal existence of Spirit, in which Spirit expresses and speaks itself as it is in its essence and its Being" (*JS*, frag. 22). And this spirit of a people which language helps to shape is "*the absolute universal element*, the ether, which takes in all individual consciousness; it is the absolutely simple life, simple substance" (*JS*, frag. 22). Language articulates the common cultural and political sphere upon which and out of which the spirit of a people first comes to be at all. It is in this sense that language must be thought as "the pure existence of Spirit" (*VGP*, III, 107). Spirit has its subjects all of whom both have a voice and are expressions of the expression of Spirit in culture.

For Hegel, the fundamental truth of Spirit is its binding power, and the same must be said of language since "the language is the existence of Spirit" (*PG*, 458). Language shares this characteristic binding power with Spirit in that language is effective in the inwardness of our being while being active in our outward behavior. It is thus as overcoming the isolation and privation of the subjectivity of particularity that language unifies man with his fellow man and with his world as well. In fact, language shares this characteristic with work, for "language and work are expressions wherein the individual no longer holds to and possesses himself, rather in them the inner is able to come outside of itself" (*PG*, 229). Yet, to say that the binding, or unifying, power of language is to be witnessed in its power of expression would be not only an inadequate explanation, it would be quite wrong, for language conceived as expression is language which remains on the level of representation. Hegel was quite aware of the inadequacies of language conceived merely as expression and, hence, representatively. If we are to understand the true being of language as Spirit, then it is necessary to recognize it as both shaping and shaped by the essential core of Spirit itself. Language is not merely a means of expressing Spirit, it is rather the real articulation of Spirit in a culture. Not surprisingly then, the highpoints of culture, and the turning points of history can be recognized in the new dimensions of language found in those periods. Thus, it is as a critique of representative language that Hegel introduces his analysis of the Greek tragedies and the concept of tragedy in general.

Hegel introduces the concept of tragedy as overcoming the narrative, representational language of the epic. We find in tragedy, says Hegel, a "higher language ... which brings closer together the dispersed moments of the essential and active world" (*PG*, 510). The language of tragedy is no longer a language which merely describes or represents the action of the tragedy; rather, the language itself is of the very essence of the action. This is why language, for Hegel, must be recognized not merely as the expression of Spirit (as the Spirit of a people) but as the embodiment of Spirit. The language of tragedy is itself the embodiment of the tragic combat. Only once we recognize that tragedy is found in the mutual hostility of two ways of speaking and judging about what is right and necessary can we be in a position to recognize that something more fundamental is at stake than that which is referred to as the conflict of duties. In the language of tragedy the essential agony of Spirit, its dialectic, is spoken out. However, it must be recognized that language as the embodiment of Spirit does not encompass the whole meaning of Spirit, it is not "larger" or "more original" than Spirit; rather, language is only one manner in which Spirit is embodied and given voice as the Spirit of a people. The arts, political action, scientific discovery, and war are other ways in which Spirit realizes itself and is realized in the world. It is in this sense that language, for Hegel, has the meaning of being disclosive of the element of Spirit which, though shaped by language, is itself more than a merely linguistic element within which a people lives. More precisely, language is the unity of a people and so is disclosive of Spirit insofar as it is a gathering together of the dispersed moments of the essential and active world. In short, we find in language evidence for the conflictual unity that characterizes the Hegelian notion of Spirit as Absolute. Language not only expresses this conflictual unity, but as the embodiment of it, language points beyond itself to that which builds the larger context, or element, for the thinking of what is. In this sense, it must be said that language, for Hegel, points to the Absolute as ground. Hegel's own language, and the legendary peculiarities and frequent untranslatability of his philosophic prose, must be seen as part of his own self-conscious effort to speak in ways appropriate to the dialectic. It is quite important to bear in mind that "Hegel's whole discourse enacts a refusal of fixity, of formal closure. . . . In Hegel, reflection and utterance are in constant motion on three levels . . . Hegel rigorously subverts the naive linearities in order to communicate the simultaneities, often conflicting, and inward recursions or self-corrections of his proposals."[70] Hegel's sense of language is too sensitive to the conflicting and complex character of Spirit for it to contribute to the objectification of Spirit. The authentic language of Spirit, in identifying Spirit, identifies it as the conflicting identity of differences.

Once again, precisely at the point at which Heidegger offers his evidence for the need and truth of the thought of the ontological difference, we find Hegel interpreting the same evidence in fundamentally the same manner, but as evidence for the thought of the Absolute. But this similarity makes the third question which resulted from our analysis of Heidegger's text *Identity and Difference* all the more pointed: is the Hegelian concept of the Absolute as a conflictual unity in truth evidence for the inescapability and insurmountability of the thought of the ontological difference? How does Hegel's concept of Spirit as a conflictual unity differ from Heidegger's notion of the ontological difference?

VII

Heidegger characterizes the notion of the ontological difference as being best witnessed in the event that he calls *Ereignis*. There, in the mutual appropriation and belonging together of man and Being, the original and lasting difference between Being and beings, and between Being and thinking, is disclosed. The significance of the ontological difference is that, owing to it, one must recognize the irreconcilability of the struggle of Being and beings, of presencing and the present, of Being and thinking, and therefore the thinking of what is, i.e., philosophy, must, if it is not to be forgetful of its true task,

recall and preserve this irreconcilability, this unhealable homeless- NB
ness which first and always calls thought. Thus, Heidegger's critique
of metaphysics finds its most comprehensive form in his critique of
the traditional concept of identity and of the notion of ground both
of which reify and so render static the originally ecstatic openness of
Ereignis. In this way metaphysics is said to forget that which is to be
thought in attempting to heal the homelessness of thought. For
Heidegger, to extinguish the inner difference and struggle of that
which is to be thought is to deny the very roots and origin of thought,
which it is the task of philosophy to think. The question that we
must put to Hegel is: does Hegel deny this original and perduring
difference that Heidegger contends is witnessed in the more radical
thought of what is, or does the Hegelian concept of the Absolute bear
witness to the inescapability of the ontological difference? How far
can the Absolute, as the identity of identity and difference, preserve
the truth of those phenomena that Heidegger points to as testimony
to the enduring and insurmountable presence of the ontological
difference?

It is not enough simply to say that the Hegelian concept of the
Absolute must be understood as the unity of conflict in order to say
that Hegel does make a real effort to preserve the true nature of
conflict and of difference in the Absolute. It is clear that Hegel makes
some effort to think through the conflict between thought and Being
as essential to the self-identity of each, but, rather than interpreting
this inner conflict that is necessary to the life of the Absolute as
testimony to the ultimate homelessness of thought, Hegel interprets
this original, ontological difference as further evidence for the ultimate identity and unity of thought and Being. In short, the inner
difference that characterizes the Absolute testifies to the necessity and
inescapability of a final unity that builds the ground of this difference.
The real difference and so individual integrity of both thought and
Being is found in the openness of each to the other witnessed in history and Spirit. Through the contradictions and conflicts that arise
from opposing demands of each upon the other, this openness and
belonging together of thought and Being is disclosed as the prior, yet
originally, concealed ground of both. As such, the ground is not other
than, or higher than, either thought or Being but is the inner essence
of both. Heidegger is well aware that Hegel's concept of ground has
a certain uniqueness in the history of metaphysics, for with it Hegel

attempts to overcome the traditional, representational concept of ground, and of a formal and abstract concept of identity. In so doing, Hegel attempts to preserve, rather than extinguish, the original diremption between thought and Being which calls thought. But, Hegel contends that the true and more original preservation of this inner difference is only to be found in the thought of the Absolute. To understand why this is so it is necessary to recall that Hegel's concept of identity is as the identity of identity *and* difference.

This issue of the logic of identity and difference was a lifelong concern of Hegel's, and so we find several different ways in which he presents the resulting notion of identity. One not only finds a very clear conceptual analysis of it in the *Logic* (cf. *WL*, II, 26–62), but also in the *Systemfragment vom 1800* where Hegel says that "life is the unity of unity and nonunity" (*FS*, 422). One could view Hegel's entire career as the extended attempt to demonstrate the necessity, and implications, of thinking *speculatively*, of grasping the internal relation, the *logos*, which runs through all that is. To think speculatively is to understand the need to move beyond the fixed oppositions that shape and restrict the representative thought of the intellect. The warrant and necessity of speculative thought is to be found in the concept of dialectic, which "constitutes the moving soul of scientific progress" (*Enz.* #81).

The key idea in understanding the Hegelian concept of dialectic as the logic of speculation is found in the idea of contradiction. Hegel criticizes any way of conceiving what is that holds fast to the law of noncontradiction. The reason Hegel gives for this, besides the blindness of such a way of thinking to the original identity of Being and Nothing, is that it abides by an empty conception of identity, for the law of noncontradiction is but another "expression of the principle of identity" (*WL*, II, 31), and the result of this is a concept of what is as "the night in which all cows are black" (*PG*, 19). Like Heidegger, Hegel finds the traditional formulation of the principle of identity, A = A, to be meaningless, since identity is only meaningful insofar as it identifies both the specific difference and the full relations of the concept at issue. As such, the authentic concept of identity does not shy away from the contradictions that surface from the hostilities found between the specific difference and the communal dimensions of a concept. Authentic identity is achieved only once those contradictions have been confronted and worked though. Thus, the speculative dialectic must not be conceived as the avoidance of contradiction but as the more original way of thinking contradiction.

Hegel explains the relation between dialectic and contradiction by saying that contradiction arises when reflective, representational thought poses to itself its own limits. Indeed he claims that the history of philosophy up to his time presents the various stages of the development of representational thought, which reaches its highest point in Kant who, in exposing the antinomies of thought, exposed the "necessary internal contradiction of determinations" (*WL*, I, 26). Arriving at this insight, Kant is the first to recognize the limits of representational thought. However, what Kant failed to recognize was "that contradiction is precisely the rising of reason above the limitations of the understanding and the resolving of them" (*WL*, I, 27). Despite Kant's own refusal to make the speculative move, the Kantian antinomies are thus to be regarded as evidence of the inner contradiction that propels thinking to the point where the essential identity that hides within all opposition must be recognized. One reaches this point, which is the transition to the level of speculative thought, not merely in recognizing the mutual belonging together of that which stands in the relation of contradiction, but in the recognition that this mutual belonging together points to the essential *inner unity*, which is the *common* element identifying the apparently contradictory. In the antinomies Kant was able to speak of the respective legitimacies of both the thesis and antithesis; he was even able to see the extent to which the legitimating grounds of each ultimately pointed in the same direction as the other. But he was not able to speculatively grasp the way in which both the thesis and antithesis required each other, thereby serving not as evidence for the final self-contradiction into which reason must inevitably fall but as evidence for the Absolute as that identity to which all reason leads. One only arrives at this recognition with the discovery that "what is self-contradictory does not resolve itself into a nullity, into abstract nothingness, but essentially only into the negation of its particular content; in other words, that such a negation is not all and every negation but the negation of a specific subject matter which resolves itself, and thus is a specific negation, and therefore the result essentially contains that from which it results" (*WL*, I, 36). This is the structure of the process of the progressive dialectical sublation of the particular into the more universal; furthermore, "in this dialectic, as it is taken here, that is in the grasping of opposites in their unity or of the positive in the negative, consists speculative thought" (*WL*, I, 38).

Speculative thinking, unlike representational thinking that holds fast to the opposition of ideas in their ahistorical fixity, is not deceived by the apparent hostility of that idea viewed in terms of its specific difference (in itself) and in terms of its relationality (for itself). Because it is not hampered by the implicit assumption of an empty concept of identity concealed in the principle of noncontradiction, in other words, because it is dialectical, speculative thinking does not shy away from confronting the real question of the difference between the for itself and the in itself. Only because such thinking is willing to undergo the labor and struggle of confronting the idea of difference itself is it able to grasp the final identity of identity *and* difference in its full and dynamic complexity. To deny the truth of dialectic as the necessary structure of thought is to deny the circular struggle of the interplay of the in itself and for itself, and that is tantamount to denying the conceptual basis for understanding the historical life of Spirit itself. Thus, once the meaning of difference is thought radically, it reveals itself as concealing a more original identity. Indeed, all difference, i.e., all nonidentity, even the apparent nonidentity between identity and nonidentity, must be dialectically thought to the hidden point of its identity, the *logos*, which holds them together. Failure to recognize the necessity and truth of this fundamental identity is due simply to what Hegel called "the stubbornness of the logical intellect" (*D*, 26), and this failure results in the incompletion of the task of philosophy, which is "to posit as life the diremption in the Absolute—as the appearance of the Absolute, the finite in the infinite" (*D*, 25). Difference, finiteness, are not abolished but come to be understood as the lifeblood of Spirit's infinity.

From this concept of dialectic as the progressive sublating confrontation of contradictions, it is clear how the Hegelian concept of dialectic[71] is tied to the notion of the Absolute as an identity. So long as nonidentity remains as more fundamental than identity, and so long as the fixed oppositions found by the representing intellect remain in force, the full extent and complexity of that which appears remains hidden. Attentive to the multiple dimensions and dynamics of Being as Spirit, the dialectic does not entail the extinguishing of differences but their sublation, that is, the uncovering of the fundament upon which difference can be intelligible *as* difference at all. For this reason the Hegelian concept of the Absolute does not appear as other to difference or the abolition of it, but as having internalized all difference by being the inner identity of difference. Thus, at the end of the *Logic* Hegel says: "The absolute Idea alone is Being, lasting life, self-knowing truth, and is all truth" (*WL*, II, 484). To admit the truth and priority of the Hegelian concept of dialectic is to commit oneself to the final end of that dialectical process: the identity of the Absolute in the full self-transparency of self-knowledge. Dialectic, as "the regressive grounding of the beginning and the progressive determination of the same" (*WL*, II, 503), is, for Hegel, the demonstration for the necessity of the fundamentality and ineluctability of the Absolute as the real outcome of radical thinking of difference.

VIII

Both Hegel and Heidegger point to, and criticize, the dominance of the traditional concept of identity and of the law of noncontradiction in the history of philosophy. Both argue that representational thought, namely, thinking governed by the formal laws of logic, is incapable of thinking the full meaning of the original difference between thought and its topic. Both agree that the neglect of this original difference is a fundamental oversight and liability that must be overcome. Consequently, the logical concept of identity, which has played such a fundamental role in philosophy, has no positive force in either Hegel or Heidegger: Hegel reconceives the concept of identity as the identity of identity and difference; Heidegger reconfigures the relation of thought and Being by saying that they belong together in an identity by virtue of their difference. Each makes his own efforts to overcome the traditional concept of identity in order to respond to the full complexity of the difference between thought and Being. But the similarities only go so far, for the outcome of the radicalization of the thought and logic of difference is the reaffirmation of the conflict at the center of the proximity of Hegel and Heidegger. For Heidegger that which is to be thought points to the thought of the ontological difference; for Hegel that which is to be thought dialectically justifies the truth of the Absolute.

And so the same question that has followed the confrontation between Hegel and Heidegger reappears with a new focus and intensity: how is one to arbitrate the dispute over the priority of the Absolute or of the ontological difference? (In *Identity and Difference* Heidegger approaches the dispute via the theme of the radicalization of the thought of difference.) But there is another approach to this dispute that is tacitly suggested in the text of *Identity and Difference*, that is, to attend to the way in which *that which has been thought* testifies to that which originally calls for thought: "Only when we turn to what has already been thought do we prepare ourselves for that which is to be thought" (*ID*, 30). Part of Heidegger's argument is that philosophy always has its start in an inadequately recognized attentiveness to the ontological rupture that pertains between thought and Being. Philosophy develops its own special excellence not simply in the thinking of Being—that is also the task of other ways of addressing fundamental concerns, ways of speaking and thinking found in the arts and religion for instance—rather, philosophy wins its integrity among the many modes of thought and speech once it takes its clues from the subtle, yet all important, questions raised by the ontological difference. The history of philosophy, as the record of the pursuit and shaping of such clues, conceals within itself testimony for the ineluctability of the ontological difference. The step back into that history, especially into the beginning of that history before the entanglement of thinking with its own written history reifies prejudices, is the first step in the recovery of thought's true topic. That is why the only thinkers other than Hegel mentioned by Heidegger in the essays in *Identity and Difference*, Plato and Parmenides, are the thinkers at the origins of the history of that which has been thought philosophically. Not surprisingly, Heidegger's final extended work on Hegel is entitled "Hegel and the Greeks". Heidegger's critique of Hegel now takes the form of a critique of Hegel's way of thinking that which has been thought; more precisely, it is as a critique of Hegel's manner of thinking that which has been thought at the origin of the history of thought that Heidegger now seeks to separate himself from Hegel.

6

History, Heraclitus, and the "Not Yet"

The past is not dead; it is not even past. We separate ourselves from it and make ourselves strangers to it.

—Christa Wolf

The philosopher with a radical historical consciousness, that is, the philosopher for whom what is to be thought and what has been thought are finally inseparable, manifests that consciousness in the conviction that the history of philosophy remains alive as a place of unfulfilled expectations. There are several ways of giving an account of this historical consciousness, but perhaps the most basic, and most radical, is expressed by the notion of effective history. While the name and special contemporary sense it carries come from Gadamer, the essential idea behind that name is found first in Hegel, but later in Marx, Nietzsche, Dilthey, and Heidegger;[72] namely, that in both its continuity and discontinuity with the present, the past actively informs the expectations, possibilities, and matrix of the present. In a very real sense, the philosopher possessing a radical historical consciousness must hold that the past is ultimately no more determined and no more finished than either the present or future. Reflection of every sort—whether upon Being, the contemporary constellation of man or Being, or the self-reflection of thought itself—inevitably opens onto its own entanglement in history. The more radical reflection becomes, the more it discloses its own involvement in history. The history of philosophy is an essential element, part of the real stuff and phenomenality, of philosophy's own topic.

Both Hegel and Heidegger have involved themselves in an extended dialogue with the history of philosophy. Hegel's large-scale effort to reappropriate thought's past as prelude to the present is without precedent in that history and matched only by Heidegger's later effort to rethink the essential developments in philosophy's history. To the extent that both are after what could be described as an "essential" history of philosophy, it must be said that both manifest profoundly conservative tendencies. Marginal voices in that history, the disenfranchised and discounted individuals and modes of discourse, seldom count for much—initially at least—in such a reading of history. Foucault's analyses of power and discourse, which are deeply indebted to Heidegger, open avenues into such a reading of philosophy. But, even if neither Hegel nor Heidegger strayed as far as might be necessary from the idea of an "essential" history, both would need to recognize that the "essence" of history is never completely written.

There are, of course, differences in the ways in which each carries out this conversation with other thinkers: one is hard-pressed to find in Hegel the subtle and detailed interpretations of texts and topics that Heidegger developed in his lectures; likewise, Heidegger's global generalizations on the history of metaphysics are no match for the articulate and sophisticated vision of the logic of philosophy's history that Hegel formulated in his lectures. Heidegger wants to find or impose a unity of purpose and character upon the history of metaphysics, while Hegel wants to develop and stand for the best of such a unity. Nevertheless, such differences aside, both make and shape the essential conviction that philosophy cannot begin to carry out its task apart from the confrontation with its own past and the correlative sensitivity to the vitality of that past in the present. It is clear that, since both Hegel and Heidegger make an appeal to a sense of the "destiny" of thought at crucial points in the determination of the task of thought, it is necessary that the way in which each understands the effective dimension of philosophy's history be understood.[73]

The historical origins of philosophy have a special significance for both Hegel and Heidegger. There one finds the basic tenor of the history of thought to come unencumbered by the later involvement of that history with itself. As the history of philosophy becomes a web of texts, it must be acknowledged that "in script, the scream is easily smothered" (*HD*, 20). It is at the origins of philosophy, when the special call to think thought's own relation to Being was first heard, that each finds the clearest evidence for the true topic of thought.

With the one important exception of Nietzsche, Hegel and Heidegger are distinctive by virtue of the extent to which each identifies himself with the early Greek thinkers, and especially with Heraclitus. This appeal to a kindred mind is more than just that. Both turn to Heraclitus not just to find confirmation for their own positions; rather it is in Heraclitus that each finds the essential and effective history of thought most clearly articulated in that history.[74]

This embrace of Heraclitus is, in part, an effort to lay claim to his position in the history of philosophy. More is at stake in the interpretation of Heraclitus than scholarship or even the appropriation of the insights of another thinker. In this massive reappropriation of the history of thought and of individual thinkers in that history, there is one period that has a special significance for both Hegel and Heidegger, namely, the *origin* of the history of thought, for both contend that the notion of the origin offers special and privileged evidence for the truth of what each says. Heidegger is clearly aware of the extended significance that the interpretation of the origin of the history of thought has in the confrontation between Hegel and himself, for on the opening page of "Hegel and the Greeks" he announces that in this issue "the matter of thought is at stake. Matter here means that which of itself demands attention" (*HG*, 421). Furthermore, Heidegger is aware that in this struggle over the issue of thought he does not confront Hegel merely as an opponent, for Hegel's reappropriation of the Greeks is, as is the reappropriation which Heidegger undertakes, distinctive: "Hegel and the Greeks— this sounds like Kant and the Greeks, Leibniz and the Greeks, the medieval Scholastics and the Greeks. It sounds the same, but it is different. For Hegel is the first to think the philosophy of the Greeks as a whole and to think this whole philosophically" (*HG*, 422). Heidegger is well aware that the Hegelian project of completing metaphysics must return to the origin of metaphysics in order to complete the circle of history. He has also become aware of Hegel's sensitivity to the ideas both of origins and of history, and so credits Hegel with the intention of thinking the historical origins of philosophy as a philosophic matter, that is, as a question with a real philosophic substance. That is why he says that "the matter of thought is at stake." But does Heidegger give a new determination of the issue of thought that he claims is at stake here? What does Heidegger find in Heraclitean thought that is found nowhere else, yet which points again to the ontological difference? And how does Heidegger claim to have demonstrated the priority of his thinking through this issue over Hegel's reading of Heraclitus and the origins of philosophy?

I

One of the most peculiar points concerning Heidegger's analysis of the theme of Hegel and the Greeks is that his presentation of it turns immediately to a quite lengthy exposition of the impact and significance of Descartes upon Hegel. As in *Hegel's Concept of Experience*, Hegel is introduced here as a sort of super-Cartesian who represents the most extreme position of subjectivity. In line with this, Heidegger makes a remark that is reminiscent of his early purely critical remarks on the dialectic: "Dialectic is the process of the production of the subjectivity of the absolute subject" (*HG*, 424). But Heidegger admits that Hegel also represents the attempt to overcome the onesidedness of a naive position of subjectivity insofar as Hegelian dialectic is presented as speculative dialectic; that is, insofar as Hegelian dialectic is not a "transcendental, critical, limiting, or polemic way of thought, it is rather the mirroring and unifying of opposites as the process of the production of Spirit itself" (*HG*, 425). This process of speculative dialectic, which is the process of the conceiving of the Absolute, is, according to Heidegger's presentation of it, the method which mirrors (*spiegelt*) "the innermost movement in the course of Spirit, i.e., the absolute subjectivity coming to itself. The departure, progress, transition, and return of this course are all determined in a speculative-dialectical way" (*HG*, 426). In this concept of the dialectic as a method appropriate to speculative subjectivity and conceived as "the soul of Being," Heidegger finds not only a further Cartesian inheritance but also the key by which the theme of Hegel and the Greeks may first be unlocked.

The essential structure of speculative dialectic is its circular return to its beginning. By redeeming the unfulfilled promises of the past, and by exposing its own indebtedness to that past, the speculative dialectic discloses the history of philosophy in its essential wholeness. As a whole, and only as such, is it possible to disclose the essential insights of the different moments in that whole. Therefore, by presenting speculative dialectic in its fullness, "in the system of speculative idealism philosophy is completed, i.e., it achieves its highest and closes itself from there" (HG, 426). Accordingly, Hegel understands himself as the highest affirmation and fulfillment of the original promises of Greek thought. Thus, the character of the relation of Hegel and the Greeks is to be thought as the relation of completion and beginning. In Hegel we find the last and ultimate Greek thinker, and in Hegel the tradition of thought that begins with the Greeks finds and achieves its own unity. The effort to link Hegel and the Greeks is essential to Heidegger's attempt to present the tradition before him as representing a unity of thought and purpose.

In order to explain how Hegel accounts for his own relation to Greek philosophy, Heidegger sketches Hegel's interpretation of what Heidegger claims to be the four basic concepts outlining the essential matrix of Greek philosophy: *Hen, Logos, Idea,* and *Energeia.* The outcome of this explanation is, according to Heidegger, that "Hegel understands *Hen, Logos, Idea, Energeia* in the horizon of Being, which he conceives as the abstract universal. Being [here] ... is *not yet* determined and *not yet* mediated through and in the dialectical movement of absolute subjectivity. The philosophy of the Greeks is the level of this 'not yet' " (HG, 432). In further determining the character of this "not yet" that Hegel finds characteristic of Greek thought, Heidegger contends that it must be understood as meaning "not yet the level of truth," and this is what Heidegger finds as objectionable in Hegel's reading of the Greeks. What makes such a characterization of Greek thought blind to its essence is that it implies a conception of truth that forgets what Heidegger claims is the more original experience of truth, i.e., "as unconcealedness and disclosure" (HG, 433). According to Heidegger, to conceive of Greek thought as "not yet the level of truth" is to conceive of it as "not yet the level of Spirit which is Absolute," and this identification of truth and Spirit leaves unthought the possibility of the presence (*Anwesenheit*) of Spirit and the essential origin (*Wesensherkunft*) of truth. To speak of Greek thought as "not yet" the full disclosure of truth is to subscribe to a conception of truth as progressively disclosed and as the progressive vanquishing of concealment. Such a notion of truth displays several assumptions and prejudices that Heidegger contends betray true character of Hegelian thought: it falls victim to the view that the present is a privileged moment; it is ultimately ahistorical; it fails to do justice to the finite character of truth, and that means that it does not succeed in its claims to have radically thought the original ontological difference between thought and Being. All of these prejudices concealed within the treatment of Greek thought as "not yet" the full disclosure of Spirit point to what Heidegger argues is the real shortcoming of Hegel's approach to the Greeks; namely, that it is never able to account for the genesis of Spirit and for the complexities and costs of Spirit's relation to truth. Herein lies the difficulty with Hegel's understanding of the origin of thought, for against him Heidegger claims that "*aletheia* is the unthought which is most worthy of thought, it is *the* matter of thinking" (*HG*, 438). As opposed to what he considers the Hegelian conception of Greek thought, Heidegger characterizes his own attitude toward Greek philosophy by saying: "If we pay attention to the riddle of *aletheia*, which rules over the beginning of Greek philosophy, then our thinking too finds a 'not yet' here. However, this is the 'not yet' of the unthought, and not a 'not yet' which is inadequate to us but one which *we* do not yet measure up to" (*HG*, 438). The "not yet" found in Greek thought does not refer to a naiveté or youthfulness on the part of the Greek mind. For Heidegger the "not yet" is not discovered from the privileged vantage point of a present fullness of thought not yet present in the past; rather, the "not yet" found in Greek thinking of truth is the essential and unthought dimension of truth itself. The "not yet" is not a deficiency on the part of the Greeks but their true merit. It is our forgetfulness of this insight into the essential structure of truth that should be called deficient. In sum, Heidegger presents Hegel's relation to Greek thought as one that is blind to that which Greek thought has bequeathed to the history of thought as that which is to be thought.

Yet Heidegger's treatment of the theme of *Hegel and the Greeks* is less than persuasive and leaves much to be desired. Certainly the lack of attention to details would not be so easily tolerated in a lesser philosopher, but then Heidegger does not offer *Hegel and the Greeks* as a dialogue with Hegel, he offers it rather as a restatement of the fundamental difference in the direction and attitude of his thought from what he conceives to be Hegel's basic position. It is quite unlikely that Heidegger regards the theme of Hegel and Greek thought in so simple a light as it appears in this text. Indeed, Heidegger indicates that he is aware of the full complexity of this issue when he quotes Hegel as saying that "there is not one sentence of Heraclitus which I have not taken up into my Logic" (*VGP*, I, 320), and since much of the early part of Heidegger's 1943 lecture on Heraclitus is devoted to a discussion of Hegel's interpretation of Heraclitus, it is clear that he recognizes that the debate surrounding the interpretation of Heraclitean thought goes to the core of Heidegger's own debate with Hegel. In fact, given the special importance of Heraclitus for both Hegel and Heidegger, namely, that both claim that in the thought of Heraclitus we find another thinker testifying to the respective truths of the thought of the ontological difference or of the dialectic, it becomes clear why the ways in which Hegel and Heidegger interpret Heraclitus can perhaps make clearer how each claims to have thought the origins of the history of thought most radically and so sharpen the confrontation between them.

II

Heraclitus proved to be a lifelong preoccupation for Heidegger. From as early as *Introduction to Metaphysics* (1935) through the Seminar on Heraclitus (1966), we find frequent and quite extensive meditations on the fragments and thought of Heraclitus. However, Heidegger's attentiveness to Heraclitus was especially intense in the years immediately following the publication of *Hegel's Concept of Experience*. The titles and themes of the essays and lectures of this period further indicate the centrality and significance with which Heidegger regards the interpretation of Greek thought, for three of the notions that are central to Heidegger's own thought take on a special prominence in these texts: the topic of the origin, the problem of the *logos*, and the riddle of *aletheia*. The deep influence that Heraclitus had upon Heidegger's thought is matched only by that influence which Hölderlin's poetic reflections—equally inspired by Heraclitus—had upon the shape of Heidegger's own work.[75]

Heidegger's interpretation of Heraclitus, whom he considers preeminent among Greek thinkers, has as its keynote the name which Heraclitus' contemporaries and successors gave to him: *ho Skoteinos*, the dark one. The darkness of the thinker Heraclitus does not, says Heidegger, "lie in the unclear style of Heraclitus' expressions, but in the 'philosophy' itself because here one thinks in a manner with which common sense is not acquainted" (*VH*, 29). Heidegger makes the reason for this darkness of thinking clearer when he says that "the universe, in Greek *ho kosmos*, is in the essence of its Being the self-concealing and so *essentially* 'dark.' The relation of original thought to that which is to be thought is originally determined from this point" (*VH*, 31). Thus, Heraclitus has earned the name of "the dark one" not because he was intentionally obscure in what he said, but because what he said is devoted to thinking the meaning of the essential obscurity and darkness of that which is to be thought. More precisely: according to Heidegger, one only begins to approach an understanding of the essential thought of Heraclitus insofar as one recognizes that Heraclitus is attempting to think the meaning of the self-concealing, or self-dislocating, essence of that which is to be thought. Thus, of Heraclitus' name Heidegger concludes: "Heraclitus is called 'the dark one.' But he is the light. For he speaks of the lighting insofar as he tried to call forth the shining of light into the language of thinking. Insofar as it illuminates, the lighting endures. We call its illumination the clearing" (*VA*, 250). Saying this, Heidegger identifies the Heraclitean insight into the darkness of truth with Heidegger's own notion of the clearing as the essential call to the thought of Being as finite. To describe Heraclitus as a thinker of the "clearing" and of "finite Being"—words that are not to be found among the fragments left to us—is an interpretation that approaches Heraclitus violently. Nevertheless, Heidegger insists upon this interpretation without reservation. But how does Heidegger's interpretation of Heraclitus find in the thought of "the dark one" testimony for the self-concealing clearing, this finite of appropriation that is to be thought?

For Heidegger the first key to the riddle of the thought of Heraclitus is to be found in what Heraclitus named the *logos*. In order to understand how Heidegger interprets this Heraclitean notion, it is important to recognize that he claims there are two senses in which the word *logos* should be heard and that these senses must be held apart: there is the sense of the word *logos* that has been translated to mean "reason" and there is the true sense of the word *logos*. This first conception of *logos* as reason is, says Heidegger, un-Greek and so a falsification, yet in order to understand in what sense *logos* conceived as reason is a misinterpretation, it is necessary to understand what Heidegger claims is the original meaning of the Heraclitean notion of *logos*.

To truly understand the meaning of the *logos*, it is necessary to hear what the heritage of the word itself says: "We discover what *logos* is from the word '*legein*'" (*VA*, 200). According to Heidegger, this original sense of *logos* as *legein* has been carried over into the German word *lesen*, to pick and gather (as in *Weinlese*). The gathering that is referred to here is, of course, a special kind of gathering. It does not refer to a random and unselective process of collecting; rather, it is a selective and guided gathering that in its selections first lets what is gathered appear as itself. The *logos* is not assembled out of already disclosed elements, nor does it precede the elements it gathers together. It is first in the gathering itself that both the *logos* and that which the *logos* reveals appears; as such the *logos* is the name for the process by which the apparent appears. "*Legein* is to lay. Laying is the letting-lie-before—which is gathered into itself—to that which comes together into presence" (*VA*, 203). The gathering process is neither prior nor subsequent to that which appears "as a result of" this process. Rather, the *logos* understood as this gathering process is the dynamic and ongoing unifying unity that is the intelligibility of any "results." Understood in this way, the *logos* is Heraclitus' name for the Being of the apparent. But the full meaning of the *logos* only comes into view when it is interpreted in the light of that which it aims at gathering, namely, the *physis* of things.

The modern translation of the word *physis* is "nature" from the Latin *natura*; it is a correct translation, but one which nevertheless misses the real scope and complexity of the original Greek sense of the word. For us, the word *nature* generally names a determinate region of beings, i.e., what is natural as opposed to what is a product of culture or of history. It is also used in ways somewhat equivalent to the word *essence*, as for instance when we speak of the "nature of things" (cf. *W*, 237). But in the original Greek sense the word *physis* names all beings and all that found a place in the Greek world. *Physis* is in no sense merely a determinate region of beings opposed to other regions of beings; rather, it is the way in which the Being of all beings disclosed itself to the Greeks. Thus, *physis* encompassed the tree and plant as well as the stone and the stars, human being and its history as well as the gods, and the earth as well as the animals which populate it. It encompasses all of this only insofar as *physis* is understood to name both *that which manifests itself* as well as the *process of manifestation, of emerging from the darkness of concealment to the light of unconcealment*. *Physis* designates the unity of this process of *unfolding* with that which is *unfolded* in such a process; it is the word in Greek thought that speaks of the way all that has a place in the world has come to have its own special place in the region and order of appearances. The result of thinking the horizon of *physis* in this way is that the world of appearances is regarded as a unity of appearances. But this unity of appearances is not a calm or simple and uncomplicated one, for *physis* also designates the struggle, or conflict, both of the multiplicity of appearances competing for places in the world and of the different dimensions of *physis*—as both process and result—both struggling to show themselves. Thus *physis* must be understood as expressing the world of appearances as a primordial ambiguity, a conflictual unity. For the most part, our attentions are arrested and fixed upon what appears in such a way as to conceal the very process that is required for things to manifest themselves whatsoever; in other words, *physis* tends to conceal its full meaning. This, according to Heidegger, is the sense of the saying of Heraclitus, *physis kryptesthai philei*, "*physis* likes to hide." *Physis*, as that disclosed by the *logos*, by virtue of the twofold nature of this disclosure, does not disclose itself except at the price of an element of self-concealment. One might take liberties with the translation of the Greek and translate the saying as "*physis* intrinsically inclines to self-dislocation (or self-concealment)"; in this close relation of *physis* and *kryptesthai* (hiding) Heidegger claims that Heraclitus names the same original ambiguity and duplicity that Heidegger himself speaks of in his analysis of the origin as the circular struggle of concealment and unconcealment.

The Heraclitean notion of *physis*, like Heidegger's conception of the origin, is never static, but always dynamic. The recognition of this dynamism of *physis* is to be found in what Heraclitus spoke of as *eris* (struggle): "The attempt to follow that which the original thinker, Heraclitus, formed as that which is to be thought encounters fire, play, and life, and in each of these the struggle" (*VH*, 26). The centrality and importance of the notion of struggle, and its companion notions of war and tension, in Heraclitus' thought is well known; one finds these words throughout the sayings of Heraclitus, and they appear in two of the most famous sayings, B51 ("They do not comprehend how a thing agrees at variance with itself; it is an attunement turning back on itself, like that of bow and the lyre") and B53 ("War is father of all and king of all; and some he has shown as gods, others men; some he has made slaves, others free"). Yet, despite the long-standing acknowledgment among interpreters of

Heraclitean thought that the notion of struggle lies at the heart of that thought, Heidegger argues that the full meaning of this notion has gone unrecognized. So we must ask what it is that is distinctive about Heidegger's interpretation of this key Heraclitean notion of struggle. This means that we must ask in what sense it is that the notion of struggle testifies to the necessity of the thought of the ontological difference.

In order to understand the Heraclitean notion of struggle, it is necessary to recognize that with this notion Heraclitus names the tension that lies at the heart of the inner ambiguity of *physis* as both the process of coming into unconcealment and that which comes to be present in this process. Struggle, *eris*, names the inner liveliness of *physis* itself, which needs to be thought. As the character of the liveliness of *physis*, "this struggle is not only insurmountable, but it belongs to the essence of the struggle to contradict every surmounting and attempt to surmount it" (*VH*, 26). This struggle must not be considered according to the usual way of representing a struggle as a struggle of opposites, for to do so would be to lend to these opposites a priority over the struggle itself when, according to Heidegger, it is struggle itself that first lets what is come to be itself. The opposites come to be what they are out of, not before, their opposition. But, more importantly, in this notion of struggle we find the inner unity of *physis* and *logos*, for the selective gathering, which the *logos* is, gathers, collects, and releases precisely these opposites in their opposition, and in so doing holds them into this struggle as one. Rather than sublating the struggle and liveliness of *physis*, the *logos* is its locus, and as such is the common element hidden in all that appears. Thus, "the *logos* obviously does not speak randomly and isolatedly. It speaks of everything and says that it is one" (*VH*, 261). The fullness of the *logos* appears in the way it constitutes a unified locus for all appearances and in the way it reveals the essential belonging together of all diversity in this locus. That is why Heidegger says that one of our main routes of access to the true meaning of the *logos* is through attending to the last words of fragment 50, "*hen panta einai*" ("all things are one"). Once one does listen to the inner connection of the *logos* and *hen panta einai* then one recognizes "that the *hen panta (einai)* remains through and through equivocal" (*VH*, 266). In other words, the *logos* is disclosed in its full complexity and as insurmountable in this complexity.

This complexity and struggle of the *logos* is sharpest in the relation between the *hen* (the one) and *panta* (all things). The difficulty is in attempting to expose the way in which the *hen* "ones" (*eint*) and "unites" (*vereint*) all things. Heidegger indicates that there are four possible ways of interpreting the *hen* that stems from the *logos*: "the one of the number one, the one of the self, the one of the unifying unity, the one of uniqueness" (*VH*, 262). But rather than elevate one of these interpretations to the highest rank he says, "Perhaps Heraclitus thinks all of these meanings of the *hen* as he thinks it" (*VH*, 262). In short, each of these senses of the oneness that is the essential character of the *logos* is in fact an aspect of that oneness. The oneness itself is not simple selfsameness but at odds with itself, since uniqueness, unity, selfhood, and singularity need not be identical. Heidegger's analysis of the interrelation of the *logos* and the *hen panta einai* does not address this issue; it only makes clear that in it oppositions are, in some still vague sense, held into a unity.

Saying that the *logos* is a way of speaking and thinking of opposites as one sounds more like a testimony for dialectical thinking than for the ontological difference. Hegel works out the logic of such an opposition as the path to the Absolute, yet Heidegger contends that in the case of Heraclitus we find a thinker of such opposition who has recognized both the inextinguishability of this struggle of opposites as well as the incommensurability that this signals. Heidegger warns that we must not hastily decide that the *eris* that the *logos* mirrors in the *hen panta einai* is dialectical and that this dialectic leads to a sublation of the tension referred to in saying that "all things are one." He does not explicitly defend and justify his contention that the struggle of opposites, the struggle of the *hen* and *panta*, must not be conceived as the dialectic of opposites; however, we might find a clue to Heidegger's reasons for saying this in what we have already called the keynote of Heidegger's interpretation of Heraclitus, namely, the "darkness" of Heraclitus. According to Heidegger it is this dark obscurity of the thought of Heraclitus and of that which Heraclitus thinks that most forcefully testifies to the radicality and originality of that to which Heraclitus points. For Heidegger, to conceive of the inner struggle of the *hen* and *panta* as a dialectical struggle is to overlook the essential originality of Heraclitus, an originality that hides itself in what Heraclitus said: "The truth is the unsaid which only remains what it is according to that which is said" (*VH*, 180).

Thus, the reason that the name "the dark one" is appropriate for Heraclitus is not because Heraclitus was deliberately obscure in what he said, or because he lacked an appropriate conceptual language, but because Heraclitus is the thinker of the necessary hiddenness that belongs to the inner struggle of the *hen* and *panta* and the depths of the *logos*. This unspoken dimension, which can only be pointed toward by what is said, is not simply omitted by Heraclitus; it is rather ultimately unspeakable, since it is that which "likes to hide." The darkness of Heraclitean thought is the most pointed way in which the essential darkness and mystery of the *logos* is brought into view. From Heraclitus we learn that this struggle of opposites cannot be extinguished for reasons that cannot be explained, but toward which we cannot remain indifferent. That is why Heraclitus focuses his attentions upon paradoxes, riddles, and moments of transition. The key fragments in this regard are those, which like fragment 26 ("A man kindles a light for himself in the night when his sight is extinguished. Living he touches the dead in his sleep; waking, he touches the sleeper.") speak of the transition from sleeping to wakefulness, where a sudden and striking change is witnessed yet no clearly explainable transition is found. There are gaps, transitions, ruptures, and transpositions in *physis* that are sudden and, while to be taken into the *logos* of *physis* and increasing its *eris*, are nevertheless mysterious. In the end no central point, or source of life, can be found: "You will not find out the limits of the soul by going, even if you travel over every way, so deep is its *logos*" (frag. 45). In short, according to Heidegger, the proper interpretation of the sayings of Heraclitus reveals his central thought, the thought of the *logos*, to be further testimony for the inner difference which calls thought, but which itself "likes to hide."

III

Whereas Heidegger's interpretation of Heraclitus presents a view of Heraclitus as quite archaic, dark, and radically original, Hegel's interpretation of Heraclitus offers a very different view of Heraclitus. The opening announcement of Hegel's interpretation of Heraclitus makes this quite clear: "With Heraclitus the speculative form of the philosophical idea first appears: in the reasoning of Parmenides and Zeno the abstract logical intellect is at work; Heraclitus was regarded everywhere as a deep-thinking philosopher.... Here we see land; there is not one sentence of Heraclitus which I have not taken up in my Logic" (*VGP*, 320). Once again, as in Hegel's presentation of Descartes, we find the metaphor of land. In other words, Hegel locates Heraclitus alongside Descartes as one of the turning points in the history of Spirit coming into the full possession of itself. Furthermore, this metaphor of land implies that we find in the thought of Heraclitus a foreshadowing of the thought of the Absolute as fundamentum, and this is because in Heraclitus "dialectic [is] itself [conceived] as principle" (*VGP*, 320). Yet we find the Absolute here spoken of only dimly and conceptually undeveloped, and this is the reason for Heraclitus being called "the dark one."

As in Heidegger's interpretation of Heraclitus, Hegel's interpretation too places an emphasis on this nickname of Heraclitus. But, unlike Heidegger's understanding of its significance as pointing to the depth of Heraclitean thought, Hegel insists that the significance of this name "is basically a consequence of careless word order and of uneducated language [found in Heraclitus].... The darkness of Heraclitus comes from the deficiency of his grammar" (*VGP*, 322). Despite lacking the appropriate language and grammar, despite his appearance at an early and ultimately uncultivated stage in the history of Spirit, Hegel sees in Heraclitus the first to witness the thought of the Absolute, and so it must also be said that "the darkness of this philosopher primarily lies in the deepness of the speculative thought which is expressed in it" (*VGP*, 323). For Hegel, Heraclitus represents the first fulfillment of thought and the beginning of philosophy, because Heraclitus is the first to recognize and express the universal logical principle, namely, that "essence is change" (*VGP*, 323). To have recognized the universality of change, and so to have moved beyond the representational stage of thought that deals with static and unintegrated oppositions, is the merit of Heraclitus in the history of thought. In this universal principle of change, in the thinking confrontation with the demands of such a principle, Heraclitus is the first to have a sense of the higher unity of opposites disclosed by speculative thought.

Hegel cites the Heraclitean saying of *panta rhei* (all things flow) as evidence that for Heraclitus "truth is becoming, not Being" (*VGP*, 324), and this is interpreted by Hegel to mean that Heraclitus has speculatively elevated the ecstatic principle of becoming over any static conception of Being. The true significance of this for Hegel is that, by recognizing the truth of becoming, Heraclitus is the first to point to the original and fundamental identity of Being and Nothing, from which it can be understood that "'truth' is and is not" (*VGP*, 324). For Hegel this identity of Being and Nothing is the ultimate expression of the unification of opposites, in it "the completely opposed determinations are bound into one" (*VGP*, 324). This, according to Hegel, is the most difficult speculative step for thought to make, and to have introduced this into the history of thought is the greatness of Heraclitus, for it is by means of this restless identity of Being and Nothing that he opens up "the principle of life" (*VGP*, 325). To be able to speak on the basis of this principle, to grasp the fullness and multiplicity of life, Heraclitus first had to break through the inadequacies of a way of thinking that holds fast to the principle of noncontradiction. That Heraclitus does this is clear from the number of fragments speaking of opposites in the same breath: "Immortals are mortal, mortals immortal, living the others' death, dead in the others' life" (frag. 62). From the standpoint of commonsense intelligence such a passage simply makes no sense. The logical intellect represents ideas and things in isolation and opposition to other such individuated ideas and things. Such categorizing thought is incapable of grasping the true unity of what it can only perceive in isolation, consequently it is never able to reach the real life of its topic since the true principle of life is not bound by the static law of noncontradiction. To have grasped this principle of life is to have understood how all things are in flux and that "truth is becoming." This insight requires a speculative leap beyond the level of representation, and that entails the recognition of the fundamental identity of opposites. It is as having first recognized and expressed the principle of becoming and the identity of Being and Nothing that Heraclitus is said to be the first to have understood the true sense of speculative reason.

This, for Hegel, is the true significance and lasting contribution of the thought of Heraclitus: to have pointed to the inner unity that runs through apparent opposites. "In Heraclitus we see the infinite as such or its concept, its essence, expressed: the infinite, in and for itself... is the unity of opposites, and indeed of the universal opposites ... of Being and Nothing" (*VGP*, 325). The infinite referred to here is not an infinite above or beyond the finitude of opposition; it is rather the infinity disclosed by the unity of oppositions. The *logos*, which Hegel translates and interprets as reason, is not other than what it discloses. It is not reached by stepping away from the full force of contradiction and opposition, but by speculatively grasping the essential, ineradicable truth of contradiction itself. In making this step Heraclitus recognizes the inner restlessness and irrepressible liveliness of that which is to be thought, and so "in Heraclitus the moment of negativity is immanent" (*VGP*, I, 326). For Hegel, the name of Heraclitus is to be associated with the idea of negativity on two counts: as representing a break with the prehistory of speculative thought, his place in history is to be regarded as the first significant historical negation, and this is so because Heraclitus has an insight into the essential negativity at the heart of all Being. To understand this inner negativity of that which is to be thought, and so to recognize the inner infinite identity of Being and Nothing is, according to Hegel, to recognize the necessity of dialectic. Thus it comes as no surprise to discover that Hegel interprets the famous Heraclitean sayings that speak of the struggle of opposites as speaking of the dialectic of contradiction. As an example of this Hegel quotes fragment 50: ". . . that which differs with itself is in agreement: harmony consists of opposing tension, like that of the bow and the lyre." Here the word *harmonia* names the way in which Heraclitus thinks the unity of these conflicting opposites, and in unpacking the meaning of this notion Hegel mentions the common understanding of it offered by Eryximachos in the *Symposium*, that is, the view that harmony is not conflictual, for "there can be no harmony . . . [of what] is still in conflict, since harmony is concord . . ." (187b). In opposition to Eryximachos Hegel says: "The simple repetition of a one is not a harmony. Differentiation belongs to harmony; it must be essentially a differentiation" (*VGP*, I, 327). Certainly such a description of the notion of harmony as being the unity of difference would be equally fitting as a description of the Hegelian concept of the Absolute as a conflictual unity, and in this parallel Hegel identifies the essential trademarks of the key Heraclitean notions with those of his own highest thought. Furthermore, like the concept of the Absolute, the Heraclitean principle of the inner harmony of opposites is unable to be grasped by the logical understanding such as that expressed by Eryximachos, which holds opposites as isolated, and so the Heraclitean sense of harmony appears dark and obscure to such a way of thinking. From the standpoint of the logical intellect, the deepest insights of speculative thought look like a "night in which all cows are black" (*PG*, 19) and as such always dark for the understanding. This is the reason Heraclitus' contemporaries saw fit to call him the "dark one."

Hegel furthers his presentation of Heraclitean thought by saying that "in his presentation, Heraclitus does not stick with these expressions in concepts ... rather, from this universal form in which Heraclitus introduces his principle he gives his idea a more real expression" (*VGP*, I, 328). Unlike his predecessors, Heraclitus did not locate the real essence of what is in some particular existing being such as water or air; rather, in recognizing becoming as the true logical principle, Heraclitus recognizes that what this principle describes, that is, the real, cannot be accounted for by a particular, determinate notion, but that *process* itself must be the character of the real. Heraclitus is thus the first to answer to the full demands of the universality of the Absolute insofar as he recognizes that the true universal cannot have a particular place of privileged appearance, but must be the universal element of any and every appearance. Such an element is not another appearance but is found only in the process of appearing itself, and this process is best described in the language of change. This is why Hegel says that for Heraclitus "time is the first bodily essence ... time is the abstract intuition of process ... time is pure becoming" (*VGP*, I, 329). Heraclitus is thus the first to see the way in which Being has an essential relation to time. The discussion of the nature of time in Heraclitus resembles quite closely Hegel's own treatment of time found in the *Phenomenology of Spirit*; indeed, some of the passages of Hegel's presentation of the Heraclitean notion of time and of Hegel's own concept of time are worded identically.

There is, however, one significant difference between Hegel's own analysis of this abstract process of time and Heraclitus' presentation of it, and that is that Heraclitus symbolically represents it as the process of fire. Thus, according to Hegel's analysis of Heraclitus, "fire is physical time; it is absolute restlessness" (*VGP*, I, 330). Hegel finds that the need to represent this abstract process of time as fire is merely further evidence that, although Heraclitus is the first to recognize the logical principle of the Absolute, he nevertheless does so in an immediate, representational manner. Heraclitus is the first to recognize the universality and essential negativity of becoming, but he is bound by his place in history: because Spirit has not yet alienated itself into an abstract form of universality, his expression of Spirit is a concrete one, but not a concrete universal. Thus, Heraclitus recognizes the Absolute, but as he recognizes it, the Absolute is "not yet" fully Absolute, that is, as not yet a mediated immediacy. Nevertheless, at this historical juncture Hegel finds fire to be the most appropriate manner of representing this process which is the logical principle of the Absolute, for "as this metamorphozing of bodily things, fire is change, the transformation of determinations ... it is the abstract moment in process" (*VGP*, I, 331), and this, says Hegel, is the very life of nature.

Indeed we find in this phrase "the life of nature" the core of Hegel's deep identification with Heraclitean thought, for Hegel finds Heraclitus to be the first philosopher to recognize that *life* itself needs to be thought as a unity, which does not extinguish the multiplicity and inner ambiguity of that unity. To have been the first to have thought the conflictual unity that characterizes that which thought is to think, the Absolute, is, according to Hegel, the special merit and excellence of Heraclitus. To have persistently thought the restlessness of *physis* is the source of the depth of the thought of Heraclitus, for "nature is that which never rests and the universe of transition of one into another, from diremption into unity, from unity into diremption" (*VGP*, I, 332). Furthermore, Heraclitus does not merely point to this inner, restless life of nature, the principle of becoming, but he points to it as a circular process. When Heraclitus speaks of the restlessness of life as a whole, he introduces the image of a circular process: "Being brought apart it is brought together with itself; there is a back-stretched connection, as in the bow and the lyre" (frag. 51). This means that Heraclitus does not merely introduce the principle of becoming as a logical principle, but that he recognizes the essential oneness and unity that is the life of this process of nature; in other words, Heraclitus thinks becoming equally as a return: "All things are an equal exchange for fire and fire for all things, as goods are for gold and gold for goods" (frag. 90). According to Hegel, this insight into circular wholeness of the process of all things is the truly speculative thought of nature.

Clearly it is the presence in Heraclitus of what Hegel calls the principle of speculation, of the identity of identity and nonidentity, that quite early in his career attracted him to Heraclitus. It is well known that along with Hölderlin and Schelling, his fellow students at the Tübinger Stift, the young Hegel took the phrase *hen kai pan* ("the one and all") as his motto for thinking.[76] It is in this phrase that Hegel first recognized the principles of speculation that were to motivate his battle against what he saw as the positivity of contemporary philosophy. But the further significance of this motto is as a document of the very deep influence of Greek thought upon the development of Hegel's own thought. For Hegel, the Greek world represented an ideal, one that allowed man to achieve a harmonious relationship to Spirit as a whole. In Greek thought Hegel finds the youthful genius of mankind, and in this idealized world of the Greeks there was no duality; joy and beauty walked hand in hand and truth was a living source of justice. In short, the Greeks were at home in their world. At the center of the Greek world as Hegel understood it lay the thought of Heraclitus, a point which Heidegger is quick to note: "Hegelian thought is inspired by a new creative reappropriation of the original thought of Heraclitus" (*HH*, 133). And when Hegel says of Heraclitus that "the beginning of the existence of philosophy dates from him; he is the lasting idea which continues until today in all philosophers" (*VGP*, I, 336–7), we can perhaps recognize the extent of his own indebtedness to the thought of Heraclitus. This proximity with Heraclitus is what motivates Hegel's assessment of Heraclitean thought as "idealism in its naiveté" (*VGP*, I, 340).

We see then that in his interpretation of Heraclitus Hegel not only finds another thinker concerned with the same themes and with similar results, but that he finds in Heraclitus a sort of youthful, naive mirror of Hegelian thought. Thus, for Hegel, the key Heraclitean thought of the *logos* is best understood in the light of what Hegel describes as speculative reason, since in naming the process of becoming as the principle of the *logos*, "Heraclitus conceives the Absolute itself as this process, as dialectic itself" (*VGP*, I, 319). Heraclitus is the first to have understood the task and needs of speculative thought as it identifies, and identifies with, the real life of nature. In short: Heraclitus is the first philosopher because he is the first to demonstrate a sense both of the dialectical path and of the Absolute as the true insight opened up by that path. According to Hegel's interpretation of early Greek thought, it is Heraclitus, not Zeno, who is the discoverer of the inner logic of dialectical thought and so is the first to step upon the land, the ground of Being, that philosophy is to explore.

Claiming Heraclitus as his own philosophical ancestor is of special significance for Hegel and the fulfillment of his own self-imposed task of completing the Greek project of thinking the *logos* of *physis*. He has accorded Heraclitus a privileged place in the history of thought as its originator, and consequently if Hegel is to satisfy the demand of bringing history knowingly back to the promises of its origin, if he is to complete the circle of the history of Spirit bringing it full-swing to its own concealed truth, then he must establish an essential link between Heraclitus and himself. In this sense Heidegger puts his finger on the heart of the relation between Hegel and the Greeks when he says that it is the relation of completion and beginning. Hegel is the last Greek thinker insofar as he is the first thinker with a historical consciousness to embrace Greek thought as a living issue central to the contemporary philosophical project, and this by virtue of its place in the history of thought.

IV

Both Hegel and Heidegger have a special self-imposed need to draw the lines of kinship from themselves to Heraclitus who sits at the origins of the philosophic tradition. Both find something decisive at work in Greek thought, something that largely remains hidden from the subsequent philosophic tradition, and for both the project of overcoming that tradition involves the recovery and reappropriation of that hidden destiny of thought: for Hegel such recovery entails the fulfillment of the promises of the origin, while for Heidegger it discloses the essential darkness that can be neither dismissed nor brought into the light. Given what each has said about the circularity of history and the fatedness of thought from its outset, neither can get around the question of precisely how we are to understand the origins of the history of thought. What is at stake in these competing and incompatible interpretations of Heraclitus is the question of the logic of history, a logic that is most transparent at its inception.[77]

Both Hegel and Heidegger agree that the Greek world and its discoveries represent a decisive new beginning for thinking. Culminating in the Platonic formulation of the *idea*, Greek thought reached far ahead of its own time, shaping the history of thought to come. Furthermore, both look upon the twists and turns of thought after the Greek world as in large measure only a set of variations—to different degrees of seriousness and scope—upon the conceptual frame, the blueprint for which was outlined in Greek thought and language. While Hegel sees in this history a certain forward-moving progression and evolutionary logic that leads to Hegel himself, Heidegger has a reading of that history as the place of dead ends and discontinuities as well as of continuity and evolution. There are quite important differences in their respective characterizations and interpretations of the history, yet there is a significant sense in which their respective assessments of their own places in that history resemble each other: both find that history has reached a fullness and limit in their own time, and that consequently history is ripe for a contribution, the originality of which is only matched by the contributions of the Greek world. Both regard history as a long prelude, but the coda in each case is different, one the keynote of which is determined at the origins of history.

In the end, the generally oppositional interpretations of Heraclitus put forth by Hegel and Heidegger offer perhaps the clearest display of the respective prejudices and guiding temperaments at work in Hegel and Heidegger. Both interpretations clearly rest upon a large measure of bending and chopping to fit Heraclitus into the special historical place that each must recover if he is to legitimate his own claim to recapture the essence of that place. The peculiar character of this historical place in which both find Heraclitus is that in a significant respect it is without antecedents. Something unprecedented is found in Heraclitus, and it is in this radicality that both Hegel and Heidegger find a foreshadowing of their own insights. For both Heraclitus speaks of and represents the "not-yetness" of history, but while Hegel finds this not-yet finally fulfilled, Heidegger points to the darkness and cryptic quality of that about which Heraclitus speaks as evidence for the inextinguishability of this not-yetness. For Heidegger all original thought is marked by this incommensurability and untimeliness with respect to its place, context, and topic alike, and this shows itself in the insurmountability of concealment as the price of disclosure. Hegel is not oblivious to the complexity of disclosure as Heraclitus thinks it. He is fully aware of the reciprocity of the processes of disclosure and concealment, but finds that the precise nature of this reciprocity is one of negation and that this sets disclosure on the dialectical path towards its own essential release from its early enthrallment to concealment. Standing at the inauguration of this process, Heraclitus represents truth that has not-yet passed through the preliminary stages of this process. For Hegel, the greatness to be found in Heraclitean thought is as this youthful appearance of the natural idealism of Spirit.

What becomes clear in this struggle to embrace Heraclitus is that it says more about the senses of history that Hegel and Heidegger each subscribe to than it does about the special case of Heraclitus himself. Hegel finds in thought's relation to history a certain progress. Not, to be sure, a linear progress without conflict and confusion, without its prices, but a progress—one achieved by the conflicts that thought must confront—nonetheless. Heidegger, on the other hand, works according to a historical sense that does not have room for any fundamental progress. For Heidegger thought's relation to history always exhibits an open-endedness, it is always en route, but the conflicts run so deep that they are an essential element of the history of thought. As such, Heidegger finds that on the elemental questions, on the questions that touch upon the essential concerns of thought and history, there is no progress; rather, forgetfulness and concealment are just as much a part of this process as are memory and disclosure. The one enduring element of history is precisely this unavoidable and so essential "forgetfulness of Being"—this ontological difference that "likes to hide." The most elemental truth of what endures is thus the finiteness of the enduring, that it is only for a "while."

The respective appeals that Hegel and Heidegger make to Heraclitus, the invocation of the origin of philosophy as a way of accounting for the special character of its end, do share one important feature: both are efforts to demonstrate that the roots of philosophy's history—a history that by virtue of thought's relation to time is itself part of the very stuff of philosophy's topic—run deeper than the customary view that points first to Plato as the start of the tradition; properly understood, the roots of philosophy's history run to the archaic point expressed in the obscure fragments of Heraclitus. Both find a line and a unity that lasts as the defining and yet largely unthought element that constitutes philosophy as a tradition. Hegel and Heidegger share the view that the Heraclitean fragments speak of something unsurpassed and unsurpassable: for Heidegger it is the darkness and finitude of all thinking of Being, for Hegel it is the dialectic as the infinite logic of the real itself. Both Hegel and

Heidegger call Heraclitus as a witness for what each contends is the most radical and original thought. Yet, whereas Heidegger's analysis of the Heraclitean notion of the *logos* presents it as simultaneously more original and obscure than the latter-day interpretations of *logos* as reason, Hegel's analysis presents reason as the original sense of the *logos*. Whereas Heidegger finds Heraclitus' obscurity to be testimony of the originality of his thought and to the historical riddle that this thought represents, Hegel finds this obscurity of Heraclitus to be a consequence of Heraclitus' lack of the proper conceptual language of reason. Whereas Hegel finds in Heraclitus the first true representative of dialectical thought, Heidegger finds the thought of Heraclitus to represent the original inner ambiguity of the origins of thought. In short: for Heidegger, Heraclitus bears witness to the ambiguity and tension of the origins of thought, which prevent thought from ever being in the position of thinking itself absolutely; for Hegel, Heraclitus offers the first sight of land, of the fundament, upon which thought first may come to think itself absolutely. It must be said that little is demonstrated or proven in Heidegger's effort to wrestle Heraclitus away from Hegel, but much is illuminated nonetheless. In their respective interpretations of Heraclitus, both express in an unusually direct form their own self-understandings and prejudices. Most importantly, in the recovery of the origin each reveals the sense in which philosophy can be said to form a tradition that has a unity and that has found an "end": for Hegel, the end is the completion of what was previously only "not yet"; for Heidegger, the end is the release from the presumption of such a possible completion.

In the years following the publication of the essay "Hegel and the Greeks," Heidegger continued his long effort to reclaim the finite from Hegel's dialectical account of it, but the critique of these later years introduces no new themes, nor does it lead to any significant sharpening of the confrontation between them. By the time of this essay the matrix of issues over which Hegel and Heidegger have their special accord and discord has been outlined, the proximities and distances—often at the same place—have become entrenched. Though in the course of his career Heidegger developed an admiration for Hegel largely absent in his early work, the general tendency is always to regard Hegel as oblivious to the essential finitude of both thought and its topic. But the persistence of this refusal to find in Hegel real, and so challenging, elements of Heidegger's own insights into the finite should not simply be regarded as a peculiar blindness to Hegel even if it is true that Heidegger only rarely reads Hegel with the same charity and sympathy he reserves for Heraclitus, Aristotle, Eckhart, Kant, or Nietzsche; rather, this refusal should be seen as an aspect and expression of Heidegger's own frustrations. Throughout his career Heidegger sought the language and evidence that could withstand any species of metaphysical schematization. Yet throughout these efforts he repeatedly encountered Hegel making an appeal to similar, and often even the same, phenomena in his effort to demonstrate the necessity of the Absolute for thought. It is this seemingly inextricable entanglement with Hegelian thought that motivates many of the most dramatic deepenings of Heidegger's own reflections on the finite. It is equally this entanglement that bears witness to the ultimate difficulties, perhaps insurmountable, of such a task: the finite seems to invite its own overcoming in a way that leaves the finite behind, and this invitation to its other might lurk as a concealed tendency of all reflections on the finite. The question with which we are left by Heidegger's encounter with Hegel is whether or not Heidegger has gone far enough toward releasing thought from such seductions.

Conclusion
Afterthoughts

The victors—for the present—are we, the discontinuous.
—*Italo Calvino*

The temptation to ask for a victor in the confrontation between Hegel and Heidegger is a misguided one, for such a question presupposes that what is at stake is a matter of conflicting "positions." It further assumes that the topics at issue in that confrontation admit of one resolution. But it is doubtful that either Hegel or Heidegger ever conceived of what he was doing as the staking out of a position; and it is doubtful that many—if indeed any—of the true topics of thought in any day permit their own resolution in a single exclusionary way. The urge to stack Hegel up "against" Heidegger is one that arises out of the philosophically inappropriate urge to categorize views as either "right" or "wrong." This urge motivated Heidegger's first sustained encounter with Hegel in *Being and Time* and was only slowly and partially abandoned during the course of Heidegger's career. One of the discoveries that emerges from looking at Heidegger's critique of Hegel is that until we are released from that urge the task of a philosophizing that is nourished on a real historical sense cannot be answered. Until we abandon the view that essential truths can be spoken of only from the present, in terms of being "correct," "right," or "wrong," the more important dimensions of truth—the interesting and disclosive—will not be open to us. Fortunately, literature has never quite fallen victim to this urge: no one decides to read Conrad because he is "right" and to neglect Shakespeare because of his "incorrect positions." The repeated crossing of Hegelian and Heideggerian paths does not indicate any error on either part, nor does it indicate that Heidegger has not adequately advanced beyond Hegel, since in essential matters talk of advances and progress are out of place. Following Heidegger's critique of Hegel—at times the searching appraisal of a dialogue partner, at times simply a means of contrasting himself with a representative of metaphysics—outlines a set of still unsettled concerns and phenomena that sit at the center of contemporary thought that defines itself out of the proximity that emerges between Hegel and Heidegger. Gadamer and Derrida, and to a lesser extent Adorno and Marcuse, must be recognized as working out of this "between" and the questions it bequeaths. The dialogue between Hegel and Heidegger does not end with them.

In that dialogue it is the question of tradition—its hidden and unthought potential—and the task of recovering the finite that function as the conducting wires of what is thought and said. The calls of "tradition" and "finitude" are inseparable, yet it is quite clear that it is the task of rehabilitating and rethinking the finite that has served as the special focal point of the dialogue between Hegel and Heidegger. Both claim to bring "the tradition" to its "end," thereby defining the historical present, by virtue of recapturing and liberating the finite from its alienated or forgotten role in metaphysics. In doing this, in drawing the lines of a tradition that lead to today, Hegel and Heidegger have made a deep, yet conflicted, mark upon the topics and terms of contemporary philosophy. The depth of their influence upon today seems obvious; the conflict concealed in that influence arises from their own uneasy proximity.

There is certainly far more at stake today even within the narrow purview of philosophizing out of the continental tradition than could conceivably emerge out of the confrontation between Hegel and Heidegger. They are influential and so their confrontation touches upon much that they have shaped but not directly noted. At best their confrontation is emblematic of pivotal issues of the present and perhaps what will follow. It might be fair to say that the most enduring contribution of both is to be found in the ways that they have shifted our perception of what is important and what qualifies as interesting. Both have contributed views on such matters as work, time, desire, language, technology, history, and art, but their "own" views will likely not have the same staying power as their successes at renegotiating the terms and topics worthy of attention. The dialectic and the ontological difference clearly define themselves as responses to the finite. Both Hegel and Heidegger make an effort to define their own responses as somehow "dictated" or "fated" by the nature of the finite and its tradition. Heidegger defends his effort, in part at least, in terms of his own perceived contrast with Hegel and in terms of what he tries to demonstrate as Hegel's failure to decisively capture the finite in the dialectic of Spirit. To the extent that Heidegger claims to speak "decisively" about the finite—a tendency of his early years in particular—he falls victim to the same seductions of the finite away from itself that he criticizes in Hegel and in the metaphysical tradition within which he reads Hegel. The lesson of Heidegger's Hegel-critique is that evidence of the finitude of Being is neither singular nor "primordial" in an absolute sense but that it evolves and opens itself to interpretations that lead in more than one direction. History and the evolution of tradition exhibit this in the surprises of their ineradicable "not-yetness" and conflict. Consequently, the most important questions that arise out of the confrontation between Hegel and Heidegger are directed at the point from which they both influence and reflect the larger and still emerging questions of philosophizing in the historical present. Their proximity points toward the first and foremost questions of our present as, in part at least, the place of their legacy.[78]

Thus, one ought to ask about the long-standing topic of their confrontation and contributions: why the finite? Why has contemporary continental philosophy recently attached itself so single-mindedly to the recovery of the finite from what is said to be its long metaphysical abandon? What point are we trying to make when we reconstitute and reread the history of philosophy as a tradition while simultaneously looking everywhere for evidence of the essential finitude of thought? Why has philosophy recently come to focus upon its own special entanglement in such finitude so that it can no longer seem to ignore the question—framed by Hegel and Heidegger—of its own overcoming and end? Philosophy has always faced a crisis in the question of its own legitimation; the question of its end(s) and the task of fulfilling them has accompanied it as its shadow and hope. But since Hegel the question of the "end of philosophy" has moved from the margins to the center of philosophic discussions. Our era seems to define and understand itself in terms of a fundamental difference from the past: we tend to characterize our own age more in terms of a "no longer" than a "not yet"—the ends of the past are largely regarded as "no longer" tenable, not "not yet" fulfilled. But of course every age manifests aspects of this syndrome of a "new beginning," we are certainly not the first to define ourselves in this way; we are not the first to speak out of some sense of the apocalypse of speaking and thinking as it has been. Nor will we likely be the last: every age manifests a peculiar species of myopic narcissism that looks ahead of itself and sees only its own promises as prospects. The present age always exerts a peculiar force upon the past and claims a special privilege in the future. We tend to read the past as the place where traditions are formed only to lead to our present, likewise we read the future as moving in a straight line from there. Even though every age has faced the future anxiously, we tend to look at the record of thinking that lies in our own past as a past that never really possessed any other future than us. Nevertheless, since Nietzsche the effort to either repudiate or undermine perceived traditions leading to the present philosophical moment—even by reappropriating those very traditions—has been marked by a relentlessness that often seems matched earlier only by [Descartes, whose attempt to overcome the past took the form of a blanket and ahistorical denial rather than confrontation.]Recent efforts—including those by both Hegel and Heidegger—to rejuvenate and release the past from its own repressive presumption by drawing the past into a relatively stable and essential tradition are conflicted efforts. The twin tasks of freeing history and of constituting a tradition are perhaps necessary for the self-understanding of every present, but they are incompatible. The rigor and effort that we apply to reappropriate pasts and futures past for our present must be matched by the energy to let that present—however it gets defined—preserve in itself the openness requisite for its appropriation to futures not yet its own. Defining the present is as much a matter of the future as the past, but both Hegel and Heidegger tend to forget that. Nevertheless, like most thoughtful confrontations with what appears no longer tenable, both confront and thereby unravel the past in the name of some future that will no longer be like that promised by the past; both reawaken some dormant riddles broached but unanswered in that past. Most—but of course not all—of these riddles come under the heading of the finite: that which, for reasons or not, represents a special challenge to our efforts to speak and think about what is of special concern to us as human beings—about what is right, real, important, and

shared. Since philosophizing is among the most elemental and enduring human experiences and concerns, the effort to address its special
finitude is not an arbitrary topic. When Hegel and Heidegger speak
of the end of philosophy, they are each, in different ways, addressing
this question of how and why philosophy can be said to arrive at a
point from which we must describe the experience and resulting
decisions of philosophizing in a way only dimly anticipated hitherto.
In the wake of both, and that means that Heidegger must be read as
coming in Hegel's wake, we find the widespread conviction that
philosophy must prepare itself for a fundamental change, that its
present juncture is at an end. Philosophy is not only directed toward
the finite, it is itself a finite expression of the finite.

The basic tenor of many of the contemporary discussions about the
end of philosophy is often that the truly elemental experiences and
phenomena have been overlooked, or misinterpreted, in the past.
Sometimes it is said that the very idea of the "elemental" is misleading
and so must be abandoned, but both Hegel and Heidegger speak
against such a view, trying instead to redefine and refine our understanding of what elementality means and what needs it speaks of. For
both, the end of philosophy does not entail its easy abandon but a
basic reappraisal of its place, purpose, and possibilities. In this sense,
the end of philosophy represents a rejuvenation of thought's original
talents. Wittgenstein, who belongs to these discussions in an important respect, even turned a similar sentiment against himself when,
in the *Investigations*, he remarks that "the axis of our examination must
be rotated, but about the fixed point of our real need." [79] Nietzsche,
expressing a kindred sensibility, characterizes the true originality of
any thinker or epoch by saying that "It is not being the first to see
something new that indicates a genuinely original mind, but seeing
the old, the familiar, the commonplace *as if it were* new." [80] From this
point of view, the real task of thought is not the repudiation, but
liberation, of the past from the present and the present to its future.

Heidegger is especially aggressive in this respect, and it must be
acknowledged that he more than Hegel made the careful retrieval of
the past something not to be avoided. Nevertheless, there are texts
in which Heidegger seems content to point to ways in which his
predecessors neglected dimensions of such experiences as anxiety,
language, and history, and to reinterpret phenomena such as the
work of art, nature, and technology in order to separate himself from

what he sees as the liabilities of metaphysics. Frequently—especially with the case of Hegel—Heidegger seems to believe that merely pointing to the absence of a thoughtful consideration of those experiences in metaphysical thinkers adequately legitimates his own claim to have shaken the habits of metaphysics. But does merely pointing to such experiences and the absence of metaphysical reflections upon them suffice to undermine the empire of metaphysical reflection? Do such experiences, of themselves, speak on behalf of the claim that such reflections are untenable? The confrontation with Hegel on the finite, looked at more closely than Heidegger seems to find necessary, indicates that what Heidegger has done may not suffice his task. It also indicates that the challenge that metaphysics poses and the possibilities it offers ought not be dismissed hastily. Gadamer, who works in the wake of Heidegger but is unwilling to dismiss what Hegel teaches, makes this caution when he says that "Heidegger, like many of my critics, would probably feel the lack of an ultimate radicality in the drawing of conclusions. . . . [But] may one [not] look at the last fading light of the sun that is set in the evening sky, instead of turning around to look for the first shimmer of its return?"[81] In part, such a sensibility —one that is a curious mix of radicality and conservatism—seems indicated by the entanglements with Hegelian thought in which Heidegger finds himself ensnarled. Try as we might, the language and tug of the infinite cannot be so easily extinguished, since they seem to be an integral element of the hidden abundance of the finite itself. The web of finite structures and experiences is always pulling the finite beyond itself, but not only, nor necessarily, to the infinite.

But this does not mean that the confrontation between Hegel and Heidegger lends restored credence to the Hegelian claim that since the finite harbors this tendency and invitation to seeing it in terms of more than itself, it therefore must be thought only or ultimately as a moment of the infinite. The infinite as an element of the finite is but one aspect of the richness of the finite itself. It does not erase but enriches the real legacy of that which finally does not remain as itself. Adorno, who reappropriates the Hegelian dialectic, but with a renewed emphasis upon the final ineradicability of the finite itself, describes this element as a peculiar "plus."[82] The very experiences that testify to the finitude of thought—experiences found for instance in the unremitting sense that a translation has failed, that death shatters everything for us, that nature remains opaque to our probings of it, or that works of art exceed our conceptual grasp—these same experiences, like every experience of finitude, harbor just such an excess: translations fail not just by falling short of the original, but by bringing along too much; death shatters hope, but as the ancient myth reminds us, it is the dream of its postponement that first grants hope; nature remains the name of our first and last home; and of course the abundance in the work of art only increases the more we face up to our own conceptual failures before it. In a peculiar sense the finite becomes more, not more than itself but more itself and its promises, the more we let it be. That, in part, is what Heidegger wants to say when he tries to develop the proper attitude of the philosopher in terms of *Gelassenheit*: letting go. Like Nietzsche's criticism of philosophy's "revenge against time and its 'it was'," Heidegger is trying to remind us that approaches to the finite must meet the conditions for its appearance, and that the primary condition is a renunciation of our demand that the finite yield more than itself, that it yield to the infinite. Hegel, on the other hand, reminds us that nothing that does appear, appears in isolation. Relationality is ultimately the theme of all appearance, and unless we yield to the infinity of such relationality, the full force, richness, and complexity of the finite remains "beyond" our reach. The entanglement between Hegel and Heidegger, between the claims of the ontological difference and of the Absolute, is indicative of this special integrity of the finite that cannot be neglected and that leads thought beyond the finite, but nevertheless only beyond into new dimensions of the finite itself. Affirmation of the finitude of Being does not imply the closure of the possible modes of the disclosure of Being. Quite the contrary, the finitude of Being points toward the abundance of Being in its manifold forms.

Thinking that does not renounce its task thus finds itself suspended in an imbalance and interdeterminacy both with respect to itself and its topic. The strong sense that philosophy's task is to get over the differences, indeterminacies, ambiguities, and limits that it uncovers and move to the common and enduring elemental truths that first bestow a real intelligibility upon such finite topics must always be tempered by an equally strong sense of what such a task loses. When borne in mind, this peculiar price of thinking finitude renders the most excessive claims of metaphysics untenable. Claims to an ahistorical vantage point, a pure univocal language, and any attempt to

rid the true topic of such thinking of its essential ambiguity, instability, and ineradicable darkness in relation to thought all fail to live
up to their own original purpose: to make more evident and deep the
interest in riddles posed by finite being. When it subscribes to such
claims, metaphysics is inclined to obliterate the finite. But it obliter-
ates the finite in its special way of confronting finitude, and for this
reason it preserves the finite even if only in a transformed or mistaken
fashion. Metaphysics is thus not to be neglected, nor abandoned, for
it, like other modes of speaking and thinking the finite, always sits
only on an edge of finitude. The finite qua finite itself only shows itself
in such edges—but saying that is something that is hostile to the basic
conceptual frame and self-conception of metaphysics. That means
only that metaphysics has been rather poor at judging its own genius
and horizons.

The finite points beyond and away from itself—at least for the
most part—but not always in the same direction, even then not
always only in one way. Even today with all the breakdowns of long
ossified traditional disciplinary divisions, it is insufficiently remembered that "the sway of Being extends further than philosophy." [83]
Literature, art, politics, religion, and presumably modes of discourse
yet emergent, all of the modes of addressing the central and elemental
human concerns are at other such edges of the finite; often edges
sitting in tension with one another as both overlapping and competing at once. One instance, albeit a quite narrow and philosophically
localized instance, of this ambiguity permitted by the finite is found
in the entanglement of the frequently quite hostile intentions of the
Heideggerian project to overcome metaphysics and the Hegelian
effort to complete and close metaphysics in a science. The very topics,
and their peculiar matrix, to which Heidegger appeals as unim-
peachable testimony for his own interpretation of the meaning of
Being as finite—temporality, anxiety, originality, identity and difference, technology, language, representation, history—lend themselves to illuminating interpretations at odds with Heidegger's own,
but which, by virtue of their disclosive value, must qualify as part of
the true discourse about Being. It is clear that Heidegger does win a
kind of distance from Hegel, and vice versa, but in the end this
distance tends to be mitigated by and pulled back toward the commitments of that edge of thinking and speaking the finite fastened
onto by the self-reflection of such thinking and speaking: philosophy.

For all of his readiness to recognize other modes of discourse as legitimate, Heidegger does not abdicate the discourse of philosophy. And rightly so, for this means he recognizes that the end of philosophy is largely a matter of the end, as renunciation, of philosophy's dominion and its self-understanding as the crowning achievement of thought. It is not a matter of the end of philosophy as one among many contributors to the achievements of thought, some of which are uniquely contributions of philosophy. But, in the final analysis, what can be learned from this pull and proximity of Hegel and Heidegger, and what can be taken as a matter of generality, is that thinking and speaking the finite, addressing that which itself is a plurality, opens up a plurality of modes of address and discourse. The most self-aware efforts to come to terms with the finite know and accept this. Heidegger certainly understood it, and Hegel too, but only in attenuated form, and in this respect it must be said that Hegel does not measure up to Heidegger.

Philosophy always opens up beyond and away from itself. That philosophy opens up into and outside its margins, that it is one among many forms of discourse, and that it is not singular but stratified is the way it preserves the flexibility that allows it to accommodate itself to the needs of its time. When it attempts to close in upon itself, when it writes away its margins with an "essential" history, philosophy becomes rigid and so hostile to its times and tasks. Most dangerous though is that it refuses its futures. The proper integrity of philosophy is not exclusionary; rather, it contributes to and takes from the long, historical dialogue with the topics of thought. This dialogue is spoken in different ways and so can present itself as a kind of babel. At times philosophers, who for some reason have a special love for the univocal and unambiguous, forget the ultimate inescapability of this babel. The tendency is to forget the ways in which something is lost when this polyglot discourse is translated only into the discourse of philosophy.[84] The guiding ideals and basic grammars of the language of philosophy as metaphysics—ideals such as infinity, unconditionality, and totality—originally came about in order to provide a special backdrop against which finitude, difference, and the incomplete could be better seen and witnessed as what and how they are. The persistent philosophic urge to return to the Greeks and the rejuvenation to be found in them is a tacit recognition that in the early stages of the development of metaphysics its basic trademarks had yet to display the subsequent antagonism to the finite. But those ideals came too often to have taken on a life of their own and, with this, an intolerance of other lives and ideals.

Philosophy eventually fashioned itself the "queen of the sciences" and somehow above the fray that it alone was empowered to adjudicate. The more philosophy absorbed itself into itself, the less its ideals could tolerate conflicting modes of speech and thought (a process that ostensibly begins when Plato banishes the poets from the polis), the more abstract and so hostile to the rough edges of the concrete finite it became. Both Hegel and Heidegger devote themselves to overcoming this abstract life that philosophy came to adopt. The end of philosophy sought and claimed by both is the end of philosophy understood in this way. Both saw a fulfillment in this end, a lesson to be learned that could only be learned by reappropriating this history of that life in order to recover its original and long obliterated concrete, phenomenal, topic. The respective lessons about the end of philosophy to be learned from Hegel and Heidegger do nevertheless differ, and there is a sense in which Heidegger's lesson is one that is more willing and open to face the depth of the constraints of finitude upon thinking and speaking. Heidegger increasingly came to the realization that we cannot hold onto the finite and claim it for speech and thought, but that it claims us. We cannot arrest its dynamic life—that is something that Hegel knew equally well—but neither can we succeed in gathering together the fragments and edges of the finite as always splintering and differentiating itself into manifold modes of thought and speech. The trajectory of Heidegger's thought and that of Hegel's move in opposite directions: Heidegger begins his career with a systematic bid to think the meaning of Being as a whole, but increasingly points to the insurmountable manifoldness of all Being; Hegel's career, on the other hand, moves even more clearly toward an increasingly refined synoptic vision of Being seen through the optic of self-conscious spirit. Their trajectories are reversed: Heidegger moves from the urge to a closed, systematic, and exclusionary mode of discourse to a more open one willing to listen even to the poets banished by Plato; Hegel, on the other hand, moves from the Kantian flirtations of his youth to the highly refined and all-embracing system of his last years. In short: while both Hegel and Heidegger recognize the need to rescue and recover the finite from its submersion in the history of philosophy's obsession with the infinite,

Heidegger also recognizes that this recovery of the finite equally requires that philosophy let go of its proprietary claim to being the only form in which thinking and speaking of the finite can be articulated. This means, of course, that as but one among many, often incommensurate, forms of speech and thought, philosophy will have to recognize that it cannot ultimately lift itself out of the aporias and conflicts into which, and out of which, it works itself.

Nevertheless, the urge to regard the dynamic differentiation of the finite as exhibiting a dialectical logic is difficult to resist. Hegel rode with that urge to its final end. He tried to think and see the history and phenomena of this differentiation as exhibiting its own special pattern. He did not naively impose and so oppose this pattern to the finite so that the infinite and finite served as mere backdrops to one another but tried instead to see it as the pattern and internal logic of finitude itself. His sense of the infinity of this pattern is a reflection of the insurmountable manifold of finitude. But, pointing continually to this pattern and its meaning, he privileges this pattern as omnipresent and so runs the risk of concealing his own foremost concern: the fault lines and rough edges of the finite—and these are the real emblems of finitude—are paved over and smoothed out. Bearing witness to the finite, to the limits and captivity of speaking and thinking, cultures and epochs, nations and human beings, requires a certain attentiveness to such faults and edges. The peril of philosophy, or any form of addressing such issues raised under the idea of finitude, is that it is at its best in a rather precarious place, and while it may seem as if such edges are inhospitable to thought—such places where philosophy and other forms of discourse meet and speak—it is there that philosophy is true to the place assigned to it by its own topic. Historically, and perhaps temperamentally, philosophic thought and speech have been intolerant of ambiguity and aporias. One might argue that great philosophers have always zeroed in precisely at the point of ambiguity and tensions disclosed by the approach of others— even if this is done solely for the sake of erasing them. But what seems to be demanded today, and this becomes increasingly evident in asking just what finitude means for the possibilities of philosophizing, is a realization that ambiguity, tension, aporia, and even every form of disclosure do not belong solely to the province of what has long been called philosophy. It is not metaphysics that needs overcoming, it is the "fantasy of seizing reality."[85] Letting go of this "fantasy" still somehow seems like a risk and defeat. That is the sense behind Hölderlin's remark often cited by Heidegger: "Rescue grows at the place of danger and risk."

There are of course genuine difficulties posed by such a remark. The task of philosophy is not simply, or even essentially, theoretical. Philosophy has long been theory not simply for its own sake, but also with an eye to the place and meaning of such theory as one of the human ways of praxis. Speaking and thinking theoretically about the finite not only takes praxis as one of its own topics but is itself a mode of such human praxis. It is in this doubling and altering of theoretical speech and thought such as philosophy represents that the real dilemma of such theory is most evident. Praxis is a decisive and irrevocable domain, and as such seems to demand of us a kind of decision and unambiguous clear-sightedness of the ends according to which as yet undecided questions are to be measured. Praxis is the arena in which the subtle nuances between competing or conflicting theoretical judgments make a real, often fateful, difference. It is first in acting upon a discourse and living out its peculiar grammar that the stake we have in philosophic judgment becomes visible. Consequently, it is in the matters of practical judgment that the greatest dangers and genius of philosophy are revealed. The danger is that it holds fast, intolerantly, to its own ideals, forgetting that they are witnessed from but one edge from which ideals may be seen: "Summum justitia, summum injuria." The genius is found precisely in philosophy's capacity to generate and anticipate ideals that, to some degree, transcend the given.[86] Practical life seems at times to include a request for guidelines that are not found as givens: guidelines, or what Arendt called "banisters for thought and action," that are stable and unambiguous and in that way helpful in negotiating our way through the obscurities and ambiguities of practical affairs. Theory is a response to this invitation of praxis. The capacity for theory, for speech and thought that anticipates beyond the given, and the decisions of theory, the way in which it profiles the finitude and incommensurate edges of praxis, cannot be considered apart from its impact upon praxis. Theoretical praxis, like every mode of praxis in varying degrees, involves both conjunctions and disjunctions of itself, its topic, and its other; in short, it involves a species of translation the risks of which are well known. This means that full acceptance of the insights into the ultimate impossibility, or untenability, of the idea of philosophy as metaphysics might entail both theoretical and practical acceptance of the inevitable failures of their contributions to one another: both theory and praxis contribute to, inform, and take from one another, but neither can claim any leading function in their relation. The recovery of the finite, the philosophic recognition of its ubiquity, is not simply a matter of altering our philosophic "positions" and renegotiating the possibilities of theoretical understanding; it is rather a matter of fundamentally altering the prejudices and temperament that have long guided philosophy. Most of all it is every form of "final solution" that needs to be abandoned. Nothing is more hostile to what philosophy can best remind us of.

Yet such alteration is difficult to carry out. Heidegger, despite all his theoretical insight into the finitude of theory itself, could not carry forward this insight to its full consequence. To do so requires that we finally dismiss the quite peculiar presumption that philosophers are somehow "experts" in making judgments simply because the ideals that seem to breathe life into philosophy since Plato are the apparently boundless ideals of universality, wholeness, and reason. The concerns and topics of philosophy have always edged into those of politics and history, and the reverse is equally true. In many ways philosophy and political judgment provide measures of each other's deepest sense; the same is true of all of the other modes of speaking and thinking that move in circles in the same vicinity. Heidegger only infrequently and obliquely alludes to the overlap between philosophy and politics, yet when he does—in the case of the notorious "Rektoratsrede" for instance—he tends to display the long-standing philosophical prejudice that philosophers have a special expertise that singles them out as the true "leaders," [87] and that signals a failure to break through to the fullest sense of the "end" of philosophy. His own political actions as well as the texts of the period of those actions must be read as instances of his failure to call into question the meaning of finitude for the relation of those edges of the finite represented by theory and praxis, philosophy, and politics. Hegel is not the last metaphysical thinker in this regard.

Living and judging in harmony with the finite is perhaps most difficult of all. Contemplating it, driving through the conflicts, confusions, and muddiness of phenomena and events to a heightened sense of what is real and important, that is a different matter. Aristotle spoke about this difference between practical and theoretical judgment; he also claimed that talent in one domain did not require talent in the other. But Aristotle made an assumption, or decision, that in matters of theory thought was concerned with the invariable and eternal—matters that were modeled on a pattern like the movement of the stars in the heavens: orderly, infinite, unconditioned, circular. He did say that human affairs are not so orderly or invariant as the stars, and so the demands and expectations in the realms of theory and praxis must never be confused. Heidegger, on the other hand, and in a curiously inverted way Hegel too, argues that nothing in heaven or on earth is as orderly, regular, and eternal as Aristotle thought the stars to be. Instead both, to different conclusions, argue that we only draw near the true complexity and simplicity of contemplating Being qua Being once we realize that there is a kind of ubiquity to the finite that enriches both theory and praxis. Philosophy returns to its own special genius not in obliterating, arresting, or overcoming this ubiquity of the finite, but by attaching itself to it. Hegel takes this to be evidence for the *parousia* of Spirit as Absolute, Heidegger takes it to be evidence for the ultimate ineradicability of concealment as the companion to unconcealment. Heidegger's efforts to extricate himself from Hegel do, in part, succeed, but even such "success" means that Heidegger has made but one more contribution to the discourse about Being as finite. What one learns from this contribution is that though ubiquitous, the finite "likes to hide"—it also "hides" in many places, is spoken out in many forms of discourse, and appears in many shapes. If one takes seriously the entanglements and separations between Hegel and Heidegger, between these two ultimately divergent ways of speaking and thinking the finite, then one is led to speak of the "end" of philosophy. That is so not because it has become obsolete, but because it is once again to be recognized that its first topic, however it is characterized, is one that resists schematization, always seems but a prelude, and points away from itself, generating a plurality of ways of thinking, speaking, and judging.

Notes

Introduction

1. Whitehead, *Process and Reality* (New York: The Free Press, 1978), p. 39.

2. Boeder, *Topologie der Metaphysik* (Freiburg: Alber Verlag, 1980), p. 15.

3. Buchler, *Metaphysics of Natural Complexes* (New York: Columbia University Press, 1966).

4. Gadamer, *Hegels Dialektik* (Tübingen: J. C. B. Mohr, 1971), p. 85.

5. Bernasconi, *The Question of Language in Heidegger's History of Being* (Atlantic Highlands, New Jersey: Humanities Press, 1985), p. 67.

6. Derrida, "The Ends of Man," in *Margins of Philosophy* (Chicago: University of Chicago Press, 1982), p. 136.

7. Gadamer, *Wahrheit und Methode* (Tübingen: J. C. B. Mohr, 1960), p. xxv.

8. Steiner, *Antigones* (New York: Oxford University Press, 1984), p. 20.

Chapter 1

9. See "Time and Being, 1925–1927," pp. 177–186 by Thomas Sheehan in *Thinking About Being* (Norman: University of Oklahoma Press, 1984), ed. Shahan and Mohanty, for a discussion of this issue.

10. Earlier references to Hegel often seem directed more against the neo-Hegelianism of the day than against Hegel himself. Those references also tend to be far too brief to be developed substantively. See *Frühe Schriften*, p. 352.

11. The phrase is Whitehead's, but see Joseph P. Fell, *Heidegger and Sartre: An Essay on Being and Place* (New York: Columbia University Press, 1979). I am indebted to this fine book for many of these general insights on the general relationship between Hegelian and Heideggerian senses of phenomenology.

12. See C. Guignon, *Heidegger and the Problem of Knowledge* (Indianapolis: Hackett Press, 1983) for a full treatment of the epistemological dimension of *Being and Time* and other early works.

13. See O. Blanchette, "The Philosophic Beginning," *Thought* vol. 56, no. 222 (Sept. 1981), pp. 251–262, for an examination of this question of Hegel. A large-scale study devoted to this question of ontological grounds and ontical beginnings as a general question of post-Hegelian thought can be found in R. D. Cumming, *Starting Point* (Chicago: University of Chicago Press, 1979).

14. It is interesting to note that the route that Heidegger outlines for this analytic is not the only possible one. In four of the recently released volumes of Heidegger's collected works we can find alternative approaches: thus *ML* begins with the transcendence of Dasein; *L* with care; *GP* with the ontological difference; *GM* with boredom; and *GZ* with uncanniness. The presentations of these lectures do not differ in any fundamental sense from the presentation of *SZ*.

15. Heidegger's own remarks on the being of animals are few; the most extended treatment of animals as lacking "world" (*Weltarm*) appears in *Die Grundbegriffe der Metaphysik* (1929/30), pp. 261–392. For an interesting set of reflections on language in animals—reflections inspired by Wittgenstein—see Vicki Hearne, "Questions about Language," *The New Yorker*, August 18 and 25, 1986.

16. Karl-Otto Apel has picked up on this point. See his *Transformation der Philosophie* (Frankfurt: Suhrkamp Verlag, 1973) Bd. 2, p. 419, 423. I am indebted to Rainer Forst for this reference.

17. See my "Art, Artifice, and Nature in Heidegger."

18. *Physics* Delta 14, 223a 25; and *Confessions* lib. XI., chap. 26.

19. In a footnote to this passage Heidegger remarks that "with Kant ... a more radical understanding of time breaks out than is to be found in Hegel." His intent was to consider Kant's concept of time in the second (unpublished) part of *SZ*. We may find hints at what this analysis would have been in *KPM*.

20. Jacques Derrida, op. cit., p. 38.

21. "Hegel à Iena," *Revue d'histoire et de philosophie religieuses*, 1934, pp. 153–159.

22. *Ibid*, pp. 162–163.

23. Kojéve, *Introduction to the Reading of Hegel* (New York: Basic Books, 1969), pp. 134–135.

24. *Ibid*, p. 133.

25. But it is important to remember that, according to Hegel, the determination of the ground happens both from below *and* above. See Fackenheim's discussion of the "threefold mediation" in *The Religious Dimension of Hegel's Thought* (Boston: Beacon Press, 1970).

Chapter 2

26. See *Three Dialogues Between Hylas and Philonous*: "To me it is evident ... that sensible things cannot exist otherwise than in a mind or spirit. Whence I conclude, not that they have no real existence but that seeing they depend not on my thought, and have an existence distinct from being perceived by me, *there must be some other mind wherein they exist*" in *Classics of Western Philosophy*, ed. Steven M. Cahn, (Indianapolis: Hackett Press, 1977), p. 661.

27. See Birault, *Heidegger et l'expérience de la pensée* (Paris: Gallimard, 1978), pp. 519–523.

28. The present English translation does not repeat this important distinction. See "What is Metaphysics?" in *Basic Writings*, ed. Krell, (New York: Harper & Row, 1977), p. 97ff. The sentences immediately following the introduction of this distinction are also omitted, compare *WM*, 105.

29. For an alternate reading of Kant and the problem of nothingness see Watson, "Abysses," in *Hermeneutics and Deconstruction* (Albany: SUNY Press, 1985), pp. 228–232.

30. Walter Schulz argues that, despite this, Heidegger realizes that "Greek philosophy is secretly governed by the problem of Nothing." See "Hegel und das Problem der Aufhebung der Metaphysik," in *Heidegger zum siebzigsten Geburtstag* (Pfullingen: Neske, 1959), p. 70.

31. Compare *EM*, pp. 1–3 where Heidegger begins with Leibniz's question "Warum ist überhaupt Seiendes und nicht vielmehr Nichts?" and quickly shows how this question, which arises in special, extreme dispositions, becomes the question about nothingness. In this and other lectures of this period, most notably *Die Grundbegriffe der Metaphysik* (1929/30), Heidegger indicates that anxiety may not be the sole disposition in which the groundless ground of Being is disclosed. Homesickness and boredom are also mentioned as basic determinants of authentic philosophical questioning. Both of these dispositions share a feature with anxiety that will cause persistent problems for Heidegger's efforts to address the concerns of the social world; namely, each of these dispositions is individuating. One might, however, speculate about the possibility of just such a fundamental disposition that is not a splitting off of Dasein from the social world of co-Daseins, but that is a deepening of the link between Daseins. Such a disposition might be found in an analysis of grief in the face of loss, not of oneself, but another.

32. See *L'être et le néant* (Paris: Gallimard, 1943), pp. 52–84.

33. See P. Emad, "Heidegger on Pain," *Zeitschrift für Philosophische Forschung*, Bd. 36, no. 3 (1982): 345–60.

34. The question of the will and its inevitable failure becomes increasingly important during the years following the publication of this lecture. This question also comes to the fore when Heidegger tries to come to terms with his own brief Nazi activities. See H. Arendt, "Heidegger's Will-not-to-will" in *The Life of the Mind* vol. 2 (New York: Harcourt, Brace, Jovanovich, 1978), pp. 172–194.

35. Most notable in this regard are Harris, *Hegel's Development: Towards the Sunlight* (Oxford: Clarendon Press, 1972); Haering, *Hegel: Sein Wollen und sein Werk* (Leipzig: Teubner, 1929); and Taylor, *Hegel* (Cambridge: Cambridge University Press, 1975). For a fine analysis of the confrontation of Hegel and Heidegger with respect to their critiques of Kant, see Taminiaux, "Finitude et Absolu," in *Le regard et l'excédent*, (The Hague: Martinus Nijhoff, 1977).

36. Georges Bataille, *Visions of Excess* (Minneapolis: University of Minnesota Press, 1985), p. 135.

37. It is also quite significant—especially for interpreting Heidegger's politics—that during the Winter Semester 1934–35, the time of Heidegger's break with the Nazis and his own efforts to come to terms with political issues, Heidegger announced a seminar (with the jurist professor, E. Wolf) on "Hegel: Über den Staat." See A. Hollerbach, "Im Schatten des Jahres 1933: Erik Wolf und Martin Heidegger," *Freiburger Universitätsblätter*, Heft 92, 1986, pp. 33–47.

38. See also, p. 144: "Hegel versteht unter 'Zeit' etwas anderes als wir, im Prinzip nichts anderes als den traditionellen Begriff der Zeit wie ihn Aristotles entwickelt." And: "Es muss mit aller Schärfe betont werden: Zeit und Raum sind für Hegel von Anfang an—und bleiben es in seiner ganzen Philosophie—primär Probleme der Naturphilosophie" (*HP*, 208).

39. The decisive sections of the text are: 4c, 5b, 6f, 7c, 8a, 10a, 11c, 13a, 13b, Schluss.

Chapter 3

40. See esp. *N*, I, 259, 364, 390, 395, 470, 480, 547, 626, 656–57; *N*, II, 29, 201–202, 279, 471, 481.

41. See esp. *HH*, 3–4, 61, 75, 134; *HEH*, 22–24.

42. See esp. *S*, 193–194.

43. For a more extensive and broader ranged discussion of the problem entailed by these different self-images for philosophizing see my "Kunst, Kritik und die Sprache der Philosophie," *Philosophische Rundschau*, Winter, 1987. See also R. Rorty, "Philosophy in America Today," in *Consequences of Pragmatism* (Minneapolis: University of Minnesota Press, 1982), pp. 211–229 for a discussion of the ideal of mathematics and science as essential to the self-conception of contemporary Anglo-American analytic philosophy.

44. See L. Ballew, *Straight and Circular: A Study of Imagery in Greek Philosophy* (Assen, The Netherlands: Van Gorcum, 1979) for a detailed analysis of the image of the circle in early Greek philosophy.

45. Ralph Waldo Emerson, "Circles," in *Essays* (New York: Bigelow & Brown, n.d.), p. 193.

46. For an analysis of the theme of the hermeneutic circle in *Being and Time* and its later development by Gadamer in *Truth and Method*, see J-L. Nancy, *Le Partage des voix* (Paris: Éditions Galilée, 1982), esp. pp. 23–48.

47. Reiner Schürmann, *Le principe d'anarchie: Heidegger et la question de l'agir* (Paris: Éditions du Seuill, 1982), p. 22.

48. Kant possessed an equally deep sense of the insurmountability of metaphysical error in the "Transcendental Dialectic" portion of the first *Critique*, for while it is the "logic of illusion" (*KRV*, A 293), it is also unavoidable in light of the claims of the unconditioned. Kant took this deep sense of human fallibility as the key to moral thought. One can only speculate about how Heidegger might have developed the notion of "errancy" for moral concerns.

49. See esp. Diels fragments 51, 80, 90, 126. The fragments dealing with exchange and opposition, e.g., DK 62 and 88, and those dealing with fire and war, e.g., DK 66 and 53, also speak of the same process.

50. Thus, Heidegger distinguishes the origin from the primitive (a problem that remained in *SZ*, see *SZ* pages 50–52, 82, 88): "Der echte Anfang hat freilich nie das Anfängerhafte des Primitiven. Das Primitive ist, weil ohne den schenkenden, grundenden Sprung und Vorsprung immer *zukunftlos*" (*H*, 63).

51. Justus Buchler, *Towards a General Theory of Human Judgment* (New York: Columbia University Press, 1951), p. 169.

52. See *Nietzsche I and II*, and the discussion in "Die Technik und die Kehre" on *Geviert* and *Gestell*. See also Fell, op cit., chapt. 9; and Marx, *Heidegger und die Tradition* (Hamburg: Meiner Verlag, 1961).

53. E. Bloch, *Subjekt-Objekt* (Frankfurt: Suhrkamp, 1981), p. 121.

54. Hegel would have no difficulty with the first words of T. S. Eliot's "East Coker": "In my beginning is my end." Heidegger, on the other hand, would likely find the final words of the same poem more congenial: "In my end is my beginning."

Chapter 4

55. E. Bloch, *Das Prinzip Hoffnung* (Frankfurt: Suhrkamp, 1959).

56. Wm. James, *Pragmatism* (New York: Longmans, Green and Co., 1925), p. 64.

57. The concept of the ontological difference also appears as "Differenz," "Unterschied," and "Zwiefalt."

58. See Marx, op. cit., p. 132, where three kinds of justification are noted.

59. Without doubt Heidegger would agree that the issue of tragedy is one way of conceiving the issue of the ontological difference. In the essay "Der Spruch des Anaximander," which is part of the *Holzwege* series of essays, and which opens with a reference to Hegel who Heidegger calls "Der einzige Denker des Abendlandes, der die Geschichte des Denkens denkend erfahren hat." (*SA*, 298), we hear Heidegger say: "Dem Wesen des Tragischen kommen wir jedoch vermutlich auf die Spur, wenn wir es ... seine Wesensart, das Sein des Seienden, bedenken." (*SA*, 330).

60. It is not insignificant that all four of these passages deal with the concept of tragedy as it appears in the element of *Sittlichkeit*. The connection between Hegel's concept of tragedy and his social and political thought should not be overlooked. We will return to this connection in our conclusion.

61. For an interesting discussion of the dialectic in terms of its masculine and feminine components, see Steiner, *Antigones* (Oxford: Clarendon Press, 1986), esp. 17ff where he is led to the conclusion that "sisterliness is ontologically privileged beyond any other human stance."

62. It should be noted that for Heidegger too *Antigone* has a privileged place in considering Greek tragedy. See the celebrated analysis of the chorus passage from *Antigone* in *EM* pp. 112–126.

Chapter 5

63. This is the sense of the reference in *ID*, page 12: "Seit der Epoche des spekulativen Idealismus bleibt es dem Denken untersagt, die Einheit der Identität als das blosse Einerlei vorzustellen und von der in der Einheit waltenden Vermittelung abzusehen."

64. Though Heidegger does not extensively pursue it, the analysis of the treatment of the possible senses of "nothing" in this principle would be of interest, particularly in light of our chapter 2.

65. This was a notion present already in *SZ*, indeed one could find a foreshadowing of the later critique of technology in the analysis of *Zu-handenheit* in *SZ*.

66. Gadamer, *Wahrheit und Methode*.

67. See Heidegger's use of the notion of *Gleichzeitigkeit* in *VA*, esp. page 183. This, obviously, is part of Heidegger's lifelong effort to think the relation of Being *and* time.

68. Hegel also makes this distinction quite clearly in *PR*, #187. This notion of desire must not be confused with the notion of Desire by which we presented (see our chapter 1) Hegel's concept of human being as transcending the given.

69. It would also be a misunderstanding of Hegel were one to divorce the concept of work from the human task of participating in the actualizing of God in the world. I am indebted to Joseph P. Fell for pointing this out.

70. Steiner, op. cit., 19–20.

71. Here it is necessary to distinguish between Hegelian dialectic and all previous conceptions of dialectic. Hegel himself makes this distinction by contending that his conception of dialectic is the first to demonstrate that it is the dialectic of the real, and not an artificial, subjective method which is applied to the world. Hegel bases this claim on his concept of dialectic as the real inner relation that exists between thought and Being.

Chapter 6

72. See Habermas, *Philosophische Diskurs der Moderne* (Frankfurt: Suhrkamp, 1985), p. 23 for an account of the different senses of historical consciousness in each of these thinkers.

73. It is worth noting how often Heidegger refers to Hegel in Heidegger's own provocative interpretations of the pre-Socratics. See, for instance, the interpretations of Parmenides in *VA* (especially pages 227–229), of Anaximander in *H* (especially page 298), and of Heraclitus in the 1966 Heraclitus seminar held with E. Fink.

74. Heidegger hints that the issue of the origin is once again central when he says: "Doch wir lernen langsam die Einsicht, dass die 'Primitive' der frühen Denker nicht das Unausgebildete und Unbeholfen ist, sondern das Primäre des Anfänglichen und der diesem und nur diesem eigenen Einfachheit. Die Sprache der anfänglichen Denker hat den Adel des Anfänglichen" (*VH*, 27). For Heidegger, the richness and fullness of the origins of the history of thought can never be overestimated.

75. For a discussion of Heidegger's relation to Hölderlin see Fynsk, *Heidegger: Thought and Historicity* (Ithaca: Cornell University Press, 1986), pp. 174–229.

76. It is worth noting that Heidegger was quite aware of this, for he cites Hölderlin's dedication to Hegel in 1791. See *HH*, 130 and *VH*, 30. For an analysis of the place of Greek thought in the formation of German Idealism see Taminiaux, *La Nostalgie de la Grece a l'aube de l'idealisme Allemand* (The Hague: Martinus Nijhoff, 1967).

77. For a fuller treatment of the logic of history in Hegel and Heidegger see Gillespie, *Hegel, Heidegger, and the Ground of History* (Chicago: University of Chicago Press, 1984).

Conclusion

78. Such seems to be the concern of David Kolb's book, *The Critique of Pure Modernity* (Chicago: University of Chicago Press, 1986). That book only appeared as this was going to press, otherwise further reference to its presentation of Hegel and Heidegger would have been likely.

79. Wittgenstein, *Philosophical Investigations* (New York: Macmillan Co., 1968), p. 46.

80. Nietzsche, *Menschliches, Allzumenschliches* pt. 2, "Vermischte Meinungen und Sprüche" (Frankfurt: Ullstein, 1969), p. 343.

81. Gadamer, *Wahrheit und Methode*, xxv.

82. Adorno, *Ästhetische Theorie* (Frankfurt: Suhrkamp, 1970), p. 510.

83. Bernasconi, op. cit., p. 30.

84. M. M. Bakhtin has made a similar set of remarks that are directed toward literary discourse, see his *The Dialogic Imagination* (Austin: University of Texas Press, 1981) pp. 269–275.

85. Lyotard, *The Post modern Condition* (Minneapolis: University of Minnesota Press, 1984), p. 82.

86. Ernst Bloch describes this genius of philosophy in the language and principle of "hope." Though a dialectical thinker, he resisted the urge to find the results of the dialectic only synoptically: the principle of hope is to be witnessed in each and every species of transcendence and creativity, in film and fashion as well as great literature, art, philosophy, and intents of law.

87. The investigation into Heidegger's Nazi involvement, and his subsequent refusal to comment upon it must begin at this point (the *Spiegel* interview, given in 1966, and the "Tatsache und Gedanken" composed in 1945—both released only after Heidegger's death—raise more questions than they answer). See Lacoue-Labarthe, *L'imitation des modernes* (Paris: Éditions Galilée, 1986), pp. 135–173, and Karsten Harries, "Heidegger as Political Thinker," in *Heidegger and Modern Philosophy*, ed. Murray (New Haven: Yale University Press, 1978).

Index

Absolute, xi, 15, 29, 79–82, 90–91, 97, 124, 127–129, 131, 133–135, 140, 143, 148, 154, 170–171, 178, 183–184, 188, 202, 204–207, 214, 221, 228. *See also* Spirit
agony of the, 22, 79, 171
Abstraction, 49, 55, 146
Adorno, Theodor, 1, 216, 220, 235n82
Aletheia, 106, 196. *See also* Truth
Anaximander, 109, 137
Antigone, 144, 146, 148
Antinomy, 6, 79, 81–82, 114, 130, 152
Anxiety, 19, 33–39, 48, 71–75, 77, 85–88, 90, 91, 99–100, 177
Apel, Karl-Otto, 230n16
Aporia, 14–15, 64, 83, 148, 150, 151, 225
of the finite, 21–22, 122
of the present, 6
of ubiquity, 17
A priori perfect, 37
Arche, 110–111
Arendt, Hannah, xi, 226, 231n34
Aristotle, ix, 13, 25, 35, 41, 42, 53, 59, 68, 82, 97, 102, 103, 107, 128, 129, 134, 136, 137, 152, 214, 227–228
Art, x, 92, 101–106, 164, 221, 222
Atopology, 21
Augustine, 42, 97, 103

Bakhtin, M. M., 235n84
Bataille, Georges, 90
Baudrillard, Jean, 152
Becoming, 48–49, 89–90
Beginning, 21, 95–98, 100–101, 104–111, 113–122
Benjamin, Walter, x
Berkeley, Bishop, 63

Bernasconi, Robert, 229n5, 235n83
Birault, Henri, 230n27
Blanchette, Oliva, 229n13
Bloch, Ernst, 126, 232n53, 233n55, 235n86
Boeder, Heribert, 229n2
Buchler, Justus, 110, 229n3

Calculability, 41, 163–165
Calvino, Italo, 215
Care, 32–36, 57–58
Carlyle, Thomas, 125
Circle, 16, 95, 100–105, 108–118, 120–122, 139, 174, 208, 209, 228
Clearing (*Lichtung*), 18, 198
Cogito, 100–101
Commemorative thinking (*Andenkendes Denken*), 18, 165
Community, 171
Concreteness, 15, 34, 50, 143
Conflict, 83, 144, 173, 206. *See also* Struggle
Conrad, Joseph, 215
Contradiction, 69, 76–78, 81–84, 96, 100, 150, 186–189, 205–207
Creon, 144, 146, 148
Culture (*Bildung*), 5, 170, 178–182
Cumming, R. D., 229n13

Darkness, 197–200, 212–213
Dasein, 27, 31–44, 56–60, 66–67, 70–75, 105, 122, 167, 231n31
as factical 28, 97–100
Death, 35–39, 56, 86–88, 147, 221
Derrida, Jacques, 5, 8, 216, 229n6, 230n20
Descartes, Rene, 14, 97, 100–101, 107, 129, 130, 134, 194, 203, 218
Desire, 57–61, 87, 113, 119, 176–178